Tilt the Hourglass and

By the same author

SLIP ON A FAT LADY
PLUMRIDGE
WILD THING
THE SKATERS' WALTZ
SHOUT! THE TRUE STORY OF THE BEATLES
THE ROAD GOES ON FOR EVER
THE STONES

Tilt the Hourglass and Begin Again

PHILIP NORMAN

Elm Tree Books: London

First published in Great Britain 1985
by Hamish Hamilton Ltd/Elm Tree Books Ltd
Garden House, 57–59, Long Acre, London WC2E 9JZ
Copyright © 1985 by Philip Norman

British Library Cataloguing in Publication Data

Norman, Philip
  Tilt the hourglass and begin again.
  I. Title
  082   PR6064.075

ISBN 0–241–11421–7

Phototypeset by Input Typesetting Ltd, London

Printed and bound in Great Britain by
Biddles Ltd, Guildford and King's Lynn

Contents

Author's Note

The majority of these pieces were published during my 16 years as a reporter, feature writer and diarist for *The Sunday Times*. Between 1966 and 1982, I had the inestimable luck to work for a great newspaper at the peak of its glamour, prosperity and self-confidence. What freedom and opportunity I enjoyed will be evident in the range of subjects, the distances I was allowed to travel and the, sometimes phenomenal, space my editors let me occupy. I can express only inadequate thanks to those on the paper who employed, encouraged and indulged me – notably Harold Evans, its inspirational editor; Godfrey Smith, Magnus Linklater, David Robson, Nick Mason and Don Berry. I am grateful to *The Sunday Times*' present proprietor and editor for permission to collect the pieces here.

Kind Hearts and Kotex first appeared in *Vanity Fair*, New York. The 'No Comment' Island and A Day Out in Kiev were originally published by *The Spectator*. The Mad Mullah and the Flower Child, The Liner that Never Sails and Cruising to Extinction appear in print for the first time.

Philip Norman

New York City, 1985

PART ONE

Moving Targets

The Mad Mullah and the
Flower Child

I became the first – and, as of this date, the last – British news-paperman to interview Colonel Moammar Gaddafi in July, 1972. Barely three years had passed since Gaddafi had toppled Libya's puppet King Idris, placed the indolent old Italian colony under strict Islamic law and begun his first wild forays into world politics. To the West, in those still complacent times, he seemed like some mad mullah from a John Buchan novel, waving a holy book in one hand, a machine-gun in the other. The vital difference, people had slowly begun to realise, was that this mad mullah's weapons also included oil.

In 1972, London still had a conventional Libyan Embassy where diplomats dispensed coffee and politeness rather than shooting poli-cewomen dead out in the street. I was greeted courteously, welcomed in advance to Libya but warned that Colonel Gaddafi gave few interviews, even to Arab journalists, and would be still less likely to see me after the outcry in the British press following his speech 'about Ireland'. A few weeks earlier, in his attempts to raise holy war against Israel, Gaddafi had widened his support of international terrorism to include the Provisional IRA. Still, the Libyan press attaché wrote down the names of two possibly helpful government contacts in Tripoli. I pocketed the piece of paper carelessly.

My companion on the assignment was Colin Jones, former prin-cipal dancer with the Royal Ballet, now gifted freelance photo-grapher for *The Sunday Times Magazine,* a life-sustaining Cockney cynic and wit. Neither of us knew much about Middle Eastern politics and manners, though we had received a bitter two-week foretaste in Jordan, attempting to interview the supposedly media-conscious and anglophile King Hussein. All we had succeeded in doing was precipi-tating an attempt on our virtue by two of the King's air force officers. We agreed to go on from Amman to Libya since, as Colin remarked, 'It couldn't be any worse than all these camp Jordanians'.

At Tripoli airport, each of us had a bottle of brandy ritualistically confiscated, according to Colonel Gaddafi's new Islamic law. A black and white Fiat taxi (with 'taxi' written in Arabic only, according to Colonel Gaddafi's new Islamic law) drove us into the elegant old seafront city, past lines of Roman senatorial statues whose heads were all symbolically absent. Out in the bay, several large oil tankers bore witness to the tangibility of Colonel Gaddafi's power.

Gaddafi was not in Tripoli. No one, in fact, knew where he was. According to BBC Radio's World Service – that trusty source for all Middle East correspondents – he had vanished into the Libyan desert to cohabit with Tuareg tribesmen, and the ghosts of Mussolini and Rommel, for a period of mystic meditation. Alternatively, it was said, he could have been deposed by Major Jalloud, his deputy in the Revolutionary Command Council; he might now be under arrest, or even dead. 'Your timing's not much good, mate,' Colin Jones remarked drily, making me blush a blush known only to would-be foreign correspondents who get themselves into the wrong place at the wrong time.

My first call next day was at the British Embassy. I found it to be a handsome villa on the promenade, standing in grounds only slightly scarred by the regular invasions of Libyan students waving burning Union Jacks. For all its sieges and stonings, the embassy maintained the deep, unhurried calm of a rural police station in the 1950s. One almost expected to see posters offering a reward for the capture of Colorado Beetle. The Libyan telephone operator had been trained to say 'Hullo – Bri'sh Embassy heah' as if he were speaking from Sunningdale or Thames Ditton.

Upstairs, I spent ten minutes with a blue-shirted man, described by his official card as 'Second Secretary (Press)'. It was strange to realise, even before I had sat down in his office, how keenly the Second Secretary was looking forward to the moment when I would get up again and leave. He said he had no knowledge of Gaddafi's whereabouts, and could not be of help to me in any way. The embassy was in a state of perpetual trepidation, chiefly caused, I learned later, by fear that the Libyan Customs might confiscate the bar supplies sent in via its diplomatic bags. The message, relayed by the Second Secretary, deafeningly but wordlessly, was 'Don't rock the boat, old boy'. At last, to his evident joy, I made an excuse and left.

My most promising contact was an elderly Yugoslavian who worked as a copy-editor for the official Libyan news agency. He was a gentle, genial man – a typical solid 'sub' – whose response, when I telephoned him, was a resigned 'Yes – they all come to me'. He was so wonderfully helpful, I felt I might have a story even if, as seemed highly probable, I never got anywhere near Colonel Gaddafi.

The Yugoslavian had been at work on the night of Gaddafi's coup in September, 1969. He told me how quick and efficient it had been – and how totally bloodless. No one from King Idris's regime had been executed or incarcerated beyond the initial take-over period. The old King himself had been allowed to go on living in Tripoli until he died naturally in his bed.

The picture I received was not of a demented mullah but of a modest, ascetic career officer who might be the figurehead Libya needed after centuries of being trodden over by itinerant armies from Rome, Turkey, Germany and Britain. I heard of the cruelty visited by Italian colonial rule, when immigrants from the mother country were promised fully-equipped houses – 'down to three boxes of matches in the kitchen' – while surplus Libyans were disposed of by being pushed out of high-flying aircraft. Several of Gaddafi's own family had, indeed, been murdered in this unspeakable way.

I asked the Yugoslavian if he knew where the Colonel might be. 'You can find him everywhere,' was the reply. ' . . . and you can't find him everywhere.' All my informant knew was that, in the past, Gaddafi's sudden disappearances had always portended something big. He might be in the desert, as rumour said, drinking sour milk with his Bedouin cousins. He might be preparing to nationalise all the American oil interests in Libya. He might just as easily be walking round Tripoli icognito – he might at this moment be sitting on the very next seafront bench to ours.

With zero hope, I called on the first of the 'government contacts' given to me by the Libyan Embassy in London. His name was Ibrahim Gwil. He had something to do with the 'Green Revolution' which Colonel Gaddafi had promised to Libyan agriculture. He was a tiny, quiet, round-shouldered man with a smudge of a black moustache. His only suggestion was that I should meet his brother, a prominent Tripoli lawyer. His brother, a jokey-looking man with a Zapata moustache and a habit of winking roguishly, asked if Colin Jones and I would care to spend the next day at the beach.

Colin, half under his breath, said, 'Ay-ay – more camp Arabs!'

I looked reproachfully back at Mr Gwil.

'Go to the beach with my brother,' Mr Gwil said. 'In a few days, I think you will have your appointment.'

We spent the next day with Mr Gwil's brother at the seaside chalet complex just outside Tripoli where Gaddafi subsequently accommodated his friend and fellow Muslim, Idi Amin. Our host wore an American sailor hat and winked with increasing frequency as the afternoon wore on and several bottles of pre-Gaddafi, Libyan-produced vin rosé were drunk. The Colonel's Koranic prohibition law apparently held little sway among the moneyed classes. Mr Gwil's brother told us that the bestselling book in Libya was a slim work by an American oil company executive entitled *How To Make Gin*.

Several times, in mounting exasperation, I asked Mr Gwil's brother if he had any idea where Colonel Gaddafi might be.

'My brother Ibrahim will arrange,' he said, winking again. 'In a few days my brother Ibrahim will arrange you your appointment.' But, if this was the casting-couch, so to speak, Mr Gwil's brother

13

made no attempt to press the matter. Even Colin Jones had to admit that Libyans were not as camp as Jordanians.

The next morning, Mr Gwil took us to Tripoli's old royal palace, a folly of white marble, colonnades and goldfish ponds which – I learned with sinking spirits – was the headquarters of Colonel Gaddafi's Cultural Revolution. In one Italianate salon, a figure in faded blue denims was sitting at an antique desk. 'Now,' Mr Gwil said, 'you will make interview with Sadeg.'

We had apparently stumbled on Libya's one and only hippie. As well as blue denims, he wore a purple T-shirt, several strings of beads, a silver neckband and American baseball boots. His hair was a tight-curled Afro cloud. He was lanky and laid-back, and spoke English almost without accent, flashing prominent white teeth.

His conversation grabbed one right from the beginning. 'When the wolf has eaten and made love,' he said in answer to my first question, 'then the wolf's troubles are over. When Man has eaten and made love, then Man's troubles *begin* . . .'

We knew him only as Sadeg – the Arabic word for 'wise'. What he was to Gaddafi and the Libyan revolution, we never did fully ascertain. He told us he had lived in Switzerland and America before returning home to assist in the Colonel's programme of cultural regeneration. We knew him to be a writer, a poet and a rock fan, particularly keen on Crosby, Stills and Nash, and Cat Stevens.

As a mouthpiece for Gaddafi, Arab fundamentalism and the justice of making holy war on Israel, Sadeg should have been at the UN. There was not one of Libya's madcap policies, from merging with Egypt to cutting of thieves' right hands, that he could not make sound utterly plausible. Israel, at the time, was regularly bombarding the refugee camps it alleged to be Palestinian terrorist bases in southern Lebanon. Sadeg did not inveigh against Israel. His tone was of the flower child, bemusedly reproachful. 'Bombing women . . . and little children . . . now that's not *nice* . . .'

Entertaining as Sadeg was, we still seemed no nearer seeing Gaddafi or even discovering his whereabouts. We spent most days out at the 'tourist village', meeting friends of Sadeg who were Gaddafi's political opponents under suspended prison sentence. At night we sat with a circle of these sun-worshipping penitents, our virtue still unthreatened, drinking wine or illegally-distilled white lightning and listening to Sadeg's Cat Stevens albums.

After ten days, having heard no further from Mr Gwil, I called Colin Jones to my hotel room and said I thought it was all hopeless. To cheer me up, I asked him to tell me about the time in the Royal Ballet's *Cinderella* when he played a mouse drawing Sir Robert Helpmann's coach and accidentally tipped it over. At that moment, the telephone rang.

'He'll see you,' Sadeg's voice said.

14

'Who? Colonel Gaddafi?'

'Yeah,' Sadeg replied.

Sadeg navigated our hired Volkswagen out of town about three miles to a sprawling army barracks. His blue denims led the way, unchallenged, through a system of courtyards where adolescent soldiers in full camouflage equipment drilled under shrieking sergeants. We passed along a green hospital-like corridor and climbed a raw concrete staircase. At the top, someone greeted Sadeg with an odd little chirrup of a voice. Sadeg turned to us, grinning. 'Did you hear that!' he exclaimed. 'That is how Muammar Gaddafi says Hello.'

We were shown into a long conference room, its windows filled with a flaming Libyan sunset. Halfway down, three men sat along a low couch before a coffee-table with a battery of TV microphones which, even in that stressful moment, had an unconvincing, unconnected look. I recognised Abu Bakr Yunis and gold-toothed Bashir Hawadi, two subordinate officer-members of the Revolutionary Command Council. The third was a boy of about 15, white-faced, a stenographer's pad on his knee. To the left of this trio, tapping a pencil on a plastic chair-arm and shifting his knees restlessly to and fro, sat Colonel Gaddafi.

Though not yet given to dressing like an Italian film star, jacket slung round his shoulders, he cut a sufficiently hedonistic figure, clad in his sleek grey safari suit and giving off a faint odour of expensive after-shave. The familiar, furious face was darkly handsome though preternaturally haggard. Two deep lines, like black sickles, clove savagely up through his cheeks to his tiny, watchful eyes. Throughout the two hours to come, he never sat absolutely still in his chair.

I knew that Gaddafi had once spent six months on an army signals course in Beaconsfield, Kent, and was widely suspected of speaking perfect English. He chose, however, to answer my questions in Arabic, using Sadeg as interpreter. Muslim fire and fundamentalist mayhem would thus be relayed to us across the table in the mild, jivey accent of Libya's only flower child. Gaddafi understood all I was saying, as he occasionally revealed by smiling a sardonic smile. Now and again, he suddenly spoke English in that odd, dulcet voice, like the chirp of a pea in a whistle.

Where does one ever begin? I asked, if having visited Beaconsfield, whether Gaddafi thought he would ever go to Britain again?

He shrugged his thin shoulders.

'*Momkn*' he said.

'Maybe,' Sadeg translated.

One's great fear at such times is of asking a question so hopelessly inept that the interview terminates after only minutes, bringing ignominy worse than if it had never taken place. I tried to forestall this by mentioning the Koran, which I had been reading spasmodically. At various points, I had found exhortations to compassion and

15

brotherly love much as they appear in the New Testament. Through Sadeg, I asked Gaddafi how that squared with his avowed ambition to wipe Israel from the face of the earth.

Gaddafi chirruped for a moment or two. Sadeg leaned forward, the way I had seen him do while listening to Crosby, Stills and Nash.

'The Koran is not a book sent to one religion, like the Christian religion or the Jewish religion,' Sadeg murmured in translation. 'It is a book sent to all men. The Koran understands the nature of the human heart. It orders us to use violence when it is needed, and peace when it is needed.'

I began to frame a question about the Arab leader whom Gaddafi most loathed and had sworn to eliminate by every possible and implausible means.

'King Hussein . . .'

'Of Jordan?' Gaddafi inquired archly in English. There was a titter from the others.

'How can you be enemies when his grandfather, Sherif Hussein, is a hero to all Muslims?'

'This Hussein's grandfather *did* lead a revolution in Mecca,' Sadeg translated. 'He should be known, not for what his grandfather did but for what he has done. He claims to be of the Hashemite royal family. I read in history that, in a battle, many of these Hashemites were extinguished, and their servants took their name. This Hussein may be descended from the Hashemite family. He may be descended from some of these servants.'

It was probably as close as one could ever get to a Muslim fanatic indulging in sheer bitchiness.

I was framing my next question when, to my unutterable dismay, Gaddafi got to his feet. So it was all over. What had I done? How would I live it down? Gaddafi, however, merely led the others to the far end of the room, where a muezzin had become audible, echoing through the deeper sunset. Each of them took a mat, knelt down and said their evening prayers. Then Gaddafi led them back to the interview.

He stayed there, fidgeting, tapping, for almost two hours more. I asked him if he could really carry out his current scheme to amalgamate Libya with Egypt, despite the latter's seeming inclination to find an accommodation with Israel. Though rumour had it that President Sadat was being driven to distraction by his turbulent younger ally, Gaddafi insisted that a merger between two such dissimilar Arab states was absolutely possible.

'In your country,' Sadeg translated, 'you have the English people and the Scottish people. The Scottish are the only ones in your island who can pronounce the letter r. I have been in Britain and I saw how they were treated. You make jokes about them. You consider them as Bedouin.'

'Do you dislike the British?'

'I do not dislike the British. I dislike certain accidents in the history of the British.'

It was time to take the plunge.

'Did you mean your promise to send arms to the IRA?'

'The whole world is sending arms to the Jews,' Sadeg translated.

'Is that the same thing?'

'It is the same. Both are armies in occupation.'

'Did you mean you intended to send weapons into Ireland?'

The long sickle-shaped dimples opened in Gaddafi's cheeks.

'In Arabic, there is no verb. No past and no present. In Arabic, one can simply say "Arms for Ireland".'

Sadeg leaned forward and murmured. 'I don't want to press him any further on this.'

So it continued after the sky had flushed to darkness outside: that odd little chirruping Arabic voice shadowed by Sadeg's murmurous one as Gaddafi's pencil drummed on his chair-arm, his two subordinates sat motionless before the unresponsive microphones and the boy secretary scribbled symbols frantically on his steno-pad. We heard the whole incantation of hate against the nation Gaddafi sought to annihilate while, at the same time, never recognising its existence. Relays of fruit juice were brought in, in little glasses decorated with nursery bluebird patterns. Colin Jones crawled about the floor, his two Nikons buzzing and snapping.

In the second hour, the atmosphere became noticeably friendlier.

'Do you dream?' I asked.

'Why do you ask me this?' Gaddafi said in English.

'I've heard that you dream of becoming as great as President Nasser.'

He smiled and returned to Arabic.

'I dream very little,' Sadeg translated.

'What are your pleasures?'

'Talking with relatives,' Sadeg translated. 'Talking with friends. Going into the country. Praying. Reading the Koran. The Koran gives me . . .' Here Sadeg paused and leaned forward. 'This is what we say in Arabic – soul comfort. Because when you say "Al-lah", your soul will settle down in peace.'

'Are you afraid of anything?'

'No. When you fear God, you cannot fear anything else.'

I admit to feeling oddly moved, as well as light-headed with relief, when the interview broke up at last, and Gaddafi dwindled with his aides down to the other end of the conference room. As we learned soon afterwards, there had, indeed, been a move within the Revolutionary Command Council to demote him from his supreme, enigmatic power. Gaddafi had responded by going into the desert to sulk like Achilles, in a somewhat blacker tent, until all Libya seethed

17

with stories that he was dead, and his colleagues, fearing a popular uprising, had no choice but to beg him to return. The opposition had repented. Major Jalloud, his fractious deputy in the Council, had reaffirmed eternal allegience.

We drove from the barracks and dropped Sadeg at the tourist village. 'Didn't Muammar Gaddafi sit still and have his picture taken like a good boy?' Sadeg chuckled, melting into the darkness. We never saw or heard from him again.

Early the next afternoon, my bedside telephone rang. A British voice of extreme cordiality said, 'Hullo – it's Bob here.'

'Bob?'

'British Embassy.'

It was the Second Secretary (Press) transformed into overweening cordiality. He asked if Colin and I would have lunch with him beside the ambassador's swimming pool. The meal featured cold chicken from Tupperware containers, fine wines from the diplomatic pouch and a barely concealed official interrogation about our meeting with Gaddafi.

Euphoric as we were, and slightly drunk, we began to tease the Second Secretary. I told him that Gaddafi had been wearing yellow shoes. 'Imitation crocodile, they looked like,' Colin added. How would we assess his physical and mental condition? I said that the Colonel had looked 'tubercular'. Colin said he'd played with a ballpoint with a chewed-up end. All pretty childish stuff. We discovered later from a girl at the embassy that everything we said – down to the yellow imitation crocodile shoes – had been solemnly communicated to the Foreign Office in London and to our other embassies throughout the Middle East as hot, new anti-Gaddafi intelligence.

My consuming worry was that Gaddafi might repent of the inter-view and devise some way to confiscate the tape recording and notes I had made. Our Yugoslavian friend in the Libyan news agency hinted that our hotel rooms might be bugged. 'Don't do *anything* against the law,' he warned us. 'Don't drink. Don't even have a little traffic accident.'

His words were prophetic. On our last day in Libya, an Indian woman backed her Mercedes into our hired Volkswagen and slightly dented one wing. No one else witnessed the incident. But we still had to return the damaged car and risk complications that, at best, might delay our escape; at worst, consign us to a Libyan jail, our world scoop haplessly snatched from us.

The solution was easy, if rather unkind. We waited outside the car hire office until the manager went to lunch, then we returned the dented Volkswagen firmly to the very small boy he had left in charge.

At Tripoli airport, our confiscated bottles of brandy were returned to us intact. I remembered how, when I had dropped some money at the Leptis Magna Roman site, it had been found by two Libyans and left for me at the curator's office. I reflected that, from Mr Gwil onward, Libya had not treated me with anything other than total honesty.

I breathed a sigh of relief – that proved premature – as the aircraft taxied off and our stewardess's voice began, 'Welcome aboard this Libyan Arab Airlines flight from Tripoli to London . . .'

There was a commotion at the rear of the cabin. A man lurched up the gangway, shouting, 'London! I'm not going to London! I want to go to Rome!'

Our stewardess spoke to the pilot. In a moment, the plane had wheeled round and was taxiing back to let the Rome passenger get off.

I doubt whether British Airways or Pan Am would have done as much. It is one of several reasons why I still think rather fondly of Gaddafi's Libya.

1984

The Most Powerful Woman
in the World

The avenue is deserted. It joins the circle, which unites five more empty avenues, and runs off silent again into fog. New Delhi has excluded India somehow; for all the teeming horizons there is a ghostliness here about its heart. Cyclists go in pairs, their cockades slowly nodding with the pedals. A cow undulates patiently from the mist. Only when a car enters the circle, and misses a cyclist, and the cyclist skims beside the cow, is it still India unmistakably: still almost collision.

The queue forms beside her garden wall. In the pale air, colour so suddenly intervenes that people are barely distinguishable amid the vividness of their ceremonial clothes. Gujerati women, gold shaking at their ears, carry on silver-hooped wrists babies with eyes enlarged to damp coals by the black *kajal*. Sikh boys, delicate half-faces from their holy Amritsar; a sheet of Hariana brahmins tied up in mufflers; schoolgirls with shy garlands; a professor, a Chief Minister, a madman. They are admitted to her garden, and like flowers, cover a lawn tender with the sun of New Delhi winter.

She does not flow along like smart Indian ladies. From an inner garden, she approaches with that purposeful and tripping gait which suggests slippers rather down-at-heel. The sari, muted red, the shawl, muted green, appear almost dull against the sea of enraptured colour awaiting her: no jubilant oils dress her hair with its broad plume of grey rising from the forehead. Only gradually do you perceive her knack of wearing grey hair as if it is a jewel.

This ritual of *darshan* – greeting – takes place every morning that Indira Gandhi is in her capital. It was the institution, however, of her father Jawaharlal Nehru. In those days, before he began to disintegrate, Nehru seemed to glitter with the freedom that had just been won. Government could almost be served by looking upon him. Nehru always wore a fresh rose. Nehru's daughter does not. Her beauty, like her power, is preserved with ice. For each bed of worshippers on the grass, her *namaste*, the peace of folded hands, is slightly made; the smile is very slight; her cheek has the impatient click of a lozenge in it, for her voice is not strong.

Each morning brings its numerous personal petitions. Here is a lawyer from Allahabad, the Prime Minister's own home town, with a whispered intrigue against the judges of Uttar Pradesh. Here is a farmer from Bihar. His land does not yield him sufficient: with that typical Indian candour, he desires a loan. The *swami* in the tangerine robe proffers a cheque of bright pink for the National Defence Fund. During the war with Pakistan, a small bank was set up on the lawn to receive all the contributions. Now she reaches the delegation from Hariana. All rise, muffled in their scarves. They have a grievance against the Chief Minister of their state. The depth of it, as of much else that is Indian, can be expressed only with English. 'Backdoor', 'Underhand', 'Equal opportunity', and other impassioned anachronisms float out with their mother tongue. It is the song of corruption which, under Mrs Gandhi – as always in India – remains constant as the colourlessness of the sky.

But chiefly, they wish to stare. So an Indian must salute all that is new, very strong or holy. For Nehru's daughter, for the daughter who grew greater than her father, the stare has the intensity of plucking fingers. It is as if she can sense the comparison. She gives the shawl a twitch, hiding her plump, flawless neck. She hurries forward leaving the Hariana delegation to be hustled from the garden, as all previous petitioners have been hustled, still smiling their curtailed compliments. The carpet of people is rolled swiftly up after her, leaving only some scarlet rose petals, only its empty mats, behind.

She has given India nearly enough to eat. Nehru could not claim as much, nor the Mahatma himself. But to weigh the power of Indira Gandhi even in that accomplishment is to imply some variance in it. To the people who come into her garden, to the 580 million other people beyond, it has grown in seven years to some element, like sky or gold or mud, or into some fresh deity. Her enemies, no less than her admirers, liken her to the *Trimurti,* the Hindu concept of God as three. She is Brahma, creator of a new India, Vishnu, preserver of its democracy, and Siva the destroyer, as she destroyed the army of Pakistan.

She is stronger than ever Nehru was. The two-thirds majority commanded since 1970 by her Congress Party in parliament, make her a dictator such as her father never dreamed of becoming. Nehru at the height of his power could not have signed a treaty with Russia as his daughter, almost irritably, did, nor could he so ferociously have waged war on Pakistan. It is power of the purest sort, deprecated with every gesture, increased with reluctance and unwillingly wielded; worn always as an absence of jewellery. Her voice expresses that power by its very smallness. At a soft sound, like a cat's spring, the clamour of the whole subcontinent ceases.

Outside the garden wall, however, beyond the capital's empty avenues and its Edwardian acropolis of pink, India seemed far from pacified that morning. Two-thirds lay under the drought which is foretold, if not anticipated, one year in three. Thirty universities were closed because of student agitation. There was riot and murder in Andhra Pradesh and, among the Nagas, only a delicate peace. Floods had made 30,000 homeless in Madras. A Goa hospital was suffering a plague of snakes the largest of which a resident encountered 'as he was retiring, asleep under the bedsheet'. Another of India's Victorian express trains had crashed at night mail speed, killing a boy and girl, and – as might have happened in Staffordshire in the 1850s – an official of the railway company had presented £25 to each of their families.

And all was as it had been yesterday. The specific of some crisis is more readily understood, perhaps, than illimitable normality; than India's multiplying moment. New skyscrapers climb on wooden skeletons up towards the sun. The plains roll outward, restless, frying, piling mud on mud. No conclusion may be drawn from them without interruption just as when you try to say something to an Indian he always interrupts. There is drought; yet no greater luxuriance of water could be imagined than spouting from the wheeled drums or shimmering among green leaves in a pan-seller's bucket. There is hunger; even as variety of food through the bazaars exhausts selection – food in piles, pyramids, cushions, like silver, basketwork, snow, or like dirt picked out with limes. The moment trembles with the almost collision, with patience expressed in a shout of impatience. The very sky seems only a white reflection of their eyes.

To feel for one Indian, I suggested, surely must drain the heart of all feeling.

'No,' Mrs Gandhi said, 'I don't see why. I think that the only reason I'm able to survive this with equanimity is that I'm just myself, regardless of the situation in the country. I know the condition of the people. There's nothing I can see that I don't know about already. It's not that you don't feel it but – it's like a nurse and illness. You see it in perspective.'

Her emotions are assuredly not her father's. Each mannerism is almost self-consciously a reaction from some luminous style of his, and from the years which she devoted to serving him as housekeeper and hostess. In leadership's outward flourish she is so little practised as to seem sullen. Her speeches are flat and passionless, though they have improved since a despairing Indian journalist nicknamed her *Goongi Gudiya* – Dumb Doll. There are wells of Nehru charm; a lovely shy girl smile which she can operate, an opponent says, 'like a steam radiator'. Then the eyes in their heavy orbs can drain of interest until her face is as empty as the long avenues. She has not even Nehru's human flashes of temper. 'If Jawaharlal flared up at you,' the journalist said, 'he could kiss you in the next five minutes. If she flares up at you, that's it. You've had it.'

Mrs Gandhi's government is pledged to the slogan *Garibi Hatao* – Abolish Poverty. For a principle it is breathtaking indeed. Not to improve, for mere improvement cannot show upon the surface of the land. People with hands beckoning to their mouths still wear the dreadful, bright, supplicant beggar smiles. People still lie along the streets in the nightly rehearsal for death. To make war on dimensions, past as well as present, to defeat not abnormality but that infinite commonplace, to scout the very will of the Gods is what Mrs Gandhi has promised to do.

The style is typical. By that utterance of supreme autocracy, a rebellion is somehow ushered in. It is a no more than typical Indian paradox that, in her absolute power, she can still seem somehow an anti-establishment figure: she will make it, the inference is, in spite of politicians.

Politics anywhere tend to be obstruction of the truth by voices. One is nevertheless unprepared for the distance at which Indian politics can exist from everyday concerns. Thus, it is in the nature of all political parties that, no sooner formed, they must divide; must wriggle and split again until dissenting sub-strata of philosophy threaten to choke the country like traffic. To study the papers in the last state elections was to witness a peep show both brutal and absurd – returning officers 'belaboured', pistols discharged, objects thrown down wells, menaces, bribes, sheer terrorism; a dance of hieroglyphics, which the papers never explain; a tumult as of men all through the subcontinent throwing their shoes about.

Even her skin seems ivoried to be free of all party colouration. 'The value of this' – Mrs Gandhi indicated the morning ceremony in her garden – 'is not just that I see a few people. The value is that I am available to anybody who wants to see me. Now yesterday morning, one who came is one of our most vehement opponents. In fact, obnoxiously so – he uses very bad language. He's a Member of Parliament, of the Jana Sangh party. He came up to me in the House and said, "My family is here and they very much want to see you," and so he brought his family to see me.

'Now I am not basically interested in politics at all. I don't enjoy what most people mean by politics – manoeuvring and things like that, I simply can't stand it. I don't think it's a nice thing to be at all, what the world thinks of as an "adroit politician". If you can manage better than others, it's because you can see things clearer.'

Such tasteful aloofness is born, however, not of abstinence from the political arts, but of surpassing excellence in them all. That plume in her hair is an outcrop of cold steel. The Congress Party, of Nehru,

23

of Independence itself, is also broken in two. She broke it, to assume the power she now has. In all the futile fragments of her opposition, the saddest is that in which the elders of the Nehru Congress are put out to grass. One such was Morarji Desai, formerly her Deputy Prime Minister. He, with others, procured her succession to Lal Badahur Shastri in the belief that she could be moulded, and then discovered her poinard in his back. 'She is not a Communist,' Desai says feelingly, 'she is a Fascist.'

Nobody can withstand her. All they may do – Communist parties, Socialist parties, all the bits of parties – is to join hands with Desai and the fag-end of the old Congress, hoping to create some obstruction or another. The President of India in his pink palace is but a theory of constitutional supremacy. The state governments, with isolated and ill-starred exceptions, belong to her. She personally controls the Atomic Energy department and the Information ministry, giving her total control of All India – or 'All-Indira' – Radio.

There are times when the whole huge weight of her power seemed exercised in one small scowling grudge. When, a few years ago, she deprived India's princes of their British Raj pensions, the gesture did not seem inappropriate: what seems odd was her remark about the princes to parliament. 'They are going to have to be men,' she said.

Some of her critics charge that, through Indira, the whole chemistry of India has been upset. By her wilfulness, she upsets that tolerance – that almost collision. If there was filth before, it was redressed by India's world-wide trade. Trade, under Mrs Gandhi, does not prosper. She decrees self-sufficiency of manufacture for a land unable yet to produce a satisfactory razor-blade. The Indian black market is almost like a new subcontinent. One might sometimes suppose the whole race to be all one sidelong currency-tout, beginning with an offer of Parsi girls, concluding with an entreaty for any products by Gillette.

In India, under Indira, corruption is deemed ordinary as sun, silk or crows; political life clamours with outrage over it each day of the week; the Parliament corridors, murmur about it is as incessantly and nervily as the pigeons coo among the Lutyens cupolas.

Corruption is not proved, of course, by allegations. What gives credence to it is a sigh; that note of resignation in so many voices otherwise unrelated. Morarji Desai, from his ascetic's cell, says there is corruption, so does Piloo Mody from his beautiful study. A vast, cloaked man followed by two red setters, Mody is attempting to revive the Swatantra, the party of free enterprise. He also owns *March of the Nation*, the closest which a craven and dehumanised Press can muster to *Private Eye*. But ordinary malpractice is scarcely news any more. 'This is how it works,' Mody said. 'I am an official.

I pick up the phone and say "You want that contract for two hundred spindles. It will cost you sixty thousand rupees." Next morning, the money is there. It is all going on under her beautiful nose.'

Her private life is exemplary in lack of adornment. The royally plain things furnish it; fresh flowers, a flat gold watch, an Afghan hound, a Siamese cat. In the fight for Independence, she says, she learned not to rely on possessions. She has given even her bungalow to the state; for the dispossessed maharajahs, therefore, Mrs Gandhi's eyes are quite dry. 'We're allowing them to keep a palace each' – her voice thickened in scorn – 'with *huge* grounds. They've all got business, practically. And I don't have anywhere to live when I'm not Prime Minister. I have to make some arrangement.'

Her existence as a leader is solitary; though perhaps no more so than it was as a leader's child. She has much of Nehru's passionate intellect. She read history at Oxford and studied under the great Bengali poet, Tagore. She used to write and to dance. Her position now, admitting no weakness, can admit no inclination to either, no favourite god or even book.

The past hangs on her. It is even an increase of her beauty; she has that air of trapped youth which an unhappy childhood can occasionally bestow. During the Independence struggle, her father was imprisoned by the British for a total of nine years: her grandfather, her frail but indomitable mother, were often both away from the house. That bleakness in her eyes, at moments of boredom or mistrust, somehow reveals the child she was: the long-limbed, argumentative girl whose confidences were few, whose letters from her father were destined to become works of popular history.

'I had a lot of love in the sense that I was sure my parents loved me, but there was no opportunity for them to show it. I felt protective towards them. I miss my father,' she added. 'And my mother.' Her mother died in 1936.

She spent a generation alone with Nehru. Though her political career in that time advanced to presidency of the Congress Party, it was as his aide, hostess and housekeeper that she chiefly existed. Her single-minded devotion to her father eventually caused the break-up of her marriage to Feroze Gandhi, a journalist and MP (unrelated to the Mahatma).

'Were they happy years with Nehru?'

'No, certainly not.'

'Why?'

'Well – I don't know why. Every woman has to keep house and you do it the best you can. I won't say they were unhappy years or anything like that. Just not very special.' Her eyes, which had emptied, grew attentive again. 'Now, we got Freedom in that time. Now that was a very special period.'

'How do you think of Nehru?'

'He was a good companion.'

'Would you like to be married again?'

'No,' she said.

'Don't the crowds worry you?'

'No, I like crowds. I was brought up in crowds. When I was a very very small girl I used to make way for my mother and father. I like crowds and I can handle them.'

'Were you often in danger in the years of Freedom movement?'

'I've been involved in lathi-charges many times. It's a long stick. You can have your head broken.'

'Were you frightened?'

'At times like that, you're so *angry* . . .'

'Did that make you hate the British?'

'Well, you know, we never thought of them as English men and women. This was Mahatma Gandhi's teaching – we are fighting against a theory, not against individuals. At the height of the Non-Co-operation Movement, any Englishman could walk along the street and not be harmed.'

'Are you ever afraid now?'

'I'm sure everybody fears something. I don't fear anything to do with my person – being physically hurt or dying.'

'How can you endure the strain?'

'I'm able to be calm or empty my mind in the midst of a crowd, in the midst of anything. I can be making a speech and my mind is not there.'

'–but do you feel exhilaration as well as strain?'

Her eyes looked mocking.

'Well – *obviously*. But it's very difficult to separate the two. Because I think that, if you feel deeply enough, whether it's happiness or sorrow, it's the same thing. It's the range in between that one lives with most of the time.'

'What are your faults?'

'Me? I don't know.' She smiled her beautiful, her oblique smile. 'I have plenty.' She disclaims, however, the Nehru irritation. 'It's very seldom. It just comes and goes.'

'Do you laugh?'

'I think it's much nicer to laugh than to weep. I like my humour dry.'

'How do you revive?'

'I have a bath,' she said. 'I have an Indian bath, you know. I have a very nice brass container which keeps the water, and then you pour it over you. You sit outside.'

'You can't doze in that kind of bath.'

26

'No,' she said. 'I don't like dozing.'

It is the concomitant of continuous power that it must always be rumoured to be weakening. Nevertheless, at the end of 1972, Mrs Gandhi could observe from her eyrie an unusually firm pattern of unfavourable omens. While her majority prevailed, the glow had dimmed which was on it after the war with Pakistan. In Parliament she had lost the support of the main Communist Party. (India, characteristically, has two.) In Maharashtara, Bihar and Rajasthan, the familiar herald-marks had brought on the inevitable dust-dry epidemic. It was famine, however much her tame newspapers might call its victims 'the scarcity-hit'.

The state elections were over, reaffirming her authority in a burst of almost supernatural scandal. Voters by the million, so it was claimed, had been bribed or intimidated; more than one returning-officer went manifestly in terror of his life; a certain Police Chief actually left town for fear that the incorrect candidate would triumph. The public outcry was such as to cause even Mrs Gandhi to admit a need in the Congress Party for 'organisational changes'.

But her Opposition, its spirits reviving with the drought, whispered of choicer vexations. Often it has been foretold that, just as Mrs Gandhi split the Congress, so it must one day split again underneath her. According to Desai and Piloo Mody, and to A. B. Vajpayee of the Jana Sangh, the People's Party, that disintegration had begun. She could no longer control those Right and Left forces which she had previously kept in balance. Dissent was espied in the states, drifting even up to her Cabinet of loyal Kashmiri brahmins. Uproar was growing, too, over the involvement of her elder son, Sanjay, in shady business ventures with overt Prime Ministerial patronage. It was rumoured there was a bold young element ready to utter its rebellion to her face, at the Plenary Session in December.

'She told me the other day,' said A. B. Vajpayee, 'that, with the student troubles, with the economic condition, things are getting worse.'

A white rabbit played round his feet as he spoke.

'She's quite clever, the lady,' added A. B. Vajpayee. 'She is e-smart. She is e-sly. But she knows nothing of economics, and that will be her downfall.

Calcutta, venue of the 74th Plenary Session of the Congress Party, and of that possible insurrection, stands in such a fog of cindered filth as to suggest that all mankind has agreed at once to burn potatoes. Through the archways of its former pomp, even India seems to exaggerate: the trams are beaten shapeless as by huge

27

children; wall-slogans have the eternity of cave art; the pimps are more assiduous, the beggars more charmed to see you, their limbs more neatly and imaginatively severed by the begging syndicates. Calcutta awes even Indians. Yet curiously it is at present more peaceable than Delhi and, compared with Andhra Pradesh, it is tranquil.

The conference is beckoned from the city, through pavilions of green, white and orange, to Bidhan Nagar – Salt Lake – and makes its new city there. Upon the dry plain is deposited a dressing, fresh yet perennial, of stalls, sweets, glittering flies, frying batter, cane-bottomed chairs, Series E. Morris motor cars, tin fences, trampled leaves and silhouetted urine: it thrusts with faces as of living avenues, crossing, re-crossing, faces and shirts, each wearing a rosette in Indira Gandhi's image but intent above all upon the errand of its own survival.

The proceedings take place in a barn. It is possibly a marquee, yet resembles a huge silo; for its ground is covered with straw; animal-pens mark its distinctions of place; a mealy dusk, like a mill's, hangs round the chandeliers. The only truly ceremonial figures to be beheld are the party's high officials, elevated on a coloured dais: a frieze of linen laps as pure and clean as white marble. In the centre sits the Congress president S. D. Sharma. He bears a strong likeness to the late Oliver Hardy. The front rows consist of senior MPs, reclining on sheets. Lesser delegates, penned up behind wooden barriers, strain to see and hear through the mealy gloaming.

Speeches are delivered to the President's left, through a microphone with a decorative halo round it. The halo bears the words 'Chicago Radio'. One speaker leaves, another arrives; once more 'implement' and 'mobilise' and other inedible words of theory float from the mother tongue. It is the platform itself which is the event, like a picnic or like snow. For much of the time, the Prime Minister is not there. She re-enters from behind. With her sari of green silk, the plump white picture breaks. She wears a headscarf. She settles on to her knees among them.

'The party is an old corpse in a new coffin!' Dissent assumes sudden outline on the grainy air. 'Bogus elections – bogus voters . . .' The renegade countenance is obscured by 'Chicago Radio'. ' . . . have resulted in a bogus party! – expenses of one candidate would put even an unscrupulous man to shame!' The Congress Party is taxed with failing to honour pledges made at its last session, and with offering war and drought for alibis. The party is flayed, voice by voice, a little above her shrouded and reposeful head. This is not, however, disintegration: nothing Indian can be destroyed by mere speech. Through the fieriest peroration, the huge silo buzzes, laughs, hawks, stirs upon its straw, occupies itself with that time-honoured national pursuit of attending to nobody but your neighbour.

A rebellion might succeed by infiltration of the central party mechanism, the Congress Working Committee. Of its twenty-one seats, ten are open to election at the Plenary Session. Suppose, for instance, that Chandra Shekher could carry his discontent into that enclave? He is leaving the platform now; a strong, young, scowling bearded man. In the packed white linen of the retiring-room, he is seized by a supporter whose glistening face is daubed with orange betel nut juice.

'There's blood in him!' the supporter cries. 'Blood!'

On the second day, the Prime Minister speaks.

The clatter stills; the roads become empty but for the ranks of khaki police. This is the realisation of her power: this sudden silence. The barn, packed motionless, drives dust of a moving herd up to the chandeliers.

She appeals for party unity.

Journalists turn away, grimacing, in their enclosure. Some murmur *Goongi Gudiya* again: Dumb Doll. The roads grow restless again. New Congress, old or whichever Congress, the party machine flaps on like sandals towards the camp-fires of night, concerned, as all the land is, to feed itself, to maintain itself in almost collision. The beggars are already asleep, silhouetted against the lights of the ornamental fountains.

Her power, inaudible as a cat's spring, is exercised overnight.

The next morning, twenty-one members of the Congress Working Committee are proclaimed. For ten elected seats, thirty-five candidates have filed valid papers but twenty-five of them have been 'persuaded to withdraw'. The elected ten are for her, Chandra Shekher among them. Ten more are nominated in accord with her wish. The President is her personal appointee.

The President enters and passes, with the bare feet gravely before the penned assembly. It smells as appetising as a mill. In front of the dais a red and white female choir, whose handbags and shoes are massed nearby, sing a patriotic hymn with the assistance of a lone violin. The President ascends to his place of authority. She enters from behind, as if to create no stir. Her sari is white, or is it gold? In this line of the great, only she has no belly. The hymn abates. They squat: she kneels with hands folded in her lap, looking out upon her majority like a Bloomsbury girl by the fire. Power has kept her chin firm and young.

1973

Thank You, Plum

'Dear Mr Wodehouse,' I wrote without much hope in March, 1969.
'I have read every one of your books but *A Prefect's Uncle. The
Sunday Times Magazine* has asked me to write a profile of you . . .'
The first statement was untrue, the second only half true. I had at
the time read scarcely any of P. G. Wodehouse's 100-odd books.
The bit about *A Prefect's Uncle,* one of his early school stories, was
merely cunning verisimilitude. I had cajoled the assignment as an
excuse to get to New York in order to travel back on the new QE2.
It was a desire admittedly implanted by a Wodehouse novel, *The
Luck of the Bodkins.* I hoped to enter my cabin like Monty Bodkin
and find the mirror decorated with a lipstick inscription reading 'Hi,
sweetie!'

Wodehouse replied within two weeks, typing the letter himself on
a machine symbolically ancient yet robust.

> *Remsenburg,*
> *New York 11960*
>
> Dear Mr Norman,
> *That's fine. I will look forward to giving you lunch any day after
> your arrival. The slight catch is that our maid comes only on Monday,
> Wednesday and Saturday and on the other days, we go to the inn at
> Westhampton Beach about six miles from here. If you come by train,
> the station is Speonk and we would meet you there.*
> *Do you really want* A Prefect's Uncle? *It is a pretty bad book. But
> I can give you a copy.*
> *Yours sincerely,*
> *P. G. Wodehouse*

My research was, as always in those days, precipitate. The chief sub
editor told me what P. G. stood for (Pelham Grenville). From a
Portobello Road stall I bought a cardboard carton full of Wodehouse
in the familiar orange or red bindings, end-papered with plaudits
from long defunct journals, often endorsed by printers' notes like
'17th impression, completing 85,250 copies'. The chief sub lent me
his copy of Richard Usborne's *Wodehouse at Work*, then – and now
– the only comprehensive biographical study. Wodehouse, despite

30

his enduring public, despite the acclaim of Orwell, Belloc and Evelyn Waugh, had somehow missed recognition as a 'major' literary presence. Even ardent fans, knowing him only as a benign, smudgy face on the back of a Penguin book, presumed him long dead. He was 87, living in Long Island, still writing novels at the rate of one per year.

In Richard Usborne's book I found helpful appendices of Wodehouse images and similes, which showed me what I had been missing all in a rush. 'The Duke's moustache was rising and falling like seaweed on an ebb tide . . .' 'Jeeves coughed that cough of his which sounds like a sheep clearing its throat on a distant mountainside . . .' 'Corky spun round like an adagio dancer who has been caught watering the cat's milk . . .' 'He felt like a man who has been chasing rainbows and one of them has turned round and bitten him in the leg . . .'

There were also Wodehouse's letters to an old school friend, Bill Townend, later published as the book *Performing Flea*. (Sean O'Casey had sneeringly called Wodehouse 'English Literature's performing flea'.) The book includes diaries kept by Wodehouse of his capture by the Germans in France in 1940, his subsequent internment and the ill-advised but harmless radio broadcasts he made over the Nazi network. Ample vindication came later from Orwell, Evelyn Waugh, Malcolm Muggeridge and many others. Even so, I found, there were booksellers who deliberately marked down Wodehouse first editions out of a belief that he ought to have stood trial as a war criminal. It explained why Wodehouse at 87 had received no public honour; why this creator of a world timelessly and dottily English had, since 1947, lived in America virtually in exile.

The train from Pennsylvania Central to Speonk, Long Island, dawdled all morning round a circuit of dreary towns with names like Jamaica and Barbados. At Speonk I caught a bus, wedged in the back seat next to a fat woman eating cookies. She had finished the packet by the time we reached Remsenburg, a lone bus stop set down amid the forests of deepest Long Island. Wodehouse, his wife Bunny and an old black, grey-muzzled labrador stood waiting for me on the grass verge.

The face was as benign, as smudgy, as on all those Penguin books. What I had not expected was height. Wodehouse at 87 still stood well over six feet tall. He wore a flowered shirt; big, heavy brogue shoes; a cavernous tweed jacket he himself might have likened to 'something run up by Omar the Tent-maker'. His voice had a fruity timbre peculiar to middle-class Englishmen born before 1900, it was – as Wodehouse said of Beach the butler's voice – 'like good, sound port made audible'.

Bunny Wodehouse, a little, skittery woman of 84, drove us away in a wide American car that seemed partly to owe its impetus to hitting, then bouncing off the roadside verges. She called Wodehouse 'Plum' or 'Plummy' – the usual thing if you have been christened Pelham. She buzzed and fluttered around him in a way that plainly had not changed, nor been asked to, since their courtship before the Great War. Once when she was waving her arm at him, Wodehouse seized it, kissed her hand and cried, 'Bunny – you're *crazy!*'

This being their maid's day off, we lunched at the inn at Westhampton Beach. Prompted by my chief sub editor, I had bought Wodehouse a copy of W. S. Gilbert's *Bab Ballads,* the comic verses he mentions so often in his letters to Bill Townend. 'Oh, I say–' Wodehouse beamed, as if we were study mates at Wrykin, '*Thanks*'. Amid the mock-Swiss decor, over the elongated plates of American seafood, he began to talk about meeting Gilbert at a lunch party in 1900. The young Wodehouse committed the solecism of laughing before the famous librettist had quite finished a funny story he was telling. 'I didn't think Gilbert as a person had very much humour,' Wodehouse said. 'He used to pretend there was a certain sort of wasp that followed him around while he was playing croquet. I always thought he was rather a small joke man.'

After lunch, Bunny Wodehouse drove us, slowly and rebound-ingly, to a home for stray cats which Plum and she had endowed soon after moving to Long Island. The big, slow man scooped up a tiny kitten, shutting his eyes with pleasure as its paw clubbed his freckled head. I said – quite genuinely now – that I'd loved his short story about Webster, the ecclesiastical cat corrupted by a sojourn among wild young Chelsea artists. 'Yes – I was reading that again the other day,' Wodehouse said. 'It's *jolly* good, isn't it.'

Their home was a bungalow at the end of a grassy track named Basket Neck Lane. According to Wodehouse, he had never planned to settle in so remote a place. He and Bunny had come out from New York one day in 1952 to see his old friend and collaborator, Guy Bolton. Wodehouse and Bolton went for a walk and when they returned, Bunny said: 'I've just bought a house'. Bunny, it appeared, always used to choose their homes that way, in Mayfair, Manhattan or Le Touquet. Nor had 17 years at Remsenburg dispelled her restlessness. House guests like Malcolm Muggeridge have described waking before dawn to hear Bunny moving round like Lady Macbeth, polishing table tops, even shifting furniture.

The house was full of rather impersonal sun parlours with French windows leading to lawns and the encroaching woods. Three cats and two further dogs greeted our arrival. Bunny at once picked up and began to use a little roller gadget for removing crumbs from tablecloths and sofa-arms. 'You're not to be too long with Plummy now,' she told me. 'His serial starts at four, and he's got to have his sleep before the Boltons arrive.'

I followed Wodehouse's ambling form into the little garden study where he worked and, apparently, slept. It was occupied by a table, a chair, a typewriter, a dish of pipes, a manuscript in progress and a ceiling-high bookcase. An inner recess contained a child-sized bed with a yellow counterpane. Wodehouse peered along the shelves, took out a copy of *A Prefect's Uncle* and wrote inside it, 'To Philip Norman, all the best from P. G. Wodehouse'. He had been talking about an obscure early novel, *The Swoop,* published when he was still a Fleet Street gossip columnist. He discovered a copy – a pristine 1910 paperback – autographed it and handed it to me. My eyes hovered covetously on a first edition of *Psmith in the City,* beautifully stamped in dark blue and gold. Wodehouse reached out for it, then hesitated. 'Oh – I think I've got just that one copy,' he said apologetically.

The manuscript in progress was to be a new Blandings Castle novel. Wodehouse, in his later years, had forsaken Blandings, and Bertie Wooster and Jeeves, for light comedies about young Englishmen in New York or American gangsters at large in an England imperfectly remembered, where people drank cocktails in pubs and asked for tea with 'cream'. Blandings Castle, however, seemed as immune from anachronism as from all the perils of modern aristocratic life. Evelyn Waugh rightly observed that Blandings was Wodehouse's Garden of Eden. 'This one's called *A Pelican At Blandings,*' Wodehouse said. 'It's going to be *awfully* good. Lady Constance is away, and so Emsworth doesn't have to change for dinner. He's having it on a tray in the library – leg of lamb and roly poly pudding with lots of jam.'

Interviews with Wodehouse in the twenties describe him occupying just such small, modest rooms, variations on the school studies at his beloved Dulwich. 'I don't mind where I am,' he said, 'as long as the work's going right.' I asked if he laughed out loud much at what he wrote. 'Not much,' he said. 'When you're alone, you don't do much laughing.'

We returned to the main house. Bunny had gone upstairs to an evidently separate bedroom. Wodehouse settled himself in an armchair, a black cat on his knees, and began pushing tobacco with his forefinger into his pipe. I sat forward ardently and began to interview him. We started with his school-days and his apprenticeship in the Hongkong and Shanghai Bank. My questions, imbued with the anxiety of spanning 87 years and 20 immortal characters, were less than transfixing, I saw. Wodehouse patted the cat on his lap. His eyelids drooped. Then he sat up suddenly, looked out of the window and exclaimed: 'Ooh, look! A pheasant!'

I still had not reached the Great War when Bunny Wodehouse

came back, carrying a tea tray in a haphazard style reminiscent of her car driving. Tea over, she shooed Plummy upstairs to her room where, every afternoon before his sleep, he watched a dire American TV soap opera called *Edge of Night*. I asked if I might stay and continue the interview after Plummy woke up. Bunny seized the crumb-roller again and pushed it agitatedly round the sofa-arms. 'There's no time,' she said. 'We've got Guy and Virginia Bolton coming for dinner at seven.' With shamelessness possible only at 25, I said how much I had always longed to meet Guy Bolton. 'Oh, very well,' Bunny said. 'You can stay – on one condition. You must promise to decant the wine.'

While P. G. Wodehouse slept and his wife rattled around on frenetic, unspecific errands, I stood in their kitchen, wondering how best to transfer the two bottles of Mateus sparkling rosé into the cut glass decanter which Bunny had handed me. In the end, I poured it through a kitchen sieve, removing much of the sparkle thereby.

Then for an hour, as the woods changed colour, I talked to Plum's sister-in-law, Helen, a comfortable-looking, much less elderly woman who had appeared in one of the sun parlours. It was 'Nella' who really kept house at Remsenburg, procuring Plum's favourite biscuits and fruit cake and the English kippers he still liked for breakfast. She told me how difficult it was to get domestic staff nowadays and how their casual manner grated on a household which once employed almost as many servants as Blandings Castle. 'We had one maid who, when Plum and Bunny had guests, used to put her head round the door and say, "If you want anything else, just holler".'

The Boltons arrived at seven, to be given cocktails by Bunny, using a special glass-frosting gadget which covered person as well as glass with a fine, cold film. Guy Bolton, a handsome, laconic man in his eighties, collaborated with Wodehouse on dozens of musical comedies for Jerome Kern, Sigmund Romberg, Florenz Ziegfeld and George and Ira Gershwin. Between 1927 and 1929, together or singly, Bolton and Wodehouse had 19 opening nights on Broadway. Virginia Bolton had formerly been married to the man who discovered Rin Tin Tin, the wonder dog. 'That dog was on six thousand dollars a week,' Bolton said. '– *and* a percentage,' his wife added.

For dinner we had leg of lamb, Lord Emsworth's favourite, accompanied by semi-sparkling Mateus rosé. The talk turned to butlers Wodehouse had studied for his prototype Jeeves – W. S. Gilbert's butler; various aunts' butlers; the *two* butlers employed by Edgar Wallace, one for day, one for night, so that – as Wodehouse observed at the time – 'you can never go into Wallace's house and not find buttling going on.' Guy Bolton spoke sadly of George

Gershwin's death, aged 35, from a brain tumour, not long after finishing a game of golf with him and Wodehouse. 'In fact, a golf ball hit him on the head while we were playing. We've always wondered whether that had anything to do with it.'

At midnight, I stood in pitch darkness on a length of railway track which the Boltons had assured me was Speonk station. My train did not reach Penn Central until almost 4 a.m. Sitting with assorted drunks and a nervous black ticket inspector, who started to read *The Swoop*, about Clarence Chugwater the boy scout who saves Edwardian England from invasion while everyone else is watching the Test match. Suddenly, with a pang of remorse, I realised something. I had forgotten to ask Wodehouse how it felt to be an exile.

Three days later, I entered my stateroom on the QE2. There was no 'Hi Sweetie!' written in lipstick on the mirror. There was, however, a note, mystifyingly recommending me to pick up my 'Bon voyage gift' from the purser. It was a box of cigars with a card inside: 'Happy crossing, from Plum and Bunny Wodehouse'.

My profile, 'Thank You, Plum' was published the following July. Wodehouse wrote to me that it was 'a magnificent job' (it wasn't) and that I had been correct in portraying him as Lord Emsworth, 'for he is, of course, drawn from me. I wasn't very keen on the photograph', the letter continued, 'but I suppose I'm at the age where it's impossible to have a photograph of me that looks like anything on earth.' He added, just as he used to in letters to Bill Townend: 'I've done two chapters of my new novel but am finding it as great a sweat as ever . . . Even now I never have any confidence in a character until he or she has played at least one good scene . . .'

A small controversy arose from my report that Wodehouse had disliked Ian Carmichael's playing of Bertie Wooster in the BBC television series. Tart words were exchanged by the series' producer and me in *The Sunday Times* letters column. I learnt subsequently that Wodehouse had written to Ian Carmichael, assuring Carmichael that he'd said nothing of the kind. The correspondence was closed by a letter to me from Dennis Price, who played Jeeves in the series, gracefully conceding my accusation that he had a 'pasty' face.

Soon afterwards, I acquired a job lot of the *Strand Magazine*, Wodehouse's main British fiction outlet from 1915 to the Second World War. Jeeves and Bertie, Lord Emsworth, Archie, Ukridge, Mr Mulliner and The Oldest Member thronged the pages year after year in short stories or novel serials, usually with the Gilbert Wilkinson illustrations that Wodehouse himself considered definitive. In the mid-twenties, writing for the *Strand* here and the *Saturday Evening Post* in America, not to mention his Broadway shows and

Hollywood scriptwriting, he must easily have grossed £100,000 a year. Presumably Bunny spent it as fast as Plummy earned it.

There was also the mystery of why a man so quintessentially child-like himself should have remained childless. Bunny, by a former marriage, had a daughter, Leonora, whom Wodehouse adored and who died before she was 40 after a routine surgical operation. One senses her presence in Wodehouse heroines, Stiffy Byng and Bobbie Wickham, with their boyish bobs and freckles and their penchant for getting chaps into scrapes.

Meanwhile, we kept up an intermittent correspondence. I sent him books by Henry Cecil, his favourite mystery writer, and, on his 88th birthday, a card decorated with dried autumn leaves. Still shameless, I sent him my first novel, *Slip on a Fat Lady,* for which he instantly provided the quotation 'extremely original and very funny'. Would that it had been either. He was, he said, 'plugging along' with the new book eventually published as *A Pelican At Blandings.* ' . . . my work has suffered lately from having to watch a series of terrifically exciting baseball games on television. Excuse illegibility. I am writing this in the "thinking chair" with Blackie the cat on my knees . . .'

His 90th birthday was marked by a new Jeeves and Bertie story, *Much Obliged, Jeeves,* a copy of which came in to *The Sunday Times* for possible serialisation. It was simply a photocopy of the manuscript Wodehouse had typed himself, with corrections in a hand still neatly firm. In *Private Eye,* Auberon Waugh castigated the Heath Government for failing to commemorate Wodehouse's 90th year with the knighthood that would, surely, have removed, once and for all, any lingering impression of banishment.

It was not to happen until Labour returned to power: in the 1975 New Year Honours. I wrote to congratulate Wodehouse, uncertain – as others must have been – whether he really would want to become 'Sir Pelham'. I remembered the feeling about Pelham Grenville which had inspired Bertie Wooster to remark: 'There's some raw work pulled at the font these days, Jeeves'.

He sent me a postcard dated 20 January 1975. He was 94 and hard at work on a new Lord Emsworth book, *Sunset at Blandings,* destined to be unfinished when he died on 14 February 1975.

Dear Philip,
Many thanks for your letter. Much obliged, as Jeeves would say.
> *Yours ever,*
>> *Plum*

>>> 1981

In a Ticklish Spot with
Bessie and Dicon

It was 2 a.m. in the elegant, multi-galleried vestibule of the Hotel Osterreichhof, Salzburg. Richard Burton's voice rose to the topmost gallery, charged with its inimitable Celtic passion. 'Look, baby,' he shouted. 'Don't mess with me. Either use that gun or put it away.'

Sitting in a circle of high-backed armchairs, we made a curious group. Burton and his childhood friend Brook Williams, son of Emlyn, wore Nazi officers uniform which they had not changed after the day's filming of *Where Eagles Dare*. I wore the thin jacket I had brought from London, unprepared for snow in Austria in December. Next to me was the young assistant director in whose care Burton had been left for the evening. And opposite us sat a heavy-chinned American, pointing a fat, black object which was, indeed, a revolver.

That day in 1967 had already been an exotic one for a 24-year-old, lately covering inquests in Newcastle-upon-Tyne and now given the job of interviewing Burton and Taylor for the *Sunday Times Magazine*. I had spent it mainly carrying Elizabeth Taylor's Pekinese around the corridors of an Alpine castle and, at intervals, being fed cheese and chocolate biscuits from her plump little Italian Mama fingers. Ever and again, as we waited, high up in the castle keep, Taylor would look down into the courtyard below where Burton was filming, and would squeal excitedly, 'Hello *Boofy!*'

She called him 'Dicon', he called her 'Bessie' and even then, before their first divorce, the repartee between them was crisp. Burton would refer pointedly to Taylor's developing stoutness, not helped by her purple roll-neck sweater, heavy mink cape and pale blue stretch ski-pants. At one point while he was talking to me, he indicated the World's Greatest Sex Goddess and murmured: 'Look. Isn't that belly disgusting?'

Because I was young, I suppose, and manifestly harmless, I was included in the circle of dressers, makeup men and bodyguards which surrounded Burton after each take, reviving him with mulled wine and listening to his rich, incessant monologue. After one scene, he was trying to remember the words of the Radio Luxembourg 'Ovaltineys' song. After another, he told us his brother Ivor had once accidentally left £2 million worth of Taylor diamonds in a paper bag under a parked car in Switzerland, and had gone back 10 minutes later to find them still there. Most of his stories, however, began with the words, 'When I was on Broadway, playing Hamlet . . .'

After filming ended for the day, I was put into a long black Cadillac alone with Elizabeth Taylor to continue the interview which, with one thing and another, I had not yet nerved myself to begin. As the car gushed down through the mountains, I began to be afflicted by my old enemy, travel sickness. I tried to combat it by keeping my eyes fixed on the road ahead. The smell of the Pekinese also began to be oppressive. 'I'm sorry I'm not looking at you,' I said wanly to Elizabeth Taylor. 'If I do, I'm afraid I'll be sick . . .' Too late I realised what I had said. But she simply threw back her head and guffawed.

The Hotel Osterreichhof had been taken over by the film unit. Everywhere I looked, I saw German field grey, high collars, Iron Crosses, jackboots and the faces of villains familiar from every British war film from *Cockleshell Heroes* to *The Dam Busters*. The maddest-looking one, with the blackest circles round his eyes, turned out to be a veteran bore who would not stop talking about his car. Anton Diffring, the most familiar of them all, looked just as cold and remorseless sipping a Martini as he did when shooting Robert Beatty in *Albert RN*.

At dinner, Burton, in his own Nazi uniform, became almost incoherent with laughter over the line from P. G. Wodehouse about someone having 'spun round like an adagio dancer caught watering the cat's milk'. He and Brook Williams then discussed a stage musical they had always wanted to co-produce, entitled *The Bad Taste Revue*. It would end, Burton said, with a musical skit about the mass murderer John Reginald Halliday Christie. 'We'd have all the headless corpses coming out of the cupboards for a finale, and singing a song called Cupboard Love.'

After dinner, Taylor got up, slung her mink round her shoulders and said sharply 'Come on, Dicon'. Without further ado, she began to climb the long staircase, through the galleries. Burton, however, lurched into an armchair and called for more brandy. Brook Williams, the young assistant director and I lurched into armchairs around him. This was where we suddenly found ourselves joined by a man pointing a gun.

He appeared, suddenly and inexplicably from among the neighbouring armchairs, pulled up a low stool up next to Burton and introduced himself. Burton nodded briefly and looked in the other direction. The man remained there, smiling ingratiatingly. Burton decided to ignore him, and embarked on another story about being on Broadway, playing Hamlet.

'You and I, Mr Burton, ought to get on well,' the man on the footstool interrupted. 'I'm from Wales, too. I'm a *Selt*.'

Burton looked steadily at him.

'No,' he said. '*I'm* a *Selt*. You're a sunt.'

I was drunk myself, and found the next few seconds rather hard to follow. The man had apparently got the joke, for he was now behind Brook Williams' armchair, gripping Williams tightly round the throat. Burton was on his feet, yelling 'Don't mess with me, baby.' That was when the man put his hand inside his coat and drew out the plump, black object I have described.

The gun did not seem to alarm Burton, who remained in a boxer's stance, inviting its owner either to use it or put it away. In the armchair next to mine, the young assistant director entrusted with his safety, watched with inarticulate horror. I remember wondering vaguely what would happen if the gun did go off and, inconsequentially, whether Burton's film stand-in was the same as his understudy.

Glancing up to the topmost gallery, I saw Elizabeth Taylor on her way furiously downstairs. No one else seemed to notice her until she had arrived in the lobby. Barefoot, clutching a leather coat around her scarlet chiffon nightdress, she hissed, 'Richard! Will you come to bed! Your voice is echoing all over this hotel!'

The man with the gun stopped pointing it at Burton, stuck it awkwardly inside his jacket again and advanced on Taylor, grinning weakly as if unsure if it would be proper to shake her hand.

'Forgive me . . .' he stammered. 'I'm sorry. I didn't know . . .'

'I'm *sure* you didn't know,' Taylor said caustically, pushing him and his gun aside. '*Richard!*' she repeated. 'Will you come up to bed this instant!'

Burton replied something ungracious in Welsh.

'Come on, Dicon!'

Burton spat out more Welsh. Taylor spat out Welsh in reply. The man with the gun stood in between them as they argued in Welsh, looking utterly star-struck.

Taylor was the first to return to English. 'Come up now,' she said. 'Or don't bother to, ever again.' With that, clutching her leather coat around her, she stomped upstairs, all the way to the topmost gallery.

Again, the action became difficult to follow. I remember that the man with the gun took it out again and ordered Burton, Brook Williams, the assistant director and me to sit together on a low bench while – presumably – he decided our fate. I remember the young assistant director kneeling before him, literally praying '*Please* put that gun away . . .' Then, all of a sudden, the man with the gun had disappeared. I learned later that he had gone to the gents, first ordering us not to move. Two Welsh Nazi officers, an assistant director and I all scattered for separate elevators.

Next morning, when I awoke under my unfamiliar quilt, I lay for some time, wondering whether it had really happened. I decided that it had, but that it was of little use in the profile *The Sunday*

Times Magazine expected me to write. I thought that, on the whole, I ought to say nothing about it.

Standing in the lobby later, I watched the Burtons leave for France with their dressers, their hair stylists, their bodyguards and their Pekinese. As she swept past, Elizabeth Taylor saw me and – goodness knows why, but it was nice of her – gave me a kiss on the cheek. Burton looked wrecked within his white sideburns. He winked at me and murmured out of the corner of his mouth, 'It was real. It was a Webley Four-Eighty.'

1984

Under the Anxious Guns

Children form the spearhead battalion. Fully briefed and equipped with posies, they are marched through the woods, down to a field as safe and empty as only a hundred hidden sharpshooters can make it. This will be the Queen's first sight of Northern Ireland when she lands by helicopter – children, deployed along the path with clean hair streaming, and clean white socks and happy faces, and the boughs of fir trees, coolly tossing and nodding above.

Among the trees lies Hillsborough Castle, an historic British stronghold made infinitely stronger, then masked with a placidity considered soothing to Royal eyes. Yet all that one sees in the quiet estate evokes its counterpart in the city shut out a dozen miles away. To see the militiamen, so upright and proud, is to remember frightened soldiers in Belfast, pushing and rubbing themselves like cats around the corner of a street. To see lawns and bushes and white walls is to think of cars burnt out after a 'quiet' night in Falls Road, or empty houses in Short Strand, blind with grey concrete, their disease made more pitiful by the flutter of life in a shop still open.

Life in Belfast is a fearful and endless guessing game. Last week they were trying even harder to outguess the tacticians in murder. The Queen's visit would coincide with the sixth anniversary of internment. Was that governmental lunacy, or was it perhaps a stroke of inscrutable genius? The previous week there had been car bomb hoaxes all over the city. Did that mean the Provisional IRA was running short of explosives? Or did it mean the air was being deliberately cleared, as gravel is raked over, for some large atrocity to suit the occasion?

The anniversary of internment passed off with only cars burning and dustbin lids beaten in the early hours. A woman from Donegall Road, on the edge of the Republican ghetto, said it made her ashamed of her sex to hear what Catholic girls were shouting at the soldiers.

She was serving in a coffee shop, empty at mid-morning on the eve of the Queen's arrival. The whole city centre, where the Queen could not go, had a dead and empty and apprehensive smell. A boy petrol-bomber had been shot by the army, and a boy soldier had

41

died in ceremonial retaliation. Only one soldier. In Belfast terms it was a sign that moderation was being exercised. But to what ultimate, excessive purpose?

Long investigation had produced 2,500 people fit to be near the Queen at Hillsborough Castle. Parted from their cars a mile away, they were taken to Hillsborough by coach, frisked in the old court-house and permitted, at last, to resemble garden party guests, the men stiff-collared, their wives steadying unfamiliar hats. All that the scene lacked was the society photographer who might have identified them. People in Ulster have died for much less than attending a garden party.

Under the anxious guns, the sedate ritual has begun. But for the army marquees it could be happening anywhere, with a placid, welcoming land outside. The Queen's turquoise coat, so defiant of camouflage, seems designed to add to the fantasy that we are in a place far from Ulster. That the face ever smiling under the turquoise hat seems tired is the least of anyones worries today. Did the Queen have a say in the measure of her risk or in the measure of her freedom from risk?

Other people watched, by special concession, outside the gates to the castle drive. The gates are tall and dazzling white, as thickly ornate as pastrycook's piping. The people stood on kitchen steps, on picnic furniture or velvet-coloured dining-room chairs, or sat on shoulders, clinging to spears and patterns in the ironwork. An elderly woman perched doggedly at the rounded end of a bus. They were rewarded, at length, with a glimpse of royal turquoise at a window. They turned away with the sort of faces you see in Ulster – faces robbed of small hope. A female reporter on an English liberal newspaper felt this to be fitting treatment for Hillsborough people. 'They're just a lot of Proddys,' she said disdainfully.

Big Highland soldiers stood about the lawns, eating ice cream with tiny spoons. And in Belfast, round the entrance to Castle Road, the bricks flew like meteorite showers as the army halted the Provisional Sinn Fein protest march; drunks zigzagged helplessly among the combatants and old ladies walked arm in arm beneath sniper fire. A young British officer fell with children like a swarm of birds on him, kicking him, then fleeing from the still figure on the road.

Later, at Palace Barracks, the television was on in the officers' mess. The riot sequence, when it came, had the bland unreality of a film about wildlife. 'There's David,' his friends said as the officer lay hidden among kicks. In the tall, twilit mess, the subalterns might have been students at some agricultural college. Another joined them, running and dishevelled. A company commander had just been shot in the chest by a sniper. He had an even chance of surviving the night.

Meanwhile on the Royal yacht, the Queen was meeting the leaders of the Peace Movement, whose first anniversary had attracted little attention otherwise. Then *Britannia* sailed floodlit up the North Antrim coast. Motorists flashed their lights at her from the shore.

People were more thinly-spread the next day when the Queen went to the New University of Ulster at Coleraine, far to the north. Chosen for its position in Ulster's quietest zone, the arid campus still presented vast possibilities to an IRA assassin. In the previous fortnight, with army and police positions already established, two bombs on long fuses had been discovered in the university buildings. On the morning of the visit, two further bomb warnings were received by telex. Army disposal squads were out again, like husky teams, among the hundreds of specially planted white-washed trees that gave screening from sniper-fire.

Anxiety, increased by Prince Andrew's arrival, was made most manifest among officials of the Northern Ireland Office, some of whom were reduced by their duties almost to the point of tearfulness. Luckier correspondents in the 600-strong press party were issued with photostat passes on which only the scribbled amendments might have deterred a forger. The rest were placed in a compound during the Queen's speech and instructed not to eat or drink in view of the adjoining Royal garden party enclosure.

Events here seemed to derive sterility from the college concrete. The Queen looked at a cake and unveiled a plaque and attended a lunch which excluded the Rev Ian Paisley – he made his own waves by slapping police inspectors on the back and honking 'C'mere Mother!' to a shorter, laggardly wife. There was a youth festival – its displays omitting the youthful pastime of brick-throwing – and music from the Royal Ulster Constabulary band. Nowadays, this band seldom plays at anything other than funerals. Meanwhile, a pistol and five rounds of ammunition had been dug up on the campus perimeter. As the programme neared its end, most of the 850 policemen on duty emerged from cover and stood stiffly among the artificial saplings.

Her helicopter had scarcely swung out of sight when the sirens came cawing across the still meadows. It was not the bomb – that did not explode for several hours more. It was a squad of ambulances rushing to the 40 people stricken with food poisoning at the youth festival. As yet, the IRA had caused fewer casualties than the caterers.

1977

The World of Charles Atlas

Charles Atlas puffs out his cheeks and chest like an ebony bullfrog; at 76 he is sensationally fit and brown against the leg veins and coffee-coloured straw hats of people his age who go to West Palm Beach, Florida, to die. He swims in the salt-water pool on South Ocean Boulevard or runs by himself along the endless, booming beaches. When his wife died four years ago Atlas almost gave up his body-building business. 'I thought "maybe I'll join a monastery. Devote myself to study and give the monks or brothers some callisthenic exercises; spend my life like that".'

But he is still at such a peak that Nature seems to be holding him there at pistol-point: cantering at the edge of the surf, eating vastly, talking in his earnest mixture of Palermo and the Bronx. Although his bathroom cabinet is filled with patent medicines, Oil of Camphor, Bromo Seltzer, Pepto Bismol for the wind, the most severe illness he ever has is the sniffles occasionally, after exercise. 'My one habit is chewing – helps to keep the wrinkles off my neck.' And he has discovered, to his distress, that he is still highly attractive to the blue-rinsed, dollar-rinsed widows of Miami. 'I've had proposals, sure. Here and in New York City. One of these ladies wanted me to go to Europe with her as her companion. "Forget the business," she said, "forget your pupils. How much you want? Fifty thousand?"

'I went to an engagement party over there in Miami and it was full of these widows, the poorest worth maybe ten million dollars. Suddenly this pair of arms grabs me and a voice says: "Boy! What I could do to *you!*" And then three of them took me upstairs. They say they want to show me something; I thought it was a picture or a work of art. That wasn't it in the least. "Ladies!" I said to them, "but ladies, I am seventy-six years old!" '

That kind of thing has troubled Atlas deeply ever since the 1920s and the foundation of his muscles-by-post empire; since the days when he did, in all probability, own the finest physique in front of a plate camera. Impotent fathers often approached him to sire perfect babies in exchange for money. One of the offers was two thousand dollars. 'And I said No, I could not betray my dear wife, not for ten thousand. I was a virgin man until I met my dear wife. As a young boy I used to have these nosebleeds and the doctor told my mother

44

"sometimes the body makes a little too much blood; when he is married that will take care of it." I never went with any other girl. When I was married the nosebleeds stopped.'

He *exists*. Three generations of the back pages of pulp comics have carried his advertisements; a strong man with a big smile that seems to touch the innermost nerves of flabbiness and cigarette addiction; a keg of muscle, legs planted wide apart in hot, white sand, asking only a five-day trial to turn a sprat into a tiger-man; a big brother abruptly serious as he stands above the strip cartoon, the enduring parable of the runt on the beach who had sand kicked in his face. Those who believed in his existence have always been assailed by rumour – that Atlas was helpless in a wheelchair, for example. Or that the muscles of his 17-inch neck became so big that they choked him to death.

He is still in effective control of one of the world's original and most successful mail-order businesses, with the smallest overheads. And he promises, 'I'm going to live for a long, long time.' Despite the old-fashioned big drum manner of his advertisements, all the exclamation marks, slogans ('You Too Can Have a Body Like Mine') and skilful, unsubtle imagery suggestive of chiselling brawn from weak fluid, the vital thing is that Atlas's system of exercises *does* improve the body; at least, it does so given supreme patience, application and stamina on the part of the student. The Atlas Dynamic Tension method is simply the basis of isometric exercise, the matching of one muscle with another of equal force. Mr Atlas had the good fortune to copyright the name before science approved officially of the method.

A commonwealth of moral teaching goes with it. 'Live clean, think clean and don't go to burlesque shows.' The advice, like the big smile, is timeless. Until quite recently the Atlas course of lessons warned against listening to too much Jazz or Ragtime and urged 'Banish all evil thoughts from your mind.' Atlas himself believes passionately in a world of golden innocence created by muscles judiciously applied. 'Nobody picks on a strong man. England and America . . . we must keep ourselves strong. I do the course myself, religiously – Sundays, every day. Now if I don't keep myself well, how can I take care my pupils? They say, "Ah what the Hell that guy! He's a has-been." '

He is careful to do most of his exercises when the other residents of his apartment block, faltering in Bermuda shorts, have gone indoors for the evening. 'If they ask me for advice, I tell them, don't overdo it. What the Hell, they my brothers and sisters. I'm not showing off by this. It's my religion. We are created in God's image and God doesn't wanna be a weakling. Jesus held a tree on his shoulders. Sure, he dropped it a coupla times but nevertheless he carried it. He was pretty well-built, Jesus Christ.'

45

Atlas feels very close to his students: up to 45,000 new ones a year, a third of them from the United Kingdom. They are said to have included Rocky Marciano, the heavyweight boxing champion; and Joe DiMaggio, the baseball hero; even a member of the British Royal Family who wanted to avoid having sand kicked in his face. Atlas says this was the Duke of York, which would mean George VI: Charles Roman, his partner and the source of the brilliant slogans, says it wasn't – 'He's getting his dooks mixed up.'

Letter-writing machines in the New York office controlled by Roman deal with the bulk of the student queries, easily classified under headings like Bad Breath or Dirty Acts. Questions of a more intimate nature are dealt with by the strong man personally. He has intervened over many a fallen young girl and seen her properly married. 'And young fellows – some things they won't even tell their fathers, they ask Mr Atlas. They won't even tell the local physician. They get to maybe sixteen, seventeen years old and they get gonorrhoea so they write to Mr Atlas: "I dunno what to do, I'm despondent." I say "Tell your father. He was a young man like you one time. Maybe he was in the same category."'

'I make a fine living. I do as good as any lawyer or judge, but I'm very economical.' He has an apartment on Long Island, as well as the one in Florida where he spends the winter by himself. On the verandah, where the surf wind blows the brocade drapes out, he keeps a fixed bicycle. Otherwise, his surroundings are strangely impersonal – brocade chairs, a huge TV set he seldom watches, a huge, gold-brocaded, lonely-looking bed.

His past feats of strength included lying on a bed of 700 nails, eating a banana as three men stood on his chest (women fainted), pulling a railcar or string of automobiles or – his speciality – bending a 100-pennyweight steel spike into a U. 'I haven't tried that feat of strength for many years now. I wonder if I still could do it. Only I don't wanna strain myself. We lost a lot of strong men that way – Hackenschmidt, Eugene Sandow.' At the same time his physique was once so classically perfect that sculptors competed for his services as a model: the Palm Beach apartment has a bronze statue of him in his forties, still with a 32-inch waist. Atlas liked modelling and is sorry he missed Michelangelo. 'Yeah, he was a fine artist, it's too bad he's passed away.'

In Florida he seemed a little isolated, but his telephone rings constantly. When it is not bodybuilding students it may be members of the Mafia, who have a boom town in Miami, recalling that Atlas was born Angelo Siciliano and asking him to parties. This is no new vexation either. In the 1930s he had to decline a Mafia credit card. In the 1920s, when he was staying in Chicago, Al Capone sent him a case of champagne and an invitation to dinner. Atlas pretended to have a bad cold and the hit-man sent to fetch him was most sympathetic. It happened again recently; a social call from a noted Mafioso. 'This guy drove over to see me. I thought he was a movie star. Soft hat, thirty-dollar shirt – and two guns he had.'

His advertisements are correct in claiming that Mr Atlas himself started life as 'a seven-stone weakling'. Brought to New York from Italy by his mother when he was 10, he was considered too sickly even to ride a bicycle. They lived on Front Street, Brooklyn, and he was kicked around by Irish bullies. After school he worked in a ladies' pocketbook factory where the superintendent, a Mr Welch, could pick him up with one hand. 'He was six foot seven. "Charles," he said to me, "you got a lotta talent." He was the only man I ever met who looked good with whiskers, although I wore some myself in later years to distinguish me from F. D. Roosevelt. Some of the framers at the factory didn't like it when Mr Welch put me over them. One day he picks up a chair in his hand and remarks "Anyone who harms this boy I'll beat his brains out."

'When I'm still at school I went with some of the children that had been well-behaved to a museum. And I sat down amazed at the statues of Diana, Apollo, Hercules, Atlas. I asked Mr Davenport, the teacher: "Mr Davenport, did these guys really live? Do you think a skinny kid like me could get like that?" Mr Davenport took me to the YMCA but I thought "Jeez, how am I going to afford the fees?" So I started to go and do a lot of stuff in my own room. I saw the cat in the morning doing all kindsa tricks – stretching back and forth. I thought maybe I'll go to the zoo and see what the lions and tigers do.

'I got up very early as I had to walk all the way up to the Bronx, Prospect Park – it was five cents car fare then. And here comes a lion out of his cage, stretching himself and rolling and yawning. The tigers did the same thing. I thought I should apply this to the human being. So I hit on this idea of pitting each muscle of the body against the other. The beauty of this is that, the stronger you grow, the more weight you can add. These muscles whirl around, you know.

'Next thing I know is, Jeez, I'm looking good. I changed my name from Siciliano to Atlas after the Atlas Hotel in Rockaway, Long Island. In nineteen-twenty I was on Coney Island. I had bought myself a nice green bathing suit which was cut to show my chest muscles. Suddenly a guy starts going after me, following and watching me. His name was Mr Arthur Lee; he had talent you know, good sculptor.' Subsequently Atlas posed for works including Energy in Repose, Patriotism (outside the headquarters of the Chicago Elks), and the water centaur in the fountain outside the State Capitol of Missouri. 'I posed for Mr McManus, who was carving The Arms of Civic Virtue and for Mrs Payne Whitney who was sculpting the soldiers, sailors and marines for the Fifth Avenue Triumphal Arch. Mrs Whitney had a son. His name was Sonny Whitney, and she says

47

to me "Mr Atlas, can you do anything for my boy? He's so lean."
I says "Now what you do is, to build him up, give him a good
breakfast every morning, like I have. Two soft-boiled eggs, big glass
of milk, a coupla slices of home-wheat toast and I'll give him some
callisthenics."'

He always had a deep horror of violence. One of the studios he
used to visit had a handyman who baited Atlas for two years before
he turned. 'I said "Listen. I'm gonna be sorry for what I do to you,
you're gonna go to the hospital, I'm gonna *hoit* you."' He clouted
the man and felt sick for two weeks afterwards. Thereafter he made
a point of apologising when people trod on his toe. He was a dandy,
in spats and expensive suits, carrying a cane with a dog's head
handle on which the jaws used to move. The only violent incident he
remembers after he hit the studio porter was on the subway, when
Atlas offered his seat to an old lady and a big truck-driver sat there
first. He picked the trucker up and shook him gently. 'There's an
old saying, the tongue is mightier than the sword. I reasoned with
him. You can do anything if you got a good lingo.'

He then became a Coney Island strong man. 'I worked for a Mr
Henry Brill who had the finest show on Surf Avenue. I bought myself
a pair of tights and a leopard skin and I had to ballyhoo outside,
myself: "Come see Atlas do feats of strength, see the magician, see
the boxing midgets." I did a kind of muscle dance. There were many
thousands of people there; nevertheless some men were stronger
than me. Mr Henry Brill would offer five hundred dollars to anyone
that could bend the railroad spike like me. One night – I think it
was in Binghamtown, New York – this fellow got up, and by golly
the platform creaked you know. He was an Indian weighing two
hundred and fifty pounds. He thought it was a straw to bend. But
he stopped bending halfway and the metal cooled: he couldn't do it.
When I bent it in a U this guy took me on his shoulders. A lotta
people kept those spikes for paperweights.'

He won the title The World's Most Perfectly Developed Man in
1921. The competition was sponsored by *Physical Culture* magazine
whose owner, Atlas says, still owes him nine dollars. 'These young
fellows today think all you need is muscle to get in the magazines.
In those days you hadda be perfect inside and out.' Atlas took the
cash prize of 1,000 dollars instead of a test to play the first screen
Tarzan. He began his course in a tentative way: it was almost a
disaster, thanks to his habit of giving lessons away for nothing.

Charles Roman – 'a very very fine young fellow' – intervened. He
was an advertising executive, newly-graduated and assigned to make
something of the Atlas account: he went on the strong man's payroll
in 1929 and the punch-lines he subsequently composed have become
engraved on the medicine ball of history. The story of the man who
had sand kicked in his face has passed into the literature. Roman,

however, is very modest: 'The success of that strip simply demonstrates that the public is the best judge of a slogan. They invented the line "Quit Kicking Sand In Our Faces". Originally the caption to that strip was "The Insult That Made a Man out of Mack".'

Roman, as slim as a fox, does the Atlas exercises himself every day. He is nearing 60 but has kept a 32-inch waist. He runs the paper warehouse side of the business: America and most of the world's land masses are handled from his office in East 32nd Street, New York, where the foyer, with its ersatz Greek columns and statues of Atlas, looks rather like a long-lost stage set for *Oedipus*. This office and the one in London, established in 1936, are staffed mainly by middle-aged women. They are just big stationery stores – endless shelves of the Atlas course in the seven languages in which it appears. The best customers are New Zealand and Latin America, where a former Peruvian War Minister is now among those who won't have sand kicked in his face: the only serious failure was in Africa, where Roman tried to give the course away to natives, an altruistic gesture he now much regrets. The method is entirely postal; no salesmen. 'I can't think of who it might not suit,' Roman says, 'unless somebody isn't well. It's for everyone. Another profitable market that springs to mind is Newcastle-upon-Tyne.'

Though the beach-bully in the strip cartoon no longer wears a chest-high swimming costume, Roman has kept the advertisements virtually the same as they were long before the last war: Atlas at his oldest, in white trunks, is about 44: some of the shots, in a leotard, date back to about 1930. Atlas himself would like to have some current snapshots printed – 'show that an old guy of seventy-six can still be in good shape' – but Roman firmly disagrees with that. 'To whiten his hair would not be meaningful because he is almost a living trademark.' Roman also refuses to print the more ecstatic testimonials from Atlas students, because he thinks no one would believe them.

A further legend persists: that Atlas will eat only fish, prunes and gruelly substances. In the warm bath evening at Palm Beach he put a gigantic dinner away, his teeth champing on most of a London broil of steak, hot biscuits, mashed potato and asparagus, in which he praised the sulphur. He refused salt, warning that it could cause impotence. He drank root beer and diet cola and a single glass of skim milk to keep his waist trim – once he would consume six quarts of milk a day. If he catches a chill he treats it with hot water and lemon juice, a remedy to which he was introduced by Dr Harvey Kellogg, health expert and offshoot of the cornflake family. 'Fine gentleman, Doctor Kellogg. He lived to be ninety-two. He dressed all in white and took a snow bath every day: fine gentleman.'

The true measure of his fitness was his ability to talk for eight hours practically without stopping: he guffawed and preached and banged my knee with his fist. He has an extraordinary memory for names. He truly did once have sand kicked in his face, on Coney Island: the girl he was with was called Bella Marr. Outside, the first pink sheets of a Florida storm lit up the palms on the boulevard before the wind howled them down into bow-shapes. The ancients in the apartment building called in their poodles. Atlas stood out in the downpour to say goodbye. 'I don't mind the rain,' he said. 'It does my hair good.

'Some people say I should get married again; some say I should marry Miss Lucas' [a friend of his daughter who was helping him close the apartment for the summer]. 'I think I'll read a few books on astronomy and try to look into the future. I don't know what it will hold, but without Jesus Christ you can do very little,' he said. 'I've had a clean life: it couldn't have been any cleaner.'

1969

The Candidate

'To begin with,' Edward Kennedy said, 'I want to ask all of you some questions; and just so I'll get it straight, I'm going to note 'em down.'

He groped in his pocket uneasily. Alone on the gymnasium floor he faced a student audience packed high against him in the grandstand. His collar chafed against the gymnasium colours of segmented violet and blue.

'How many of you think that each of these headings I'm going to mention is the most important? Number one, the resumed bombing in Cambodia.'

Some arms were raised in the stand, but not many. Cambodia could evince little anguish, it appeared, in the saplings and springtime of Massachusetts.

'Number two,' Kennedy said, 'inflation; economic and tax reform.'

All arms were raised violently.

'Three – ah – Watergate.'

A titter but a modest show of arms.

'Let me ask you this,' Kennedy said. 'How many out there think that more people in your school are using drugs today than used 'em five years ago? Now we'll leave out marijuana for the moment.'

'Ooh'; in disappointment.

He grinned, as he suddenly can. 'It's all right, we'll come back to it,' he promised.

'How many,' he continued, 'believe that the United States ought to make do with an all-volunteer army?'

Everybody thought this.

'How about no army at all?' a girl's voice said.

Kennedy was nonplussed. 'And . . . and how many of you are going to volunteer?'

He scanned the reply.

'Eight gals, four guys.' He fidgeted slightly inside his shirt-collar as the joke approached. ' . . . I can see why the guys are volunteering!'

It was a time in American politics when distinction was measured according to one's distance from the seat of power. In Washington

51

lawyers engaged lawyers: in Times Square, New York, the crowds, the yellow cabs scurried back and forth as above them, in letters of light, marched the information that America for some years past had been entrusted to the government of small-time crooks.

Somehow it was satisfactory that, while the Watergate scandal grew to its delicious crisis, Edward Kennedy should be thus pastorally engaged in his constituency of Massachusetts: addressing colleges, nodding at small town Fire Chiefs, campaigning a little superfluously across a countryside of spinneys and ponds which will remain secure to him for as long as he bears his name. What is more satisfactory than to see one's sins eclipsed by larger sins?

The chance of death draws back a little. Since the 1968 Presidential election, the threats received at his Senate office have dwindled to a desultory handful each week. So it may continue until newspapers and television renew their insistence that, because his two brothers were murdered, he also must be. Americans do not think: they react. For the present his only shield is a dented sports car, shadowing his black limo' among the saplings, beside the ponds. And death, in any case, seems less possible in Massachusetts. 'We've been over this landscape so many times,' he said. 'My father, my brothers, myself. The country's almost like an extension of the family.'

'Do you think much about being killed?'

'Secret Service cover was extended to me through the Presidential campaign. I was grateful for that,' he said, 'for the sake of my mother, my children. You'd be a fool not to acknowledge that a – ah – possibility was there.'

'Are you brave?'

He gave his sudden grin.

'Hell, no.'

In the photographs, standing together, they are almost indistinguishable. A President, an almost President, their kid brother: three shining busbies of hair, three wide-awake smiles, three white ties and waistcoats from a lost age of rich boys. Time has accelerated since then, of course, shifting gear ever more rapidly towards the dark ages; yet some events, because they lie outside even Man's illogic, can never retreat into the past. Dallas seems only a second ago, and the shape of Bobby's mouth. If so for us, how much more for the one who is left?

His conversation is full of allusions to his lost brothers.

'My brother President Kennedy used to say "A rising tide lifts all the boats." '

'My brother Bobby joined the parade that day . . .'

'My brother Bobby said . . .'

'You must miss both of them still.'

He stared into the open briefcase on his knee.

'I do.'

He is curiously unmarked. His face, with its easy blush, has an Irish ingenuousness that has survived his disgrace for cheating at Harvard; survived his broken back; survived even Mary Jo Kopechne's death at Chappaquiddick which very nearly assassinated him in scandal. Nor is he so much like his brothers, save in the pictures. On his own he seems to have different eyes, different hair; a frame bulky yet somehow unfinished, like his nephew Joe's; an air not of residual agony so much as constant reluctance, as if he endures political life with barely assumed good grace, because someone told him he must.

The inheritor, he remains in some odd way the cadet. At a ceremony in the Kennedy Centre for the Performing Arts, in memory of John, journalistic awards are made in memory of Bobby. And Bobby's sons are growing up fast, with clerical grey suits and gold manes of hair. Joe Jnr is as tall as his uncle now; the Kennedy voice through the crowds saying 'Nice to see yuh' belongs to Joe. Thus the master of ceremonies acknowledges the heads of the clan:

'Rose' – a wide hat, an undefeated smile.

'Ethel' – sunburned arms.

'–and Teddy.'

Public health is Kennedy's most passionate, and therefore best articulated, concern. A platform secure enough for any man, in his case it comes again to personal matters; to his own braced spine, his mentally handicapped sister, the necessity to get up in the night and minister to his little boy's asthma. His purposes, however, are less parochial. The bill which he has placed before the Senate is the most ambitious yet for the nationalisation of health insurance in America. It would abolish at a blow Medicare and Medicaid, the limited official schemes, not to mention those private insurance companies who are loathe to retire from an industry worth 80 billion dollars a year.

The main purpose of this trip to Boston was to chair an inquiry into the Nixon administration's further erosion of public health facilities. The inquiry was convened in the gracefully domed auditorium of Massachusetts General Hospital. The plaintiffs who faced Kennedy were curiously representative. There was an old lady with blue hair, a black lady with fluffy hair and, that universally middle-class figure, a man in a brown suit and yellow shirt. 'I was swimming in fluid,' the blue-haired lady told the tribunal, speaking directly to its chairman. 'Without the health centre I don't know what I'd have done, I sincerely don't. Yesterday I had another meeting with the doctor. The last words he said to me were "take it easy".'

'Where will you go for treatment if this facility closes?' Kennedy asked.

'That means I'll have to go to the City Hospital. Taxi fare is two dollars,' she added, 'and ten cents. Now I hear it's going up again.'

The yellow-shirted man said, 'We're upset, we're frustrated and we're frightened. They want to take our hospital away. They want to take it away. They want to put a price on the right to breathe, on the right to enjoy your family. If the President can have three or four White Houses, then let us in Allston-Brighton have our fifteen or twenty health centres . . .'

He was interrupted by a stirring of pleasure at the grin which appeared on the face of the chairman.

'I didn't do that too hard did I?' Kennedy asked.

'We have to depend on Senator Kennedy to rally the people in Washington,' the man said. 'We're looking to you because we don't have anybody but you.'

For the Government an Assistant Secretary then testified; a grey but decent man, uncomfortable in defence of policies that were manifestly indefensible.

'How do you put a dollar price on this?' Kennedy demanded at one point. 'How much money do you save by leaving that woman up in her home?'

The Assistant Secretary replied that the health services were to be curtailed because the Government said so.

'Why don't you take on the pharmaceutical industry?' Kennedy broke in. There was another murmur of anger and delight. Kennedy banged his hammer. 'We've got to have order,' he said.

'–Not too much,' he added.

On the shuttle plane back to Washington he travelled unguarded, save by the truculent handmaidens of American Airlines. Next to him sat another of Bobby's sons and a fat man; in front sat a little brown and white nun. He scanned *Time* magazine, in which his own misadventures have accounted for so many painful acres, appreciating that H. R. Haldeman, Nixon's disgraced White House Chief of Staff, had recently been the subject of *Time's* adoring cover story. Kennedy's opinion of Watergate came now, gangster-fashion from the side of his mouth.

'It was so incompetent,' he said, 'and stoopid . . .'

Then he enquired, 'What else you covering in the States?'

'Soul music.' He brightened.

'I like all of that stuff,' he said. 'Roberta Flack, Al Green, Dion – not Dion the guitarist, I mean Dionne Warwick. And Neil Diamond. I know he's not black, but he's sensational too.'

'When do you miss your brothers most?'

'The most obvious is when you see their children.'

'After they were killed, what was it that helped you more than anything to carry on?'

'My family,' he said. 'Their family. The whole family.'

54

'But didn't you feel a temptation to hate the whole world?'

He hesitated. 'I suppose that was felt – very sharply. They were probably the two best friends I ever had. With my father, there weren't three men that I admired or cared more deeply about. I – I sensed – ah – enormous feeling of loss. But there was really too little time to be dwelling on my feeling of loss when Bobby had eleven children that needed looking after; and in President Kennedy's case, John and Caroline.'

'That must be a great responsibility.'

'It's a responsibility,' he said, 'But it's a joy. It's not a hardship.'

In his Senate office he keeps a letter written by the 14-year-old John F. Kennedy from Choate School to his mother. 'It is the night before exams so I will write you Wednesday . . . PS. Can I be godfather to the baby?'

'I can remember him taking me out in his PT [torpedo] boat. The war was still going on. I was going to school in Florida and he'd been up for the weekend. We had to get up around four-thirty, five o'clock to drive down. I waited in the car and the boats finally went out at about eleven. Of course time never passes for a child, it just seemed like eternity. I remember it was a training run – just took hours and hours. I kept on asking when they were going to go faster and faster, until finally, around four in the afternoon they were able to put the full speed on. I can remember that one of the men was chewing tobacco. He spit, and it went all over my little white shirt. Then my brother brought me to the bus terminal and I came back in my T-shirt with all these little brown splotches over it. That was – I don't know how many years ago, but it's always something – very special.'

'How do you assess your brother's Presidency now?'

'He was able to get an extraordinary sense o' hope to the country. I think that people really felt in nineteen-sixty – old or young people – that America was the hope of Mankind; people really believed that. If you went to a college audience today and told them America is the hope of Mankind, they'd snicker at you. There was a sense that problems could be solved; that Government was interested in people and people's needs. There was a sense of charity and justice.'

Does it not appal him that the murder of his brothers, far from being dreadful aberrations, have merely seemed to intensify a habit? Today in America, more than ever before, guns are the voluptuous expression of constitutional liberty, twinkling archly at the hips of janitors, of traffic police, aching to be exercised upon a misdemeanour. In a supermarket a notice reads: 'Attention burglars and stickup-men. This store is electronically monitored by armed guards with periodic shotgun stakeout in back room.' Which came first, suspicion or the thief?

Kennedy's association with the anti-gun lobby has done little but to add righteous deer-hunters to the list of his possible assassins. 'There are still a hundred million rifles and shotguns, thirty million handguns, two and a half million Saturday Night Specials –'

'Saturday Night Specials!'

'Yeah,' he said. 'They just use 'em Saturday nights.'

'Doesn't that depress you?'

'I get depressed when I see those people from Allston-Brighton – that old lady. It isn't only violence that depresses me.'

On the question of the Presidency, and if he will dare it, a veil drops again, the voice rises, his wager with death sealed off by a half-completed sentence. And why not? Which of us knows, or should know, what he will do three years from now?

'Members of the Senate have had a much greater impact in the country,' he said, 'than many Presidents. Daniel Webster, though he could never be elected President, had an enormous impact on the Abolitionist movement prior to the war between the states; and Calhoun from South Carolina at that time in the Secessionist movement; and Clay and John Quincy Adams.'

'Are you ambitious?'

'I want to do well at what I'm doing – do well as a Senator from Massachusetts – be effective in achieving the goals that I want to see accomplished, and I intend to pursue that. It doesn't focus in terms of ambition, on any particular office or any particular time.'

'You wouldn't run for President just because your brother did.'

'Of course,' he agreed. 'No. That's true.'

'But you do want to see a big change in the country.'

'I do.' He nodded. 'Yes.'

He added, 'There was a passage from one of my brother's speeches – President Kennedy's. I can't quite get the words of it. It's either from Jefferson or the Greeks.' He called out to his secretary. 'Angelique, have you got that little quote-book of my own?'

The words of the quotation remained inexact. Their sentiment was clear, however, on his mind.

'It's something like, "I study Government so that my son can study Philosophy and so that my grandson can study the Arts".'

Now it was a time in American politics when distinction was measured in confidence to set foot outside one's own office. All through the White House the handsome young aides sat immobile behind their button-down collars as if.to freeze, as hares do, might make the catastrophe depart. Shortly, Richard Nixon would appear on television, a tremor in his voice, to accept responsibility for Watergate and to deny it. Could one imagine Kennedy as President? Can one imagine the President as President?

Kennedy was out of his office; seated in a vaulted committee-room to hear the grievances of another minority. At this time, too, there were still Indians defying the Federal forces at Wounded Knee, their fury taking them long past the moment when it would have been glamorous to capitulate. And it was Indians who confronted Kennedy, from Arizona, Illinois, Oklahoma, in college dress and tennis shoes which gave only emphasis to the sternness of their faces. He sat by himself in front of them.

'Your Kennedy Fellowships only deal with young children,' the Indians' spokesman complained. 'They don't answer the needs of Indian students. We need your help . . .'

'Well, you got that,' Kennedy said.

He walked back to the New Senate Building along the marbled pavement, past the nonchalant blue-coat guards. 'I wanted to ask them how they felt about Wounded Knee,' he said, 'only I had to leave.'

The lift-doors closed, operated as usual by a courteous Ivy League young man.

'God, they get screwed!' Kennedy said. 'There were seven Indian lawyers! Half a million Indians with seven Indian lawyers, three Indian doctors. The dropout rate is eighty per cent. before they even get in college, did you hear that? And thirty per cent. in college; what do you have left? My brother Bobby proposed a fund. of eighteen million dollars for Indian education in nineteen-sixty-eight, it was impounded, it's just been released and they still can't get it! These are the people who get hit – and the people yesterday in Allston-Brighton. They have imagination, they develop outreach programmes . . . that old lady.'

Time accelerates because we peer farther and farther ahead, to governments four, eight years hence, and so let the present go by merely as rehearsal. But for the unlucky ones it is always the present. Edward Kennedy, because past and future hold equal terrors for him, belongs to these. A new Attorney General had just taken up his mission to bring the law of America back to life. He telephoned Kennedy, as a member of the Senate Judiciary Committee, hoping to secure his vote at the hearing which would confirm the appointment. Kennedy counselled him to deal gently with the Indians at Wounded Knee.

He can rise as far as he is welcomed. At Suffolk College in Boston the students met him with a brass band, a spotlight that fell upon the flag. He walked up on to the stage, the band playing, and addressed them almost without discomfort. Then he said: 'I want to ask all of you some questions; and just so I'll get it straight, I'm going to note 'em down. How many of you think that each of these general headings is most important? Number one, the bombing in Cambodia.'

Arms rose in a unanimous display.

57

'Number two, inflation. Economic and tax reform.'
A modest concern.
'Three, Watergate.'
Everybody.
'How many think that there should only be an all-volunteer army?'
He scanned the response.
'And how many are going to volunteer?'
There was no interruption. The joke was delivered easily.
'Twelve gals,' he said. 'Four guys. I can see why the guys are volunteering!'

1973

The Splash of a Hockney

David Hockney fulfilled one requirement, at least, of a big star. He was late. A single milk bottle, its topknot as gold as Hockney's own, stood unclaimed on his doorstep. Two tranquil young men, in the next door studio, said they had not seen him, then returned to their work of producing Hockney etchings in surroundings with the ungarnished neatness of a kitchen by de Hooch. In the centre, the big-wheeled iron etching press stood, mangle-like, awaiting its burnished plates. 'David's brother came in,' one of the young men remarked. 'He's an accountant. He said we could use this place to print money. David said "Why bother?" '

Hockney himself appeared shortly afterwards, running contritely down the path between the studios. He explained that he had been caught up at the BBC, appearing on the early morning programme *Start the Week*. He was half dressed-up in a brown velvet suit, a red pullover, odd football socks and ruined plimsolls. A cigarette-hole in the red pullover seemed to have been positioned with some care. He led the way into his own studio, which is largely unfurnished save for work in progress and his photograph albums, bound like encyclopaedias in green and gold. The Sunday newspapers lay where they had been dropped, near a cold electric fire with artificial coals. The first thing that Hockney did was to take a Havana cigar from a box and light it. In so familiar a countenance, this had a startling almost desecrating effect.

Few people know that he lives here. They think he is in Paris still, using Balthus' studio in Saint Germain. He spent two years there but found it growing oppressive. He felt inhibited from putting a canvas down on the floor to work on it. And people kept calling in for tea. If he went out to the cafés or to La Coupole as well, he found it difficult to get up for work the next morning. So back he has come to London again, for all its disadvantages, and its intrinsic failure to inspire him. The secret of his return is known only to viewers of the *Russell Harty Show,* the *Book Programme,* and, now, the *Sunday Times*.

Hockney insists, with potent sincerity, that his public life is only vexatious to him. When he mentions *A Bigger Splash*, the film that was created around him, he goes 'tut' and rolls his eyes as if referring to troublesome in-laws. He has evolved an alibi to prove he was not even in Swinging London, let alone its figurehead. And the autobiography, *David Hockney by David Hockney*, published this week? That's a *picture book,* Hockney insists. He was worried about the autobiographical bits. Thames and Hudson went behind his back and got snapshots and school reports from his mother. Still, nobody reads the text in art books, do they? One finds oneself believing him utterly.

He is long accustomed to maintain that his work is grossly over-rated. He mocks, if not too loudly, the world which has elevated his pictures to one of the few remaining dependable currencies. Recently he heard that a little drawing he did as a schoolboy for the chief programme-seller at St George's Hall, Bradford, in exchange for some fish and chips, had been sold by the recipient at Christie's. 'It said in the *Bradford Telegraph and Argus* it had been lovingly kept in a drawer, tied up with ribbons. Why "lovingly?" Why wasn't it on his wall. I think that's sad. It'd almost be better if he'd said he hadn't liked it all that much.' Here, Hockney brought out sketch pads from his art college days, not used in the autobiography. There were half-drawn figures in cafés and at bus-stops; and the chicken run that was at the top of his road. 'You'd never know I did these would you?' How modest he is, one thought. Then one thought; but *is* he?

These days, he insists, he leads a quieter life than ever. His pockets are still full of soggy-looking French francs. His brother looks after all the finance. Since 'Peter' ceased living with him, he has few domestic possessions, no furniture to speak of: he tidies his own studio and sweeps his floor. He lives mostly on slices of Hungarian salami. He may not buy himself any new clothes for a year at a time. His single indulgence is Havana cigars. He doesn't like going to parties. He goes to them, none the less, entering the room in the sort of sudden hush reserved for Royalty. His demeanour might best be described as a regal slouch.

His latest project, being minted by the young men next door, is a series of etchings, inspired by 'Blue Guitar', the Wallace Stevens poem, itself inspired by Picasso's picture. Now he has four months of painting ahead of him. His greatest pleasure is, and always will be, the application of paint to a surface. Aesthetically, he prefers his line drawings, their impulsiveness and speed; he sees colours less vividly in the left eye than the right: he says, in all artlessness, that he wishes he were a better painter. He intends to winter in Los Angeles, where he has not painted since 1968. In Los Angeles, he may find a little peace, a little anonymity. One can imagine it.

1976

'This is the only decent thin suit I've got'

A baby-faced policeman rang the bell on my behalf and, after a moment, Sir Harold himself came to the door. Lady Wilson, in the background, said she thought it was the laundryman. 'He doesn't look much like a laundryman,' said Sir Harold, evidently tickled. In the front reception room, books and possessions were laid out in ordered confusion, as if awaiting removal. Sir Harold showed me into a first floor sitting-room, perfumed by smoke from his cigar. He would have a glass of whisky, he said, since he had eaten only half a pork pie for lunch. On the mantelpiece stood a silent gilt clock and a green jug shaped like a fish, the kind that gurgle when tilted. 'You can get Wilson and Heath jugs like that,' Sir Harold said. 'They don't gurgle that much, though.'

It had been a busy publication day. Big reviews everywhere, of course, including one by Professor Bernard Crick in *The Guardian*, which called Sir Harold's book 'fascinating but intellectually disgraceful'. Then a Press conference, at which Sir Harold had the Lobby journalists eating out of his hand, as of old; then a signing session at Hatchard's where, despite the donnish rebuke, they were running out of copies fast. *The Governance of Britain* is even jacketed in its author's favourite colour: dark green. He has always been fond of green. 'The trouble is, you can't wear it with a blue suit, and this is the only decent thin suit I've got.'

I said that *The Governance of Britain* – which Sir Harold describes as a handbook for sixth formers and college students – left an overall impression that being Prime Minister was jolly good fun. Yes, he agreed because you could never be bored. But he recollected one moment when he was assailed by boredom. 'It was right at the end. I'd been through a Saturday and a Sunday, and then I got this report from Shirley [Williams] about metrication. I thought 'Oh, no, I can't plough through all this.' So I simply wrote on the top, "The British public is bored by four syllable words".'

So far, Sir Harold has not been bored in retirement. It entails, he says, a 70-hour instead of a 100-hour week. Since finishing *The Governance of Britain,* he has been hard at work on his television series about former British Prime Ministers. There is a deluge of honorary posts, so difficult to refuse. Now, at least, if he makes a schedule, he knows he can stick to it. I asked whether, as ex-Prime Minister, he allowed himself any special indulgence. Yes: as Prime Minister he always had breakfast in bed, to go through the newspapers. Nowadays, it is nice to get up early and potter downstairs in his dressing gown. And to give Lady Wilson her breakfast in bed? No, he replied: she gets up even earlier.

Of all the predecessors he has studied, Sir Harold is most enthusiastic about Harold Macmillan. 'Nonchalant,' he calls Macmillan in the book, with a touch of envy. No butcher himself, he admires Macmillan's adroitness at bringing about purges which left no bloodstain on his own cuff. Sir Harold himself always got stomach pains when contemplating Cabinet changes. And he treasures the fights he had with Macmillan in the Commons. 'Great days of debating. It was gladiatorial. Then they took him from me. I was bereft. I got Peter Thorneycroft instead, and what can you do with Peter?'

What are his greatest regrets? 'I made a few bad appointments.' The bad days, he thinks, were mainly in the sixties: the 74-76 Cabinet was an unusually happy one. He regrets Rhodesia, of course, and failing to bring about an armistice in Vietnam. What, then, does he count as his best achievements? Forging an administration from a party which had been out of office for 13 years. And he is proud, above all, of having initiated the Open University. He feels certain it will still exist and be admired 100 years from now.

Sir Harold gives himself 10 more years of being busy. He will be happy to be free of worries about economics. He describes himself as an historian *manqué*. He has just finished writing about Disraeli – who, he points out, wrote novels like *Sybil* far more quickly than he wrote *The Governance of Britain*. He is looking forward to laying into Neville Chamberlain. Then, at the end of the series, he may attempt a profile of himself; a study of his political life in the third person. Just for a bit of fun, he says. But it may work out.

1976

A Soldier Far From Home

Officers of the Royal Scots Greys take their meals below the melancholy face of Tsar Nicholas of Russia, the honorary colonel in whose memory the regiment's grey berets are to this day trimmed with black. In the Mess, 20 minutes for lunch still have all the mirrored pomp of a 300-year history partly based on plunder – silver-bellied salt cellars, a silver dragoon on horseback shining in the polished lake of the table. The menu was egg-and-bacon flan, peas and mash, of which Major, the Duke of Kent remarked that probably it looked better than it tasted.

The officer in the khaki pullover, drinking Guinness with a black labrador at his feet, could have belonged to almost any Mess at this hour of the day. His face is Royal just faintly, like a worn-away Coronation mug. In common with all in his line, he has thinning hair and a faint cast of sadness round the eyes.

His morning had been spent in writing character reports on the men of the scout-car C Squadron under his command. Had he finished? 'Lord no. It's like doing school reports. One tries to think of something different to say about each one but after about ten, the same old chestnuts start to come out.' He had soldiers to interview as well; applications for special leave to consider. 'One's instinct is always to say "of course he must go home" and then, if there's a reason why he can't, one feels an awful heel.'

Like any under-exercised profession the Army has long periods of slackness masked by stocktaking. What the Greys were preparing for, however, was literally death. This summer, they amalgamate with the Third Carbiniers to form the Royal Scots Dragoon Guards. A final period of active service on patrol in Ulster had been cut short after an outcry that the Duke's own squadron was involved. Now, with men on leave or already posted to Germany where the new regiment begins service, the barracks, with their faint odours of polish and cooked cabbage, had some of the mournfulness of school during holidays. The barracks were supposed to have been built in India but two sets of plans were confused. Therefore, while troops somewhere in India curse and roast in quarters designed to shield them from the Scottish damp, the Royal Scots Greys inhabit twilit

63

corridors affording shelter from a noon-day heat infrequent a mile or so outside Edinburgh.

Like everyone else, the Duke felt depressed about the amalgamation; the loss of the berets representing the grey chargers of his regiment at Waterloo and Balaclava. He felt sorry for the Carbiniers too, a Welsh regiment whose national identity was to vanish entirely – and, being Royal, relieved that the decision to merge such disparate regiments had had nothing to do with him. He admitted that leaving the Army had crossed his mind. 'At times like this of course one does wonder if one wouldn't like a change but after a number of years it does become a way of life – more than that, it's the feeling of doing a decent job.'

In fact, the Duke has always had a desire to write, and, in 16 years of soldiering, has hoarded up journals and made tapes about subjects he would like to tackle in print. 'Unfortunately when one's voice is played back, it's not often really good enough to write down.' He said he'd like to write a novel. The thought produced a shy kind of guffaw. '*Definitely* under another name.'

He is not like his brother officers, being apparently more skilful than most, and much less talkative. Most of them have their families living with them, or nearby. The Duke can get home to Coppins in Buckinghamshire only at weekends. He fears that his children now look on him more as a visiting uncle than a father. He has a room at the Mess and a share in an orderly. The seam below one trouser-pocket had torn; possibly the result of a nervous way he has of tugging out a large coloured handkerchief with which to envelope his nose. His amusements are a record-player, Liddell Hart's history of the Second War, a comic novel or two – Waugh and Anthony Powell – and his black labrador, Flint. If it can be termed an advantage, he is of course one of the few Greys with his own full-dress uniform, which he needs for official occasions when he represents the Queen his cousin.

In the afternoon, with a smeared grey sky over the hills behind the barracks, the sense of merely killing time grew stronger. On the parade-ground the flag flew at half-mast for the latest three Scottish soldiers killed in Belfast. Some of the Duke's squadron were stripping and cleaning Ferret scout-cars employed in the brief Ulster patrol duty. A few more were taking gunnery instruction on a Saladin armoured car, its turret still fitted with the metal spike to cut through IRA garrotting wires. Every soldier wants action if he is as highly trained as the Duke, and has reflexes as swift: every soldier frets if he sees another unit getting it all.

Instead, one of the week's strategic operations was the transportation of soldiers into Edinburgh to the cinema to see *Waterloo*. And there were domestic matters to sort out; vexations of the kind that always accompany marriages between reluctant partners, very late

64

in life. Which of the regimental silver would be kept for the new combined Mess and which would be left behind in a glass case in Scotland? An ante-room was dazzlingly muddled – cheroot-boxes, band-programme-holders, a silver galleon on wheels that used to be pushed round the dinner table loaded with bottles, and scores of stamps and replicas of the French Imperial eagle that the Greys captured at Waterloo before Junot's Polish lancers overwhelmed them. The Duke repeated he was glad not to have the responsibility for sorting all *that* out.

As bright a face as possible is to be put on the amalgamation, with a ball at Preston Castle, attended by the Queen and most of the Royal Family. The Duke vetted the seating-plan with the Major commanding B Squadron. ' . . . I don't think the Queen will want to powder her nose . . . it's important to give easy access for the hard drinkers . . . I'll keep an eye open,' he promised, 'I'll hover.'

Passing by various groups of lounging soldiers, he received some textbook salutes, with fingers quivering at the right temple. Others scarcely bothered to salute at all. Ignoring those, the Duke remarked he was glad Army advertisements had stopped hinting that military life was easy. 'You can get a soft life anywhere. It's more important to offer people a bit of excitement.' A brother officer called out 'Are you playing squash Edward?' and he said, no: he had to write to his son at boarding-school. He moved off with big, unrelaxed strides and a tangible air of not being very happy – although perhaps this attends all Royal persons that one sees walking alone. He went with Flint back to his squadron office to continue writing reports on his men.

1971

'Joan, Are You Decent?'

The front door of Joan Collins' London house was opened by a bald-headed young man, wearing a short leather jerkin and a thin bow tie. In the hallway beyond, several half-unpacked statues littered the passage to a small end study where a larger man sat in profile, rather sadly, reading documents. The bald young man was Miss Collins' London publicist, an art he seemed to have acquired by memorising the dialogue of films made in prewar Hollywood. 'Take a seat in here and I'll see what Joan's doing' he said. In a moment his voice became distantly audible. 'Joan' he called. '*Joan!* Are you decent?'

The sitting room, large and lofty and as cold as the security bars to be glimpsed through the curtain-muslin, likewise recalled an earlier epoch. Before one of the two fireplaces stood a pair of thick silver candlesticks. Above the second fireplace hung a portrait of Miss Collins, veiled and challenging in black chiffon. The varied and expensive ornaments on view included a china camel with flowers growing out of its back; a cornucopia of wax grapes; a four-foot high golden palm tree; a heavy gilt music stand, supporting an ornate edition of Erté's theatrical designs; and about six Greek figures, male and female, in different attitudes of recumbent endeavour. The bald young man returned, plumped himself down among the royal blue heraldic cushions and said 'Joan's coming.' Though our interview had been arranged three days before, this was evidently a cause for jubilation.

Being much smaller than expected, and rather vigorously dressed in a rah-rah skirt, bolero and boots, she seemed less like an international sex symbol than a busy little scrum-half, until one saw her face. Off camera, it is even less believably the face of a woman rising 50. Clouds of hair drift around a complexion still exquisite, wide-set eyes still blackly ingenuous, a chin still tip-tiltedly firm. Really, the only giveaway is her voice. She speaks in the unmistakeable tones of the mid-fifties British starlet, best described as a pout made audible.

She was in London to visit her 80-year-old father, be caught unawares by *This Is Your Life* and promote her new film, *Nutcracker*. Only the shortest break could be taken from her star role in the hugely successful American TV soap opera, *Dynasty*. She had, even so, flown in on clouds of press sensation emanating from a rumour

66

– firmly denied – that she was about to divorce her third husband, Ron Kass. For some reason, the story had to be accompanied by pictures of Miss Collins, smiling and wearing a sparkly two-piece bathing-suit.

'I'd love a cup of coffee,' she said, as if this were not her own house but an hotel with room service. 'Would you mind awfully, darling?'

'Sure,' The bald young man sprang up. 'How about Ron. Is he here?'

'He's in the house, I think,' Miss Collins said, somewhat coldly.

The plan had been to talk seriously to a woman who, for all the outward Hollywood flim-flam, none the less seems sensible and down to earth, with self-deprecating humour that has enabled her to play stooge to Leonard Rossiter in a TV commercial, and to write a genuinely funny autobiography revealing, among other things, that Marlon Brando steals ice cream from refrigerators and that Bing Crosby (whom she was forced to kiss in a 'Road' picture) had nasty-smelling breath.

Being sensible and down to earth, however, clearly has limits, defined by what now seems archaic big star protocol. This meant that, throughout our conversation, the bald young man sat vigilantly four feet away, as if a perfectly lucid and literate woman could not be trusted to speak unsupervised. It meant also that, while at times Joan Collins laughed and fidgeted and even kicked up her legs, her most usual response was a guarded stare and studied petulance. One felt one's every question to be connected with her bosom-measurement.

It is a mould which she herself, paradoxically, longs to break. Her roles as the same sultry vamp in films like *The Stud* and *The Bitch* – adapted from novels by her younger sister, Jackie – have become inhibiting and, she insists, boring. Her new film, *Nutcracker* (a title designed to amuse American audiences) casts her as the principal of a ballet school, still obliged to play *Penthouse* centre-spreadish scenes in satin sheets and bubble baths. Here and there she can be seen attempting to lend humour to the proceedings. In one scene, a fancy dress gala redolent of the late sixties, she makes a nice comic moment out of pushing a jester's three-cornered hat away from her face. 'Oh, you *noticed* that,' she said, with evident relief.

She fought against typecasting since the beginning of her career, when she made films at 'Southall Studios' and was nicknamed The Coffee Bar Jezebel. 'I was never an English rose. The only other role for me in British pictures then was as a young girl who'd gone wrong.' In those days, her greatest wish was to be like the Hollywood star Ava Gardner. 'I thought she was lovely, and I liked her "screw you' attitude to life. She's living quietly in London now. I like to think of that – it's as if she's still saying to everyone "screw you".'

At this point, a tall, flat-haired American came into the room, wobbling slightly on one plaster-encased foot. It was her husband. Ron Kass, taking a break from his solitary reading of documents.

'Your fabrics are here,' he said.

'My *what?*'

'Your fabrics.'

They spoke to each other at the impersonal level of a desk-intercom.

'You ordered fabrics. They're here.'

'Oh – you mean my *fabrics* . . .'

Her success in remaining desirable to thousands of cinema-goers, while simultaneously writing books and now even producing her own films, has been aided – inevitably – by exhaustive analysis, getting to know herself and learning to be positive. She is positive in that rather arid way which denies the existence of anything quirky or even humorously uncomfortable. Thus, no films she has ever made – not even *Tales from the Crypt* – strikes her as ludicrous. No past love-scenes, or even love-costume, make her retrospectively cringe. She is positive even about the ordeal of a four-hour makeup job to transform her into the wicked witch in her next film, *Hansel and Gretel.* 'I didn't particularly like it when they gave me a hunch back, a false nose and chin and about two inches of slimy stuff all over, or when my rubber chin kept coming loose and the makeup people had to poke adhesive into it on the end of a stick. But no . . .' she flounced her shoulders. 'I'm an actress. I wear makeup.'

A diversion occurred with the arrival of the *Sunday Times* photographer. Michael Ward was an actor before he turned to journalism and, it transpired, he knew Joan from way back. The hallway echoed with 'Hullo. darling' and the sound of stage kisses. The bald young man rose from the couch.

'Right,' he said as Ward came in, still partially in Joan Collins's embrace, 'You've got ten minutes to do the picture.'

'It's not enough,' Ward said.

'It's all we can give you.'

'Then I'll go now.'

'Then we'll have to send in a photo . . .'

All this while the hapless writer looked on, believing it to be more show business badinage.

It was Michael Ward, while photographing her, who came nearest to a Joan Collins interview.

'Stand just there, darling, and put your hand on the door.'

'Why?'

'To hide the dirty finger-marks.'

'What?' she said in alarm.

'Seen anything of Max?' [Her first husband, Maxwell Reed.]

'He died in seventy-four.'

68

'No! How?'
'Cancer.'
'Poor sod.'
'He deserved it,' she said. 'The bastard.'

She was already running upstairs as we were shown, across the half-unpacked statues to the door. Her publicist feared she would be late for her lunch party at San Lorenzo. One knows how much film stars dislike to be late. In the room at the end of the corridor, her husband, Ron Kass, remained in profile, rather sadly, studying documents.

1982

The Curse of St Trinian's

The complex, very hush-hush directions to Ronald Searle's hideaway
in the mountains of the Var ended on what seemed a characteristic
note. 'Park next to the baker's. There's a lane off to the left and,
half-way down, a big iron sign in the shape of an owl. We're directly
opposite. The key will be in the door. I'll meet you at the top of the
stairs.'

A slender man in dark blue, chin-bearded like a chapel elder,
stood there as promised, saying 'Aha' with Englishness undimmed
by his 20 years' self-exile. One is as struck by his neatness and
mildness as was Noel Coward, who expected even a handshake from
Searle to leave him covered in blood.

The most joyously vengeful pictorial satirist England has produced
since Cruikshank prefers nowadays to live in a sleepy French village
containing no figure more grotesque than the occasional wild boar
rooting around its medieval arch. 'You won't *name* the village, will
you?' he said anxiously several times. It is a seclusion that will not
be broached by publication of his new cartoon anthology, *Ronald
Searle's Big Fat Cat Book:* seven editions in four countries, 75,000
copies already in print. Searle as usual has refused all TV or radio
appearances.

Even in this remote place he is never free of a dread of people
arriving unannounced on his well-concealed doorstep. The visitors,
if St Trinian's fans, are quickly discouraged. Not so easy are the men
with whom Searle shares the unique bond of the Japanese prison-
camp. 'They still turn up out of the blue with their sleeping bags.
They write to me, too. Changi left so many people half-crazy. Half
the letter will be sensible, half of it will be crazy.'

St Trinian's, that strange by-product of the Burma Death Railway,
continues to haunt its creator scarcely less. Searle finds it perpetually
irksome that his reputation in Britain still rests on those hell-inspired
schoolgirls, horned and boatered, wreaking mayhem with hockey-
sticks and dynamite. He himself quickly wearied of them and tried
unsuccessfully to destroy the school by ceremonial holocaust. He
was still trying last year when he issued a single portrait of a broken-
down hag, said to be a St Trinian's sixth former, now selling bondage
in a Port Said brothel.

70

'It's terrible to be remembered only for something you did 30 years ago – and which was short-lived anyway. There are really so few St Trinian's drawings. I didn't want to do even as many as that. To most people in England, it's as if I did nothing else.'

A generation of schoolboys would disagree, citing the gentler glories of St Trinian's male counterpart, St Custard's, and its fugitive-philosopher star, Nigel Molesworth. So would the dwindling number who recall a moment when *Punch* actually became funny, thanks to Searle's collaboration with Alex Atkinson on imaginary travelogues about America and Russia. So would the multitudes abroad who appreciated Searle's erotic studies from Paris and Hamburg, and his latter-day lampooning of all supposed sacred in the animal kingdom. Few artists in any medium have stretched themselves so wide and so relentlessly. At 62, Searle still works like a man possessed. 'He gets up at six, fetches the bread and reads the paper,' his wife, Monica, says. 'Then he works for eleven hours. It's all he ever wants to do.'

It was all he wanted to do in 1935 when he left elementary school in Cambridge and worked as a packer at the Co-op to pay for drawing-classes at night school. His home overlooked shunting yards near the station where his father had worked as a porter. Ronald's strange ambition, like his odd humour, was explained by the fact that he wrote and drew with the incorrect hand. 'In East Anglia, to say you were left-handed – 'Our Ronnie's cack-'anded' – accounted for any deviation.'

His family realised he was serious when he won a scholarship to art school and began earning money as a cartoonist for the *Cambridge Daily News* and the university magazine, *Granta*. In all respects he seemed set for the predictable repertoire – and line – of late 1930's visual humour. Then came the war.

Searle joined the Royal Engineers as an architectural draughtsman. The first months passed uneventfully, designing unusable pill-boxes and blowing up piers along the east coast. His unit sailed for north Africa but was re-routed to the Far East to strengthen the Singapore garrison. Singapore fell and for the next four years, Searle was a prisoner of the Japanese.

He spent a year in the notorious Changi camp and was then shipped to join the slave-gangs on the Burma–Thailand railway – the 'death railway', built by starving men, largely without equipment other than bare hands at an ultimate cost of some 100,000 lives, Searle, one of the more fortunate, endured malaria, beri-beri, gastric ulcers and maggot-filled sores, all in addition to his captors' ritual brutality. Each morning, he would awake to find dead friends all round him and then, since the prisoners were forced to share the Japanese Army's Shinto religion, he and his guards would kneel down together to pray to the sun.

'Survival under those conditions was a question of attitude. You had to find something to survive *for*. There was a Dutch cavalry officer who'd escaped from Java and seen his young wife machine-gunned and drowned in a Japanese air attack – he found God. There was Duckworth, who'd coxed the Cambridge boat and who looked after everyone, organised everyone, almost took on the role of martyr. That was his therapy. My means of survival was my work. I had to survive to draw; to show the world the way it really was.'

On whatever scraps of paper he could scrounge, he drew his comrades' shrunken, parchmenty bodies and his guards' faces, inexplicable in both their cruelty and kindness. The drawings, if discovered, would have meant instant beheading. Searle hid them in the only place the Japanese would not dare look – under the bedcovers of men dying from cholera.

He left Changi weighing six stone, with 200 drawings kept secret for him by dying men. Prison camp had also prompted him to produce his St Trinian's prototypes, with their lank, ferocious bodies and remorseless eyes, a weird transmutation of his captors' unfathomable urges to cruelty and destruction.

Searle is not like other ex-Changi prisoners who, even today, cannot bring themselves even to speak to a Japanese. 'They treated us like that because they couldn't understand how we'd allowed ourselves to be taken prisoner in the first place. They'd kill their own wounded in retreat, to save them that dishonour. We'd see young kids like ourselves going off into the jungle with their packs, a little portion of rice and, swinging from their belts, a little doll, to be ready to meet their ancestors. Their officers were almost as brutal to them as to us. We were all nineteen- and twenty-year-old kids from opposite sides of the world, opposite cultures: there wasn't any hope of understanding.'

St Trinian's launched Searle on his first career, as England's best-known and highest-paid comic illustrator; via magazines like *London Opinion* and *Lilliput* and *Punch* – under Malcolm Muggeridge – and the famous but dying *Strand,* whose editor, Macdonald Hastings, was once overheard by Searle, shut in an office lavatory, moaning 'Poor Mac, poor Mac . . .'

Searle married Kaye Webb, London's foremost publisher of books for children. He turned his attention to stage-design and publishing his own imprint, Perpetua. He enjoyed the friendship of such internationally-known humourists as S. J. Perelman and James Thurber.

Then in 1961, for reasons he has never fully understood, he left his wife, home, reputation and sizeable income to go to Paris and begin again. 'I still don't quite know why I did it. It was just a feeling that I couldn't stand any more and that I had to go back to zero. I thought – and I was right – that Paris didn't let artists starve.'

France responded to his work in a way that Britain never had. A few years after settling in Paris, Searle was approached by the French Mint and invited to accept a commemorative medal. He was also invited to design it. His work for the Mint has continued, both as a designer and a source of ideas for other likely medal-recipients. He is proud to have successfully proposed other radical artists like Otto Dix and George Grosz for their (otherwise undecorated) stand against Nazism. 'I even persuaded the Mint a few months ago to strike a special medal to Nelson and Trafalgar.'

Monica, his second wife, is a black-haired, fair-skinned, ebullient woman, full of bad puns, good ideas and warm, thankful life. In 1969, she was found to be suffering from breast cancer of a type then believed incurable. 'It was on December thirty-first that they diagnosed it. I had a party that night. I came in and said, "Sorry we're late everyone, we were held up. I've got cancer." I was determined it wasn't going to be hidden. It had to be recognised and spoken about.'

While Monica was submitting herself to an untried, very painful cancer therapy, the Searles' Paris landlord tried to drive them out by systematic harassment. Scaffolding blocked their apartment windows and radios played all night near the room where Monica lay. At length they fled to the Var, to a semi-derelict property that Monica, weak as she was, began resolutely to put in order.

The village is one which regards even someone from five miles down the mountain as a foreigner. Its attitude to the Searles changed dramatically when French TV showed a film about Monica and her, apparently successful, fight against cancer. 'Everyone in the village usually goes to bed at nine, but they all stayed up until midnight to watch the film,' Searle says. 'The next day, women in the shop came up to Monica and embraced her. They were enormously proud to know such a famous invalid.'

A further bond was created last August when forest fires destroyed 40 square miles round about and, at one point, threatened the village itself. Searle and Monica – despite her weakened arm – seized buckets and joined the chain which halted the fire just short of the village square. Searle felt ill for weeks afterwards from the effects of the ash and chemicals from fire-fighting planes.

Their life, though private, is far from idyllic. As a result of her cancer treatment, Monica cannot stand direct sun. Searle himself prefers to work in a studio devoid of natural light. Fearful of visitors, they none the less overflow with warmth and welcome. Their labyrinthine, unfinished house is full of guest rooms.

Searle turned from caricaturing people to lampooning animals, he says, in order to reach the world audience he now enjoys. 'Animals are an international language. With people, you've always got problems in this or that country, about race or skin colour. I notice that every strip cartoon nowadays has to contain at least one faintly tinted child.' Not that the gooey-eyed will feel themselves specially catered for in Searle's 'Particularly repellent dog glowing under the impression that it is man's best friend' or 'Baby seal under the impression that clubs are centres of social activity'. The cats in his new book are hairy heaps with nyloned legs, tip-tilted breasts and expressions of lascivious inanity. The final one in the book squats, triumphant, upon a captive world.

Among younger contemporaries, he most admires Gerald Scarfe, in Searle's opinion a more direct descendant than himself from the bloody-quilled age of Cruikshank. 'His use of line is in just that tradition, and it's fantastic. People have no right to be revolted by anything he draws. He has to draw it like that because he's *seen* it, he knows it's there.'

Searle himself works with a ferocity partly dictated by fading faculties, the long-term legacy of his years in prison camp. 'The chief effects were on the eyesight and memory. There's a thing called "Changi memory" that a lot of us developed. Lately, I found I'd even forgotten about some of the drawings I made there. I looked at them again and felt quite upset. I'd forgotten how awful it was.'

There are few original Ronald Searle drawings. Searle himself destroys most of them after publication. 'Otherwise people get hold of them and put a false value on them.' He regards himself as still struggling, needing work, ever subject to deadlines and art editors' caprice. 'I often get rejections. I haven't had a *New Yorker* cover accepted for about two years.

'You *have* to agonise. Scarfe does – I can tell when he comes to see me. I know *he* looks placid, too. That's the trick, you see. Inside, you have to agonise. If you're an artist and you ever once feel pleased with yourself, you're dead.'

1982

Jimmy Makes it to Washington

The day before President Jimmy Carter reached Tyneside, two American Secret Service agents called at Dave Gibson's pottery shop in Washington old village. The two wore light coloured raincoats and little letters G – for G-men – in their lapels; they inquired, in their quiet, courteous, menacing way, if the pottery had a telephone. Even while he strolled on the nearby village green, the President must remain close to the wherewithal for starting World War III.

A telephone now stood newly-installed on Dave Gibson's bench, amid hand-turned pottery mugs and vases. It connected his pottery directly with the White House, a fact made plain by the words 'White House' and a picture of the White House encircled in its dial. The potter looked on while one Secret Service man rang up Washington DC for test purposes. Outside, on the corner by the Cross Keys, now full of UPI and AP news agency men, yet more secret service men turned a fish-eyed stare to an ice-cream van as it passed through the village. On the side of the van was written in a brash but, under the circumstances, tactless coloured letters: 'Warning! This vehicle contains 200,000 highly explosive fizz bombs!'

Press handicaps during the presidential visit to Britain have already been widely-ventilated. But a certain local radio reporter, in Newcastle on Friday morning, could have melted the sternest editorial heart. Picture him trapped in the media corral outside the Civic Centre, simultaneously trying to describe the scene and receive instructions by headphone from his office, while 300 urgent colleagues of all nations poked lenses and meters and even camp-stools into him. His sound-recordist, a kindly man in a hairpiece, gave what help was possible.

'See the sharpshooters up there.' The sound-recordist pointed to the spots of vicious orange denoting police positions among the sooty turrets beyond the park. Six thousand people, including anti-Zionist demonstrators, obliterated the narrow ornamental garden. Select groups of pensioners and children had been led to their forward listening-posts. A brass band waited under the piers of the Motor Tax department. The podium was searched yet again, and the microphone tested for its ability to transmit Southern vowels. The presidential motorcade had left the airport by now, its progress into Newcastle charted by many remote control devices.

'They're at the New Bridge Street roundabout.'

'That's ninety seconds away. You're on air in ninety seconds.'

'Is that "Town Moor" like M.O.R.E?'

The radio reporter pulled down his headphones.

'You'll let me know if you hear them coming,' he begged the sound-recordist. 'I can't hear a thing with these on.'

'You'll know they're here when the band starts playing "The Stars and Stripes".'

'Er, what does "The Stars and Stripes" actually *sound* like?'

The sound recordist was going 'la-la-la la la la' into the radio reporter's ear as the motorcade swished along the newly-hosed precinct behind them.

The car was a black Daimler, not an armour-plated Cadillac. That much was conceded to the Carter-Callaghan *entente*. All its doors opened at once, and Secret Service men rolled out like parachutists in close order. The President, by contrast, emerged upright, with a noticeable little jump, landing on both feet, triumphant, as if he had leapt from some greater height. To Newcastle, this gesture seemed symbolic. It symbolised terra firma: reality. This was not, after all, some huge hoax. The applause, and relief, rippled all across the park to the boarding houses of Jesmond.

What of the man who has successfully defied description these many months? He is shortish, cat-footed, boyish down to the waist. His hair seems to have been sprinkled with pepper and salt. His shoes have no heels whatever. He smiles a lot. His countenance, unsmiling, resembles that of an intelligent gundog. And, for the moment, his presence gives delight and excitement. We have learned to look for much less in a world leader.

With him came James Callaghan, wearing a suit with a light blue jumper (the latter on heaven knows what advice), smiling and shaking hands with Carter yet again, after greeting him at an airport for the second successive day, seemingly infatuated with his portable President, steering him here, beckoning him there, touching him ever and again with a large, white, shepherding hand.

That his own welcome in Newcastle was more qualified did not seem to trouble the Prime Minister. As President Carter received the Freedom of the City from a perky little red-robed Lord Mayor, Callaghan sat and beamed and forgot the local election results. When Carter attempted to pronounce 'Ha'way tha lads,' the Geordie war cry, Callaghan smiled beneficently as if to say 'I taught him that'. Then the Prime Minister, regardless of circumstances, delivered an extended fireside chat. Not cheers but sour chuckles greeted this. A thousand men more expect shortly to lose their jobs at C. A. Parsons's factory in Sunderland.

76

Washington waited, six miles away, among the factories, beautified to a fault. There were new white lines on all the roads; lamp posts had been repainted and potholes selectively filled in. It was a pity, some women said, that the improvements did not reach as far as Spout Lane, where street lighting is poor and dustbin men are a law to themselves. A police horse, crossing the immaculate square, briskly defecated amid sardonic applause.

Simon Kolson, a Geordie of Russian parentage, had stood for three hours in the same spot by the pottery. 'On one leg,' he added, pointing cheerfully to the other leg that was missing. 'I'm hungry and I'm thirsty and I've enjoyed every minute.' Nearby stood a delegation from Consett Lions Club. One man, dressed as a lion, smoked a cigarette on the inside of his paw.

Approaching down the hill from Sunderland, the President's car revealed the secret of its propulsion. It was propelled from outside, by petulant little pushes from Secret Service men walking beside it like funeral mutes. So it passed the pottery, where Simon Kolson was packed behind a barrier at right-angles. 'Is that the President? I can't see. Is that the President?'

The 300 correspondents were faced with an excruciating choice. They could watch the President visit Washington Old House, home of George Washington's ancestors. Or, from yet another corral on the green, they could watch him plant a tulip tree. A chosen half-dozen scurried around him as he made his way along the crash-barriers, shaking the thumbs of hundreds of outstretched hands. Even the back of his head is televisual, being cut in three precisely-symmetrical layers.

Close behind him always walks a naval officer, carrying an attaché case. The officer is tall, dark-skinned, looped handsomely with gold braid. The attaché case is inoffensive-looking. It would be pleasanter to think that it contains documents, rather than the key-device with which the President may set in motion the end of the world.

In 20 minutes, he had done everything that Washington could hope. He had used a spade with some vigour and handed it to a rigid nurseryman for local exhibition. He had traversed the green anti-clockwise, to the anguish of the clockwise spectators; he had waved to those in windows above the Cross Keys and Consett Green Library; he had taken and held up several North-Eastern babies with every appearance of pleasure. The White House Press Corps were all apprised of the spelling of 'Ha'way tha lads'. The Washington Welfare band ceased playing 'Hava Nagila' and began playing 'My Grandfather's Clock'.

The limousine now waited, covering that inadvertent horse manure. On reaching it, he mounted the running-board to smile yet again and to wave. That smile, that wave, by their very superfluity, vanquished cynicism. In that moment, Jimmy Carter truly seemed to have risen higher than merely the running-board. Then he was gone, his limousine pushed by Secret Service men, off into the remoter worlds.

'Was that the President?' Simon Kolson said. 'I was hoping to meet him, you know,' he confided to a St John Ambulance attendant. 'I'd like to meet him. Are you a Chief Inspector?'

1977

PART TWO

Home

Poison from the Potting-Shed

After the curtains are pulled shut across the little stage, Professor Alan Gemmell unclips the slim gold ballpoint pen with which he is so apt to emphasise biological principles. Sometimes he will point it, as towards a wall-chart; sometimes he suspends it, demonstrating truths about plant-growth or gravity. Another habit of the Professor's is to interpolate sudden non-gardening allusions, aimed generally at showing the breadth of his mind and specifically at silencing, if not discomfiting, his antagonist, Bill Sowerbutts. Thus Professor Gemmell, in his beaming Scottish brogue, remarks: 'I've always wondered – what *was* the Pierian Spring?' Sowerbutts, at this moment lighting his pipe, recognises the ploy but disdains to notice it. The third panellist, Chris Brickell, gazes from Bill Sowerbutts back to Professor Gemmell like a voyager in the Lost World, waiting for the Brontosaurus to engage the Pterodactyl.

It is in other words the correspondence edition of *Gardeners' Question Time*. The team with their chairman, Ken Ford, scan the list of a dozen inquiries, selected from up to 5,000 received each week by BBC Radio 4. The sound engineers are ready. Ken Ford, a genial though tired-looking man, asks what might seem an innocent question to test voice-level.

'You first, please Alan. Perhaps you'll tell us how you're getting home after the programme?'

'Yes, Ken,' the Professor beams. 'I'll be catching the 8.53 to Euston, staying overnight in London, then back to Cheshire tomorrow.'

'Thank you. And you, Bill?'

'Yes – same for me, Ken,' Bill Sowerbutts says. 'Straight back to London – but it's not the 8.53, like Alan says. It's the 8.52.'

In 1947, as Britain scraped and shivered through post-war austerity, a BBC producer named Bob Stead conceived the idea of a radio programme based on the national mania for home food-production. A pilot edition, provisionally titled *How Does Your Garden Grow?*, went out on the then Home Service, from the Broadoak Hotel, Ashton-under-Lyne, before an audience supplied by Smallshaw

81

Horticultural Society. It was the start of a 34-year run and a popularity impervious to fluctuating fashion and BBC internal politics. *Gardeners' Question Time,* with its constant two million Sunday afternoon listeners, is – after the news – the most widely heard 'talk' programme on radio.

The figures testify, of course, to a deep-seated British passion. But *Gardeners' Question Time* numbers its greatest addicts among people to whom tips about potting and pruning have not the smallest allure. For these, the magic traditionally began in the announcement of the three-man panel: 'Fred Loads of Lancaster, Bill Sowerbutts of Ashton-under-Lyne and Professor Alan Gemmell of Keele University.' The appellation is almost heraldic – three champions from northern shires, riding forth to do battle with sharpened spade and poison-tipped hoe. 'Now . . . Bill knows as well as I do that . . .' 'Well, you see – Fred's only trouble is . . .' 'You see what Alan always forgets is . . .' The lances shiver and break over the guiltless forms of parsnips, geraniums and – especially – types of compost.

For this half-hour at least each week, the BBC remembers its once-paramount duty to give its listeners comfort and reassurance through unchanging habit. *Gardeners' Question Time* proves that Britain is, after all, chiefly composed of horticultural societies, allotment associations and green fingers clubs. An older more ingenuous excitement stirs as the 'team' – Lord Reith's own device for making knowledge palatable – holds forth in a village hall where ancient flags have been brought out in their honour, and committee ladies are even now preparing tea in large, brown, two-handled pots. The vision is as inseparable from Sunday as gravy-boats in the kitchen sink, the whisper of rain on a skylight and the smell of warm ironing.

'If it *is* a village hall,' Professor Alan Gemmell says, 'then we've probably struck lucky.' The Professor, in his 33 years with *Gardeners' Question Time,* can remember broadcasts from insecure shanties in the far Scottish Highlands and from Welsh bethels with gales rattling their corrugated iron roofs. Bill Sowerbutts recollects Sabden, in Lancashire, where a sheep gnawed through the BBC's power cable. Professor Gemmell combatively mentions nearby Rawtenstall, and broadcasting to 12 questioners and 12 other spectators. 'And there was a place near Derby where a cow put its head through an open window and mooed.'

Perpetually travelling as the team are, they never seem to reduce the backlog of 1,700 urgent invitations. Some societies wrote in 20 years ago, and are still waiting. 'It can be very embarrassing when you do get in touch with people,' Ken Ford, the producer says. 'You write to "the Secretary", and his wife writes back, "My husband died several years ago . . ." '

Not that *Gardeners' Question Time* dispenses its bounty with any but the roughest pruning-gloves. The reverence of that other peripatetic BBC programme, *Down Your Way* had no place in the Loads-Gemmell-Sowerbutts approach to questioners. Fred Loads in particular could be rather terse, as when a lady asked what to do about Dutch Elm Disease and Loads replied 'Move'. There was also the questioner whose lengthy description of an aphid he had observed on his rose bush drove Fred Loads to enquire in exasperation: 'Are you sure you didn't see its big blue eyes?'

Fred Loads's death last March robbed the programme of Lancaster's irascible knightly champion: it also caused a noticeable power-shift. For 33 years, Professor Alan Gemmell had faced odds of two-to-one in his jocular insistence that gardening is a matter of scientific deduction. Loads and Bill Sowerbutts together taunted the Professor as just a boffin rashly pitting his new-fangled Biology Chair against their respective market gardens – a boffin and a new boy, of course, since they were both on the first-ever panel whereas Gemmell did not arrive until a year later, in 1948. But now, without Fred Loads, the odds and the weapons are equally-matched.

From the bar of the Broadway Hotel, Letchworth, into its pink and white ballroom annexe, the combatants walk – as combatants always do – side-by-side. Professor Gemmell, 67, is plump, sunburned, beaky-nosed, lightly freckled. Bill Sowerbutts is 70, a jug-eared man with the solicitous stoop of a lifetime's attention to celery crops. In contrast with the Professor's tasteful tweeds, it seems a principle with Bill to dress no more formally for radio than for a day in his greenhouse. His coat, misshapen and cavernous, might be stuffed with seed-packets, even small pots. His tie bisects his clean white shirt like the seam in a broad bean.

'Sowerbutts' is an ancient Midland name, meaning sower, or planter, of a 'butt' of land. Bill's family were long-established Staffordshire nurserymen, cultivating mainly tomatoes and celery in the premier peat soil called 'Ashton Moss'. He himself planned to become a journalist on the Ashton-under-Lyne *Reporter:* it was his father's premature death that forced him into horticulture. Strangely enough, via his own nurseries, in Ashton, Hyde and Warrington, he became Britain's foremost gardening writer, producing an advice column syndicated to 50 provincial papers.

Retired now from commercial market gardening, he keeps up his journalism and broadcasts. The burden of producing cash crops, however, has fallen from his shoulders. In his own garden, near Glossop, he can permit himself to grow exotic, self-indulgent things like orchids, melons, peppers. And loofahs. 'Loofahs', he repeated. 'People allus make the mistake of thinking they come from foreign parts. I grow any amount of 'em. I grew the loofah I've got in my sponge bag. I scrub my back with it. *And* my front and sides.'

Professor Alan Gemmell, an alumnus of Glasgow, Leiden and

Minnesota universities, spent his early career in study of diseases affecting oat and potato crops and golf course greens in his native Ayrshire. During the Second World War he became a Home Office pathologist, on one occasion tracing the cause of death in a headless, limbless corpse to starch and sycamore fragments inside the dead man's cap. 'We decided in the end that the fellow must have been hit with a rolling pin.' Even now, when a diseased vegetable is described but not shown to him, the Professor will observe that it's like holding an inquest without the body.

In 1950 he received his Chair at Keele – the first in Biology at any English university. The Principal said he could continue on *Gardeners' Question Time* so long as Keele got a mention. In fairness, the billing was extended to Lancaster and Ashton-under-Lyne.

Such is the disparate power engaged by a letter from Mr W. Stevens from Swanage, opening the correspondence programme with a description of brown and black splotches on his 'Tender but True' parsnip crop. Neither Gemmell nor Sowerbutts demurs from the view of Chris Brickell, the newcomer panellist, that Carrot Root Fly has probably been at work. Brickell, a youngish man with black eyebrows that collide on the bridge of his nose, runs the Royal Horticultural Society's nurseries at Wisley, Surrey. It was a significant day in gardening's upper and lower worlds when the RHS deigned to send a representative to *Gardeners' Question Time*.

Professor Gemmell adds that 'Tender but True' are a lovely strain of parsnip. 'And "Avon Resister" is another *very* gude one.'

'– quite good,' Bill Sowerbutts amends.

Minor skirmishes take place around the enquiry, from Mr M. F. Gricks, of Timperley, Cheshire, as to whether bonemeal can harm shrubs, and over the brown blisters which Mr. Z. Jelonek, of Wendover, Bucks, has noticed on his flowering currant. The rival merits of 'steamed' or 'meat and bone' manure provoke a bitter exchange that reduces Chris Brickell to silence and makes even Ken Ford seem wary of separating the combatants. On the strength of savage last words, Bill Sowerbutts wins this bout. But then Sowerbutts slips. Replying to Mr A. Lowe, of Overpool, Cheshire, about fertilising a compost heap, Bill Sowerbutts incautiously describes the needed quantity as 'a closed handful'. As the Professor beams triumphantly at him, he amends this to 'three matchboxes full per bucket'. Professor Gemmell observes, with almost lyric satisfaction, that matchboxes come in different sizes. 'I said *small* matchboxes,' Bill replies testily.

Mr G. Smith, of Leicester, asks which variety of early potatoes the team would recommend. 'There is,' Professor Gemmell beams, 'a simply lovely one called "Irish Peace" . . .' '– how do you spell that?' Bill Sowerbutts interrupts. The Professor giggles – a weakness of his – but recovers. 'I think I can guess the variety Bill will go for. It's another lovely one called "Duke of York".'

'Is that one still available?' Sowerbutts's surprise could not be more elaborate if the Professor had suggested that they go home tonight in a hansom cab.

For Letchworth's Horticultural and Allotment Society, the visitation has come a mere 10 years after their secretary wrote to the BBC. At the Broadway Hotel, the ballroom stage blooms with potted daffodils and poinsettia around the sacerdotally scarlet BBC table-cloth. Meanwhile, in an adjacent dining room, Society officials enter-tain the team to a 5 p.m. chicken dinner. The table is covered with wine bottles which prove on close inspection, to be only cardboard dummies. Professor Gemmell's voice lilts through an otherwise fitful conversation, dilating on irises, asparagus and the reign of Edward VII.

Further along, Ken Ford recalls a terrible night, 2 March 1972, the programme's 1000th edition, when its most celebrated chairman, Franklin Englemann dropped dead from a heart attack. Ford, as mere producer, little thought he would ever fill the urbane Engle-mann's shoes. He is, in fact, an experienced farmer, whereas Engle-mann, like Freddie Grisewood before him, knew almost nothing of horticulture.

'– he'd trained as an opera singer actually,' Professor Gemmell put in.

'Remember how embarrassed he used to get?' Bill Sowerbutts added. 'Every so often we'd get this question about a variety called Englemann's Giant Pansies.'

After dinner the team and their chairman escape to a cloakroom, and the first drink of the evening. The 12 questions they will be asked are studied and roughly apportioned. Ken Ford's assistant, Tricia Thompson, meanwhile summons the 12 questioners behind a screen. A briefing proved necessary with the very first programme in 1947, when a questioner seized the opportunity to perform a brief cornet solo. Eleven men and one woman, holding a potted *Plumbago Capensis,* are exhorted not to touch the microphone or utter spittle-producing phrases like 'peat pot'. Rough fingers, clasped behind backs, nervously twist and crumple the unfamiliar crop of words written out on paper.

The team make their entrance ceremonially down the middle of the hall. Professor Gemmell carries the stricken *Plumbago Capensis,* and Chris Brickell, a potted African violet. Each in turn then 'warms up' the audience by telling a horticultural joke. A story repeated by the late Fred Loads on every programme for 33 years contained the evidently ideal elements of a vicar, a sermon and a dose of cascara.

85

'And jokes about manure, of course,' Professor Gemmell said. 'Even elderly spinster ladies seem to find the subject hilarious.'

'That,' Bill Sowerbutts said portentously, 'is because Woman is a constipated animal.'

The opening question, from Mr Victor Brown, about types of pot plant to grow in a moderately-heated greenhouse, allows Bill to mention half-a-dozen varieties, from Mignonette to Black-eyed Susan, and also to caution against the allergy-producing *Primula Obconica* that were his own father's great horticultural mistake. Professor Gemmell complains, when his turn comes, that Bill has pinched all *his* ideas as usual. The Professor has his chance with the next question, from Mr Paul Shipman, concerning mysterious holes which have appeared in some heavy-duty polythene sacks. The questioner wonders if slugs could have been biting them. 'Slugs,' Professor Gemmell says, 'don't bite – they *rrasp*. It's more likely to be mice.' The questioner replies doggedly that the marks look too small for mice teeth. And why would a mouse bite into a sack with only sand in it? 'You mustn't imagine that mice think the way *you* think,' Professor Gemmell says, possibly meaning the opposite.

Ken Ford, like a kindly courtroom clerk, unscrambles Mr J. Chamberlain's verbose enquiry into a classic gardener's question. Does it matter if broad bean seeds are planted upside-down? The team replies tersely that it doesn't. The next questioner begins: 'My hoped-for farmyard manure has not materialised . . .' 'What happened?' Ford asks innocently. 'Did the horse turn round the wrong way?' At his elbow are three prompt cards, covering all he needs to signal to the team in mid-broadcast. The first card says 'Over 50 mins', the second says 'Keep it short', and the third warns 'No questions'. It often happens that a questioner, convulsed by stage fright, asks a friend to deputise. The team must be stopped from quizzing or teasing the innocent substitute.

Mary Pearce-Martin's *Plumbago Capensis,* near death from over-watering, reunites the Sowerbutts and the Gemmell furies against this common cruelty. Likewise, the wood-like indentations on G. Wallduck's *Doyenne de Comice* pears are agreed to be Stony Pit Virus, and terminal. 'My name is Tommy Cox,' the next questioner starts boldly, 'and my problem is pests.' Professor Gemmell takes the opportunity to explain at tutorial length that fast-moving insects are generally useful to the garden while slow-moving ones tend to be harmful. Tommy Cox further asks whether an earthworm can live on after being cut in half. The Professor squashes that myth, so fostered by the scarcity of dead earthworms. 'After they die, you see, they're destroyed so *very* quickly. It's the same with birds. You very seldom see a dead bird, even though there are thousands of them flying around . . .'

'Not flying round *dead,*' Bill Sowerbutts interrupts. Having stopped the Professor in mid-flight, Sowerbutts now essays the *coup de grace.* 'Why don't you ask Alan a *really* difficult question? How does an earthworm turn round in its burrow?' The victim, under the raised broadsword, suddenly twists to one side. 'The answer is, it *doesn't* turn. It burrows round in a circle and comes back to the same place.'

The programme ends with a 'Topical Tip' from each panellist. Chris Brickell recovers from his bemusement sufficiently to recommend spraying apples against Scab. Professor Gemmell observes that sulphate of potash is an excellent general tonic. Bill Sowerbutts counsels spraying cold water to minimise cell-damage after frost. He and the Professor then escape through an emergency exit that is one entire swung-back section of the pink and white wall. Hurrying to their London train – the 8.52, as Bill said, not the 8.53 as the Professor thought – a secret is inadvertently revealed.

Professor Alan Gemmell and Bill Sowerbutts are close friends. They attend football matches together; are fond of each other's wives. They are heading for the same small hotel in Euston, and the same last segment of *Match of the Day*.

Standing on Letchworth station, they remember the *Plumbago Capensis,* how sick it looked, and the question about planting broad bean seeds upside-down. The answer, as usual, could have been found in almost any book. A plant always shoots upward, just as its roots always go down. 'Heliotropism,' Bill Sowerbutts said.

'*Geotropism,*' the Professor said. 'Get it right now.'

On the train, they talked affectionately of Fred Loads, their missing team-mate; his horticultural skill, his ability to be rude without giving offence. Before their tripartite joust, the champions of Keele, Lancaster and Ashton-under-Lyne always used to meet for a gossip at the same motorway cafeteria.

'I'd say you were travelling a lot more by train these days than you used to, Alan,' Bill Sowerbutts said.

The Professor looked mystified, as professors do when heliotropism is confused with geotropism. Or, indeed, when fertiliser is measured by matchbox or closed fists.

'Do you mean to say I'm travelling a lot more by *car* lately?'

'No, I mean to say you're travelling a lot more by *train* lately . . .'

1981

Behind the Scenes at Harrods

Christmas began in earnest for Harrods on a sunny day last March, in a corner of the Food Hall where men in black coats still take down grocery orders in decorous copperplate. Through an arch beyond could be seen sticky mounds of the 60,000 hot cross buns that Harrods expected to sell before Good Friday. A Food Hall executive waited nearby, glancing nonchalantly at his watch. In a moment, another discreetly joined him. Another arrived, accompanied by an ash-haired woman. They spoke quietly together for a moment, like surgeons who do not wish to alarm the patient. Harrods, by March each year, has already produced its next range of Christmas gift hampers. These executives were the advance inspection party.

The inspection was to take place, not in the main store but in its scarcely less magnificent terracotta-fronted Trevor Square warehouse. Harrods executives daily bless the providence of their managerial forefathers in, long ago, connecting store and warehouse by a tunnel running crossways under Brompton Road. It was to this hidden Harrods marvel that the hamper-inspection party now descended. On their right, in the white-tiled gloaming, stretched tributary tunnels named Wine Cellar Close or Frosty Way (to the cold store rooms). On their left came an incessant flow of traffic from Trevor Square: of headless window dummies, lightweight Greek pillars, hand-made suits, bespoke chocolates and boxed toilet rolls, carried by people or driven by one of the dark green electric trolleys in use in Harrods' underground since *circa* 1910.

The group portrayed in miniature a command structure that might appear military were it not so strongly imbued with the spirit of the junior common room. From topmost management there was Tony Clark, the merchandise director, an Harrodian of atypically few words with a brooding Sherlock Holmes profile. From the senior operational level there was Alastair Walker, divisional manager in charge of Food Halls, on whose rosy, jovial face can be read a willingness to sample with gusto every single item in his province. Walker had brought with him two section managers, Pam Reed and Tony Guyatt, in charge, respectively, of Food Hall aesthetics and content. Guyatt, a chubby young man, wore the black coat and striped trousers in which it was so long the Harrods tradition to retail foodstuffs. Pam Reed has blonde hair and large, ironic eyes. At Trevor Square they were to rendezvous with Richard Jenkyns, the buyer directly responsible for hampers to be sold in what Harrods, ever anxious to evoke domesticity rather than commerce, prefers to call not the Provisions Department but The Pantry.

Hampers, for Harrods, have deep symbolic significance. The first Mr Harrod was, after all, a grocer. His inheritors, through age after age, have kept alive Henry Harrod's principle that food must have primacy of selling space. Today, despite its multiplying retail fronts, despite its vast intercontinental business, despite an annual turnover of £17m in Food Halls alone, Harrods still prefers to regard itself as the local provision shop for Knightsbridge, Belgravia and that big grey house with railings facing the Mall.

The £12 hamper was the one to be presented to Harrods' own pensioners. 'I got a whole bottle of sherry in this year,' Mr Jenkyns said proudly. Approaching the £65 hamper, the buyer visibly held his breath. He had, on his own initiative, included a *Good Housekeeping* cookery book as a variation on the expected cheese crock or tea caddy souvenir. 'A good residual, that,' Alastair Walker said amid murmurs of approbation.

Tony Clark, the merchandise director, thought the £65 hamper ought to be upgraded to £75. 'If people are willing to pay sixty-five pounds, they'll be willing to pay seventy-five.' With the £100 hamper came the first permanent container: a box in the unbleached split chestnut that Richard Jenkyns, after long deliberation, had ordered in preference to traditional wicker. And so on, in finely-costed degrees of opulence and permanence, to this year's £500 hamper in its dark wood casket, replete with 21-year-old whisky and Dom Perignon champagne. That one was the model Richard Jenkyns foresaw least difficulty in selling. 'Every year I get a regular order of seven from the same man. He gives one each to his six workers and the seventh to his wife.'

Door number 3 at Harrods is colloquially The Kennel Entrance. You can hear, one floor below, the cries and yaps of customers' dogs which the store would not be so indelicate as actually to prohibit. Harrods, whatever the cost-effective arguments against it, remains the last department store with dog-kennels. It is the last department store with a private lending library. It is the last store where customers may deposit for safe keeping their fur coats or Coronation robes. It is the last store with private strong rooms, apportioned by dynastic right, whose gold-leaf walls and engraved time-locks are unchanged from the day the first deposit was entered – as a ledger, still in use, records – in 1893.

Door 3, however, has associations far above mere dogs. It happens also to be the entrance favoured by Royalty. The habit dates, they say, from Queen Mary, whose punctuality was such that if she arrived a minute early, she would order her chauffeur to drive round the block again.

Not that Harrods ever officially mentions such things. The four Royal warrants on its eastern and western curves hang there by the slenderest thread. Any warrant, at any time, can be withdrawn without explanation. No one can tell you, therefore, of the regular, extensive Palace orders for babyware; of the Princess of Wales' past appearances in the Bakery croissant-queue; or of the special procedures which glide into action whenever the Queen Mother wants to change her library book.

John Hudson, Harrods' principal commissionaire – or Green Man – ascends the staircase to vestibule Door 3 with his colleague and old comrade, George Firth. Below, in addition to kennels, the Green Men have a special robing room. Firth and Hudson have spent the hour before opening-time in brushing their bottle green tailcoats, shining their toecaps to the texture of wet liquorice and polishing their many gilt buttons.

Both men served in the Household Cavalry when the horse squadrons left Buckingham Palace for Libya, to fight Rommel's Afrika Corps. Hudson was with armoured cars. Firth tried to fool the enemy by riding dummy tanks across minefields, with a wind-up gramophone that played records of real tanks on the move.

'Both of us were Monty men,' John Hudson says. 'He used to drive up here after the war in his armour-plated Rolls. He'd always recognise my medals. I gave up wearing medals, though. The younger men haven't got 'em. People nowadays think medals are silly.'

Hudson's usual station is the pre-eminent Door number 7, facing Brompton Road and the main taxi-stop. Door 3 ranks next, with its canine guests, its intermittent Royals and the parcels still left there for collection. 'Hampers as well, there used to be. Picnics for Wimbledon and Goodwood races. Not many of those now. A few, though. Remember, George, when all the butlers and housekeepers used to come through here to pay their accounts in the Banking Hall? And prams. This hallway used to be full of 'em. The other day, you know George, I saw this great big chap on one of the escalators with his little boy. I said to the boy, "I used to look after your dad and his brother when they were left here in their pram". The two of 'em had a puppy which they would keep throwing out. It used to dangle there on the end of its lead.'

Green Men open doors, obtain taxis, dispense tourist advice and, as well as receiving money, have been known to lend it. 'I've done that,' John Hudson says. 'People come up to you with a hard luck story, "Can you lend me eighty pence to get home?" I fall for those sort of tales.'

But Green Men also minister to a Rolls Royce trade as regular as it ever was, and as eccentric. When Hudson and Firth swap stories, they are less likely to feature Monty and Rommel than the endless variety of very rich, sometimes not fully alert, old ladies.

'One of them used to come out of her Rolls every time and say, "Now, what colour worms shall I eat today? Red or white?" She was a lunatic, really.'

'One of them always came in holding a pillow up against her face, so the wind wouldn't blow her face powder off.'

'Remember the one in that Italian car? Only two cars like that were ever made – one for this lady's husband, the other for Mussolini. Her chauffeur would wait until he saw her coming, then he'd open the car door and spray all lavender water inside.'

'I said to her one morning, "I see you've got a new chauffeur, Madam", "Yes," she said. "Do you know what the other one did? He locked me inside the car and then set fire to it".'

At 10.30 a.m., Aleck Craddock leaves his office in the management wing and emerges, with a look of distinct pleasure, into a selling area. Mr Craddock is a broadly-built man with neat white hair and a smile which can only be described as cherubic. His suit, excellent yet unnoticeable, is perhaps the best index to his character. For Mr Craddock, like all floorwalkers of yesteryear, is utterly classless. Nothing about him suggests that he is managing director of Harrods, in absolute authority over its 14 acres, its 22 departments and its 5,000 staff. Indeed, as he moves about the store, he is frequently approached by customers for directions. To Aleck Craddock, that is one of the day's little rewards.

Mr Craddock is the perfect Harrodian. A provisioner by upbringing, he joined Harrods in 1954 direct from his family's business in Marylebone. Harrods made him provisions buyer at the unprecedented age of 28. He was food and restaurants section manager when Harrods still manufactured its own chocolate and custard powder, and bottled its own honey, and when Harrods' private bakery sent trolleys through the Brompton tunnel piled high with loaves still almost too hot to touch. Mr Craddock's face retains the cosy calm of a man whose main concerns used to be tea and butter and at what thickness bacon ought to be sliced. What actually concerns Aleck Craddock, of course, is the steering of Harrods safely through a world intent on proving it has no need of any department store, let alone one whose telegraphic address is still 'Everything,

91

London'; let alone one which, when the GPO introduced postcodes, devoted time and expense to securing the code letters XL.

His task is made more formidable by the boom that has so obviously passed. Harrods, through the early seventies, rode high on the tourist tide which swamped London. Those were the days when so many Gulf sheikhs packed the store that taxi drivers renamed it 'Harrabs'; when Sheikh Yamani himself took his Harrods haul to Heathrow on a commandeered coal lorry; when, at certain times, Saudi harems filled the Perfumery Department like sets of little black skittles.

Harrods under Aleck Craddock can no longer take such giddy turnover for granted. Nor will its gargantuan daily non-Arab business alone ensure its survival. Economies must be practised. But, because this is Harrods, economy must never obtrude. So Harrods still gives away its green and gold status symbol carrier bags. Harrods, to avoid disappointing one family up from the West Country, switched on its 11,000-bulb lacework of Christmas lights on a sunny spring afternoon.

Outside Mr Craddock's office hang three framed testimonials inscribed in the pseudo-mediaeval calligraphy of the Edwardian age. Harrods in those days barely descended to ordinary Press advertising. Instead, it approached three 'giants of the written word', Shaw, Arnold Bennett and H. G. Wells, to contribute in general terms to a symposium entitled *Commerce*. All three, as was intended, wrote fulsome tributes to Harrods, Wells, in particular, expressing a desire to 'study your great organisation and explain its working'.

Such praise is ironic from an author whose greatest works bemoan the hopeless struggle of small shopkeepers against large department stores. Nowadays, by contrast, a Mr Polly thrives on every corner. It is the emporium which stocks 8,000 dresses, 7,000 ties, 450 types of cheese and 150 makes of piano – serviced by 40 piano-tuners – which has become the hero.

Two years ago, Harrods' chief engineer, a tousle-haired northerner named Cliff Bulcock, approached top management with a plan for the store's biggest structural alteration in 40 years. He proposed the building of escalators on the north-west side, accessible from Hans Road through Door number 10. In Bulcock's view, new escalators were essential, to relieve pressure on the existing ones inside Door number 5, and to stimulate customer flow at westerly extremes of the fashion and furniture floors. He foresaw no opposition from what was, after all, the first London store to install an escalator, in 1898. That pioneering marvel had no steps: you stood on a plain ramp, ascending from the present-day Perfumery Hall, to be greeted by a Harrods attendant, offering brandy or *sal volatile*.

None the less, there were objections to Cliff Bulcock's plan. Sinking a shaft for new escalators would inconvenience customers. 'Management changed their tune,' Bulcock says, 'when I told them the new escalators could give them extra floor space. The escalators I wanted to put in cost a million pounds. Then management announced they were going to build new escalators at a cost of *two* million.'

To the shopper, Harrods' frontage and flanks may seem infinite; but to management they are a terracotta straitjacket. The store made its last frontal acquisition in 1911. From then on, the island site was complete. Expansion can happen only from the windows inward. It is a constant process, though unseen by any shopper cruising between departments without apparent horizons. Only Harrods executives can hear the perpetual cut and shuffle of existing space, the crash of boundaries between outmoded merchandise areas, the taut, agonised sound of extra square feet being mined and scrounged and squeezed.

The store, these past 10 years, has quietly added the equivalent of whole departments to its total selling area. Yet, to the Harrods customer – 'Lady so-and-so' as the archetype tends to be called – each major stylistic change has, rather, seemed like Harrods growing more traditionally Harrodian. So, in Women's Fashions, the former vast, empty, plush-carpeted spaces vanished under multi-coloured racks and individual 'name' boutiques. The great central Banking Hall, where butlers and housekeepers once foregathered with their employers' account-books, silently metamorphosed into perfumery counters and white marble. The lofty Meat Hall, tiled by Doulton with scenes of the chase, now teems with extra business round a central charcuterie counter under suspended masses of hams and salamis, Edwardian in appearance but plastic in composition.

Cliff Bulcock's new escalators were to be installed at Harrods' north-west corner, a point where, until not so long ago, titled people lived in service flats above the second storey. Next to Door number 10, you can still see the old formal portico to Hans Mansions. The residents had their own private service road, lined with individual dumb waiters, running under the store to a corresponding block above the present-day Door 5. Coal-chutes from the street fed bunkers, still visible in the wine-cellar, embossed with baronets' names.

The final flat-dweller above Harrods was Sir Richard Burbridge, last of the three-man Burbridge dynasty which succeeded Henry Harrod's own. After Sir Richard's departure, the elegant reception rooms were converted into offices for top management. The plan, when the new escalators went in, was to spend a further £6 million on development which would gain the store some 42,000 extra square feet. Of these, significantly, 15,000 square feet would be added to the Food Halls.

The year-long work of sinking the escalator shaft gave Bulcock frequent archaeological glimpses into Harrods' 130-year history. Behind the 1911 walls could be seen the strata of little 19th-century shops, coalesced to a single frontage some time after the Great Exhibition, growing subsequently as Knightsbridge itself did, from miry village street to fashionable carriageway. Sealed in there some-where, amid fossil walls and fireplaces, is the ghost of a pub, The Buttercup, whose stubborn title deeds long hindered the second Mr Harrod's great gaslit expansion era.

The period that saw Bulcock's new escalators swung into place, also brought Harrods disruption of a less easily-camouflaged kind. Sir Hugh Fraser, 44-year-old, hard-gambling heir to the House of Fraser group which bought Harrods from the Burbridges in 1959, was ousted from his inherited chairmanship by a fellow Fraser director and Scot, Professor Roland Smith. Sir Hugh found a friend in 'Tiny' Rowland, whose Lonrho group has a minority shareholding in House of Fraser. Lonrho, with Sir Hugh Fraser's disgruntled support, instantly launched a £158 million bid for House of Fraser with the no doubt chivalrous and altruistic purpose of restoring the hapless Fraser his birthright.

All this past summer, while Lonrho's bid was examined by the Monopolies Commission, Harrods' future has hung in the balance. Would it remain in the comfortable, canny hands of Scottish drapers and accountants? Or would it be added to other corporate prizes in the fast-growing magpie hoard of the omniverous 'Tiny'?

If Harrods could not hide the boardroom tension, at least it could hide the gaping, necessary hole in its north-west corner. By March this year, through an abyss no customer could notice, via giant cranes working on a Sunday, the new silver stairways were lowered. An opening ceremony was scheduled, significantly close to the Royal Wedding, though the escalators would actually come into use for test purposes in the July sales.

In the Meat Hall, Alastair Walker stands under the hanging show of sausages and salamis, watching the day's pies being decanted into the central charcuterie case. Nearby, at a cascade of marble slabs, set about by mermaids, ferns and fishermen's nets, Jim Lovegrove, the fish buyer, begins work on the daily tableau featuring the pick of his 3.30 a.m. visit to Billingsgate.

Today, Lovegrove had intended a halibut theme. He changed his mind at the last moment on discovering a long, thick conger eel. This he twists round a wooden stake, pushing aside its mutely remon-strating face. On either side, he arranges brill and John Dory – the fish, he remarks, with which Christ fed the Five Thousand. A lobster rampant rears on a field of burnished kippers. Had the halibut been used, Lovegrove planned to relieve its whiteness with crimson butterflies made of flattened lobster tails and crabs' claws.

Lovegrove, a calm young man of 38 with a gold earring, learned his art from the previous buyer, Mr Sneath, who started the daily display in the 1940s. It was Mr Sneath who showed him how to make the butterflies and also to write the name 'Harrods' in whitebait. He took over, with apprehension, after Mr Sneath retired, but triumphed with his first tableau, a flower made entirely from plaice.

His past displays have included a sturgeon, a 14lb lobster, once a 550lb basking shark whose head and liver were afterwards donated to the Natural History Museum. At Billingsgate the merchants save unusual specimens for him. His biggest ambition is to get hold of a sunfish. 'It would look lovely in a design. It's a beautiful gold colour. And it doesn't have a tail.'

He has never, to his knowledge, repeated a design. 'Some mornings, I'll bring the box in and look at it, and it'll be just plain old plaice, nothing exciting at all. Then perhaps I'll find a red mullet, and that gets the ideas sparking . . .'

It is universally known that Harrods' telephonist, once accepted an order to supply a baby elephant as a gift for Ronald Reagan. Less well-documented is the South American tapir, Veronica by name, which dwelt for a while in Harrods' Menagerie. A sociable beast, she would follow the keepers round as they cleaned out the cages, helpfully vacuuming up the leftovers of her fellow inmates. Her sole aberration was a tendency to bolt without warning through the adjacent Carpet Department. Customers who experienced it will probably never forget the sight of a tapir streaking towards them through the Axminster-scented twilight.

Strict new laws governing the sale of wild animals forced Harrods in the seventies to replace its Menagerie by a far simpler Pets Department, offering puppies, kittens, gerbils, dwarf hamsters and occasional chameleons. Where 300 varieties of exotic bird once screeched and chattered, there is now only one dark blue, deeply pessimistic-looking macaw.

Rita Stratta, a small, quick, humorous woman, manages the department with a staff of six. It was Rita who would pursue Veronica the tapir among the Chinese carpets and Bokhara rugs, and drive her back between two short wooden planks. 'Tapirs are just like pigs. You can make them go anywhere as long as they can't see anything on either side of them. It was more difficult when we had to pack up a porcupine. The only way I could pick it up was between two rubber dustbin lids.'

The department still throngs all day with sightseers and children. 'I think I'll just clear this lot out and give my puppies a rest,' Rita says with a briskness permitted no other Harrods manager. The sightseers are ejected, to wait among the dog baskets, budgie hardware and five foot high vermilion felt cat scratching-posts.

Rita looks nostalgically through scrapbooks of unusual pets supplied by Harrods in the past. 'That was Justin, the puma cub. A civet. A Malabar squirrel. A fruit bat. She was sweet. She used to hold her baby enfolded in her wings.'

Even today there is still the odd exotic order. 'That macaw, for instance. We were asked to get that for a VIP – I can't tell you his name. Another VIP – who's in London for the Royal Wedding – saw the Queen's corgis and fell in love with them.'

The title of Harrods' chief shoplifter is disputed between Big Fat Mama, Swivel-Eyes, The Patsy, Cannon and The Cyclist. Each has a method of operation well known to the store's chief security officer, Frank Nichols. Big Fat Mama manipulates juvenile accomplices – otherwise her 'chicks'. Swivel-Eyes is self-evidently vigilant; The Patsy acts as decoy, leading store detectives on while his accomplices go to work. Cannon, the least pleasant, specialises in threatening any store assistant who tries to apprehend him. The Cyclist chains up his bike outside and steals anything he can carry off on it. His activities have ceased since he tried the same trick at Bourne & Hollingsworth, and the security staff there took the wise precaution of letting down his tyres.

Frank Nichols, ex-Murder Squad, ex-Flying Squad, operates from subterranean offices, off Harrods' Brompton Tunnel, which have much in common with the East End police stations he formerly knew. From here issue 50 uniformed guards, the 20 plainclothes store detectives and 'till-investigators' assigned to cover a populace which daily equals that of some largish town. A further 20 'squadders', or trusties, within the departments give auxiliary help in a battle where you cannot have too many open eyes.

Merely to open the store each morning occupies Nichols' staff and auxiliaries a full two hours. Shutting down at night takes even longer. Every washroom must be visited to ensure no taps are still running. Every workroom must be checked to see that all electric irons are cold. Only the strong rooms with their engraved 1893 time locks can be trusted to look after themselves over the full span of highly susceptible night.

Store security acquired a new dimension in the seventies, when Harrods found itself listed among the 'targets' available to terrorist organisations. The store has been twice attacked*: by incendiaries in 1973 and, in 1974, by a holdall bomb left in the Houseware

* Written before the bomb explosion on the Saturday before Christmas in 1983.

Department at the height of the Christmas rush. Thanks to an advance warning, and to the building's massive inner doors, nobody was killed or injured. But from then on, not even Harrods could avoid the age of paranoid suspicion. The store now, apologetically, employs close-circuit TV surveillance; its executives, as high as Mr Craddock, spoil the cut of their jackets with walkie-talkie radio communicators.

The range of crime confronting Frank Nichols is not much less than in his Sweeney days. A few months ago, someone was stabbed in a Harrods department. Not long before that, a hooded gang with sawn-off shot-guns ambushed a payroll en route through the store's underground. The robbers took £82,000, ran out through the staff entrance – knocking Frank Nichols's deputy unconscious as he tried to stop them – and escaped in a stolen taxi. The taxi was afterwards found abandoned inside Brompton Oratory with one of the gang dead in the back. He had evidently killed himself by accident with the shotgun under his coat.

Twice a year, at its January and July sales, Harrods throws away decorum. The terracotta palace becomes a rampaging Klondike where mink coats can be disinterred for half their normal prices, and piles of costly china topple under the assault of many hands. An era rife with perpetual, suspect bargains and discounts has, if anything, lengthened the queues camped overnight along Harrods' front windows, awaiting the first day's dash and grab.

Last January, on that first Saturday alone, £5 million rang up on Harrods' tills. In the Electrical Department, where colour TV sets were reduced to half price, actual fist-fights erupted. Mayhem and congestion there, and in China and Glass, several times brought the store dangerously near total standstill.

For the July sale, accordingly, Aleck Craddock and his cabinet evolved an audacious wheeze. Why not have *two* 'first days', on Friday and Saturday? The impact could thus be cushioned without damage to turnover – for both days' takings would be reckonable against January's £5 million.

As June drew to a close, the store began, once more, to change within itself. Partitions appeared as shelters for *ad hoc* changing rooms. Concourses widened, to be divided by little makeshift wooden stalls. Display cases yielded to trestle table barricades. The store's signwriters put aside fine-brush calligraphy for runic red letters spelling CASH, ACCOUNT and CREDIT CARDS. The Personnel Department took on 1,000 extra staff.

It is only at sale time that Harrods bothers to advertise on television. Last June, its agency submitted a commercial traditionally brief. Ticker-tape writing rattled out the Friday starting-date and the news of 12 months' interest-free credit. The Harrods logo then moved upward with a space ship lift-off noise.

The commercial was submitted to Aleck Craddock for approval. Mr Craddock watched it with a thoughtfulness that made the ad boys wonder if they might have gone too far this time. Then the managing director spoke. Could they, he asked, make that final 'whoosh' a little bit louder?

Mr Craddock's eve-of-sale inspection begins, appropriately, with China and Glass. In one department, together with selected kitchen-ware, 494,000 different lines await tomorrow's spearhead assault. 'Half a million from this area alone,' one of Mr Craddock's aides murmurs. At sale time, the taboo against mentioning money is relaxed. The millions they anticipate are positively flaunted.

Special precautions are in evidence to prevent any repeat of January's carnage. The prestige lines, Royal Doulton, Worcester, Spode, have been put into separate shock-absorbing redoubts. In Royal Worcester's sector, a commander addresses his, largely student, force drawn up behind their frail breastwork of trestles and cardboard. The cash registers all wear hygienic-looking paper seals. Three sharpened pencils lie next to every order-pad. Rugs have been laid to prevent carbon paper from credit card slips being ground into the carpet. There are supermarket wire baskets and thick bales of newspaper. It is the only time Harrods wraps anything in newspaper. 'It's far the best form of wrapping actually,' the Royal Worcester man said.

The glassware stands shoulder-high, tiered fragilely on cardboard sheets. Twenty-four assistants will patrol the lines, ready to catch a crystal column should it start to topple. Somehow each year, however fierce the struggle, breakages remain minimal.

Mr Craddock listens with unfeigned pleasure as Roger Street, the glass buyer, describes the forcing down of some lines to half price or even less. 'How much do you expect to do tomorrow?' Mr Craddock murmurs. 'A hundred and twenty-five thousand,' Street murmurs back. The question is put *sotto voce* to every section manager, every buyer with an independent province, on Mr Craddock's progress downward across acres of cooking pots, of toys, of ceramic flamin-goes, of carpets, of curtain stuffs, of modern cabinets, of bedding, of towels, of luggage, of laundry baskets, of lavatory seats with frogs painted on them, of radio, television, electronic games and hi-fi. In the Pets Department – firmly exempt from all sales – the blue macaw regards the directorial party with a sidelong, sceptical eye. 'Say hello to Mr Craddock,' someone suggests faintly.

In Traditional Furniture, a trolley passes by loaded with orange juice in cartons to sustain the sales staff tomorrow. In Bedlinens, a smiling Asian sells Mr Craddock a sweepstake ticket. 'I used to be in the Navy,' murmurs one of his aides. 'This is just like Admiral's Rounds, except that there's no bugler.'

On the Fashion Floor, Mr Craddock's manner becomes more skittish. 'Where are they?' he cries, pushing like Alan Quartermain through a foliage of Burberry coats marked down to £75. 'Here we are,' the salespersons reply, giggling. Thence, with judicious levity, to Ladies Underwear, to 'name' boutiques and to the small arena created for fully-stranded black mink coats, reduced from £4,500 each to £2,225. 'How much for the Fashion Floor altogether?' Mr Craddock asks. 'I haven't quite added it up,' Pat Newell, the divisional manager says. 'A million, I think. I'm sure it's a million.'

Menswear, on the ground floor, has been cleared to a broad avenue of wooden booths overflowing with ties and bow ties. There are reductions in the Perfumery Hall, oddly empty of odour as the marble floor is cleaned. There are reductions in answering machines, die-stamped stationery, even toilet paper. An 18-roll carton is marked down to £6.84. Dental floss is reduced by 16p.

At 8 a.m., the world's press and television assemble outside Door 5. Harrods' first sale day is a spectacle of undiminishing interest in all consumer societies. The media people are taken to their customary fourth-floor vantage-point, a balcony directly below two caged models in Olympic Way tracksuits, looking down to the dark green mats which the first stampede will obliterate. The staff, meanwhile, pour in through their separate entrance across Hans Road.

It is nine o'clock. The store is suddenly outlined by 11,000 white light bulbs. Security men raise the gold portcullises. The TV crews crane lenses over their balcony.

Seconds later, one man and 20 women, all with wire shopping baskets, breast the top of the brand-new escalator and sprint thunderously round the wooden-floored aisles of glassware and Italian breakfast china. In five minutes, the Royal Doulton shop is submerged. Stacks of red and gold plates topple between grabbing hands and thrusting camera noses. A solemn young Rabbi steadies armfuls of dinner plates with his beard. Japanese women kneel on the carpet, picking over their haul like an archaeological dig.

Management is everywhere, gauging the earliest signs, reckoning the earliest returns. In Modern Cabinets, Rodney Brimacombe, one of the general managers, stands aside for the Japanese women and their clinking, carrier bags. 'A good crowd,' Brimacombe says. 'It took them ten minutes to get through Door 5, anyway.'

Back in China and Glass, a girl approaches a white-haired man in a neat grey suit and asks where she can find cushions. 'Ah, yes . . .'

Aleck Craddock says. 'You go out of that door . . . keep going, and at the end of the passage . . .'

The sale starts as a hurricane. It ends as a scarcely noticeable breeze. Two weeks into July, it has shrunk to isolated coat-racks, oddments in baskets, a few final shoes and towels and ceramic frogs. Reports from the Counting House, as Harrods prefers to call its computer systems, show turnover on that double first day to have been 13 per cent up on the previous July's. Takings from the full fortnight are up 25 per cent. Now that the excitement has passed, decent inhibitions return.

Besides, other preoccupations have supervened. The Hat Department has almost sold out of Lady Diana straws. In the Food Hall, crowds congregate daily around Jim Lovegrove's *fleur de lis* modelled from red, white and blue plaice.

Two days before the Royal Wedding, the escalators are officially opened. Professor Roland Smith, new chairman of the House of Fraser group, performs the ceremony. Professor Smith is in the tradition of tall, crop-headed Scotsmen who saw off the Boche in Flanders. To the assembled Harrodians he makes a nice little speech, reaffirming the store's future expansion under House of Fraser. The message to 'Tiny' Rowland and Lonrho is as clear as if the Professor had raised two fingers.

It is the season of giant, red-hearted peaches. Alastair Walker has brought a basketful with him from the Food Hall to add to the coffee, orange juice, toast and brioches at Aleck Craddock's morning executive conference. With the peaches, piled on fresh ferns, comes a perennial Harrods topic. The store will shortly be revising its interior again.

'We all know what we'd *really* like,' Aleck Craddock says. 'We'd like to take every bit of stock out of the store and pile it in Brompton Road and start from scratch. Even if we could do that, we wouldn't have time. All the time this plan's going into effect, we've got to keep trading. In fact, we've got to put *on* trade.

'. . . We've decided on balance that shifting the restaurants into the basement isn't on . . . our main problem, that I'd like to discuss now, is what's going to happen to the Boys' Department. Should we put that on the Fashion Floor, or should it go up on the fourth floor as part of the new Leisure Complex? On the first floor, it'd be more convenient for the parents. On the other hand, if a boy has to go for his school uniform to a place near a ladies' dress department, it may give him a bad memory of Harrods. We've got to remember that he might be a customer of tomorrow . . .'

On the roof at Trevor Square, Ernest Greenleaf, an elderly man with white specks on his ears and eyelashes, works happily in the sunshine near his white-splashed transistor radio. Mr Greenleaf is a plasterer, engaged on his customary midsummer task. He is making Greek columns for Harrods' Christmas window.

1981

Night Watch with White Watch

The Firemen's Strike was almost one day old. At Poplar fire station, in the East End of London, picket duty had passed to the Red Watch. Keith Leggitt, a blond-haired fireman of 29, was standing with the others at their brazier, trying to keep warm. A few minutes before midnight, a police car raced up East India Dock Road and stopped in front of them. A single constable got out, his face blackened, his coat streaked with mucus. 'For God's sake, come on,' the policeman said. 'People are dying back there . . .' Leggitt and several others left the picket line, grabbed breathing apparatus from inside the station and, in their own cars, followed the policeman to the fire.

At St Andrew's Hospital, an old people's home in Bow, they found four or five Army Green Goddess trucks already in attendance, and a scene to dismay any professional fireman. The fire had started in the hospital basement but the soldiers were aiming hoses at second-floor windows, where they could see smoke. Keith Leggitt was shocked to see how young the soldiers were. One of his first jobs was to disentangle 'a bunch of bastards' – fireman's jargon for hosepipe twisted and trodden into knots.

The Poplar strike-breakers, and others from Bow and Stratford, contained the fire and helped the Army to evacuate the hospital. Many patients were so old that they had to be carried out in their beds, with drip-feeds still attached. When the main fire was out, Leggitt noticed smoke billowing from a secondary outbreak around the gas meters. In such cases, the danger from gas fumes is greater than from fire, and one keeps the flames merely in check by cutting the hose jet to a spray. The Army's hoses had no means of controlling the jet from the nozzle. One soldier said to Leggitt that night what many have since repeated – they would rather be in Northern Ireland than serving as temporary firemen.

Poplar station covers an 'A' risk area of the East End – dockland, power stations, gasworks, the Blackwall Tunnel, hospitals, childrens' homes, bonded warehouses, miles of tenements and tindery lodging houses where drunks nod to sleep with fag ends hanging on one lip. And all around, the tower blocks twinkle like slum streets standing

102

on end. An 'A' risk area is one where two fire engines must be able to reach any call within five minutes.

The engines stand, in impeccable readiness, behind red gates unthinkably obstructed by parked cars. On the forecourt, a group of men in long blue jackets and boots huddle round one small blaze in a tin can. Traffic along East India Dock Road is always heavy, but one can detect the sound of more screaming horns than usual.

White Watch have come on picket – corresponding with their normal duty – under Sub Officer Tony Mackenzie. It was they who stood the last watch on Sunday night, before the strike began. With two appliances, the regulation number, they went to free a girl trapped in a lift in the tower block opposite the station. On returning, they found that two staff cars had been surreptitiously removed from the station. The cars, equipped with radios and breathing apparatus, have since been noticed with Army crews at fires in the area.

'That's our trouble,' Mackenzie said. 'That's always been our trouble – we're too naive. We expect people to play fair.'

After four days, it remains for all of them an eerie sensation to be on strike. 'I don't think any of us thought we'd really be standing here,' said Michael Gamble, age 26. 'It just seemed like a big poker game with the Government at first. Four of us went to Parliament to listen to the Emergency Debate. We sat up there listening to all the speakers and wondering what we were worrying about, because they all supported us. Then Merlyn Rees [the Home Secretary] got up at the end, and you could see: *he* wasn't bothered about us.

'Even on the night before it began, I think I said a little prayer that it wouldn't happen. Because we're putting our own families on the line as well. That's what people forget – we're putting our close ones at risk, too.'

Sub Officer Mackenzie, with 13 years' service behind him, does not need to remind himself why he is here. Age 37, with three children, his take home pay last month, including fares allowance and London supplement, was £45 per week for duties that have included being blown through a shop doorway by an explosion. From now on, if he escapes serious injury, he can look forward to the fireman's afflictions of heart and respiratory diseases and back trouble.

White Watch includes an elderly fireman with 30 years' service, and one aged 19, just a week out of his probation. Mackenzie's Sub Officer pay is almost exactly twice as much as the 19-year-old's. The man with 30 years' service earns no more than do his younger colleagues after 10 years. Recently he received what all GLC employees do after 30 years – a transistor radio.

Large, tough, straggle-haired men, mostly in their mid-20s, the rest of White Watch appear slightly in shock over the attitude of passers-by. Poplar station, like many others, displays a placard

103

requesting motorists to sound their horns if they sympathise with the strike. The freezing day is a stream of hoots and blasts and cheeps, from buses, ambulances, police cars, vans, and the long elephant bleats of articulated lorries. Some – a very few – have screamed abuse.

The encouragement is not only verbal. One lorry driver tossed a sack of cabbages to the pickets. They have received gifts of cigarettes, apples, rum and money, the latter often in tiny amounts from old age pensioners. A car stopped at that moment, its driver holding out a £1 note. Another lorry threw them the firewood for their brazier. 'And what about the hamburgers?' Mackenzie said to a long, lean fireman. 'How much did the butcher charge you for those hamburgers?'

'One-fifty – for fifty hamburgers.'

It was Thursday of what, to the strikers at least, seemed an unusually quiet week for fires. In the sky over East India Docks hung a long brown arch of smoke. Some of White Watch had been to investigate – it was only rubbish burning on a tip. About 45 minutes later, an Army Green Goddess from the Mile End base went past, driving cautiously and sounding an old-fashioned bell. An ironical cheer came from the men who can be almost anywhere on their patch within three minutes.

Their attitude to their soldier stand-ins is sympathetic. They cannot help smiling to think of the burning car which one Army team reportedly took four hours to extinguish, or of the 13 hoses which played ineffectually on a single houses in Greenwich. Pictures and film of soldiers coughing and exhausted have not moved the White Watch unduly. Every fireman returns from a job coughing black lumps and blowing filthy mucus into endlessly-ruined handkerchieves.

To give the soldiers breathing apparatus, Mackenzie says, will put them in even greater danger. A fireman at Poplar must serve for two years before he is allowed to use the Proto breathing set, and qualifies only after a fortnight of oral and written tests. Mackenzie can picture some young soldier, blind in the smoke, deaf and dumb in his apparatus, blundering about and, inexorably, running out of air.

No crash course, the White Watch agree, could inculcate the thousand-and-one tricks of body and brain with which an experienced fireman defends his life. There is, for instance, the strange, reticent walk nicknamed 'the BA shuffle', so closely does the fireman, advancing in goggles, resemble a ballroom dancer chasséing as his hand performs a vertical movement in front of his face.

In a burning building there exists an etiquette as rigid as if fire were fastidious – the delicate footfall on crumbling ground, the tactful opening of doors, the stopping and listening for the tread

104

and echo of flames, the hushed communication with a colleague in surroundings which might as well be the ocean bed. The toughest member of White Watch will admit that, in bad smoke, firemen hold hands – how fervently they seek out one another's fingers to discover if the thumb is turned up or down.

A file room at Poplar station bulges with the data a fireman must carry in his head, from the toxic properties of steel wool to knot-tying and the procedure for dealing with crashed aircraft carrying nuclear weapons. Firemen give each other incessant oral tests at the station while coiling hose or bulling up the engines' wheel-arches. They think it strange that society does not yet regard them higher than 'semi-skilled'.

Why do they bother? Easy, Mackenzie says – they do it for the sheer happiness of helping to save a life. Firemen tend to remember the names only of dead people. But Mackenzie can still see the coloured woman he pulled out of a burning room in Watts Grove. Even in his breathing-set, he could not help remarking to a colleague on the size of her breasts. Then another fireman appeared, carrying a bundle of bedding that had a baby inside it. 'When that happens,' Mackenzie says, 'It makes you feel like you want to go turning cartwheels.'

What if another hospital caught fire? 'You wouldn't see a car or a man left here,''Michael Gamble said. 'If people were dying, what could we say? "No, we don't feel like it"? We'd go. But for *property* . . . That's what Rees said, wasn't it? "We're concerned with lives, not property." '

Property of a sort, was still burning in the district. Another Green Goddess passed, following its predecessor in the direction of East India Docks. After two hours, the rubbish fire was apparently not under control.

A frail old man, leaning on a stick, was signing his name in the firemen's petition book. The effort exhausted him, and he was helped to a chair beside the brazier. He said he had served as an East End fireman for more than 40 years. He helped to fight the fire at the Silvertown munitions factory in 1917.

'What's your name, Pop?' the firemen asked.

'Bennett's my name – Wag Bennett,' the old man said. 'I can tell you things enough to make your blood boil.'

He took a key from his pocket and poked it into the end of his walking stick. Inside the shaft, like the blade in a swordstick, was a tightly-rolled red banner. The old man brandished it by the stick handle while the firemen unrolled it and read:

'I would like to know why Herbert Morrison cheated me of my 1914-18 War pension – W. Bennett.'

'They cheated you in then, and they still cheat you today,' the old man cried fiercely among the car horns. 'Go it, boys! You stick to it!'

1978

Plimsoll Power

The girls started it. Don't girls always? Karen Giles explains, 'We had this campaign you see. We decided to kick all the boys on Mondays.' 'And,' Sharon Hubbard says, 'we dance *Cats on the Rooftops* at them and at the end we pull our dresses up.' She cannot, however, explain this refinement. It's just the rule of the game.

The boys have not attempted reprisals until now – Sports Day, when all the parents are drawn up in the middle of the playing field, balancing on school chairs with some of the dexterity of large ice-creams on little cornets.

To the eight-year-old tactical mind, the codeword always precedes actual strategy. The brainwave is Richard Randal's, known throughout Windlesham School as Randal-pops. 'If any girls kick us, we'll shoe-shoe them.' This penalty consists of Randal-pops on the shoulders of a confederate, belabouring with his stockinged feet any inoffensive female, or indeed anyone inoffensive, who may cross his path. But he is no small burden, being of that gingery cast in which mirth so often co-exists with girth. His mount, after the first serious impact, falls sideways and breaks the slender line of the minority under the trees who are actually paying attention to the races.

On Sports Day the parents for some reason are always put out in the sun like that. Half-closed eyes can suggest great benevolence or perfect fascination with the heave and sprawl and clutch of the human wheelbarrows passing them. And the school forms up along the hedge; invariably a hedge containing goose-grass which sticks gratifyingly to the back of a white gym-shirt; a hedge which, being the repository for mascots, plimsolls and, occasionally, living bodies, is among the chief furnishings of the gala.

It is into this hedge that Randal-pops has at last been precipitated by his own unsteady engine-of-war. His challenge was answered at once by Karen Giles bearing on her back, like a spider under a sherry-bottle, a very large-legged girl who has disdained the chivalrous precaution of removing her shoes. Then they all collapse with a curiously languid movement sideways: legs and arms and shrieking freckles forming a mad frieze in the goose-grass.

Mr Morris, a jovial Welshman with sideburns like white earmuffs, has both insight and stamina enough to run the entire programme

107

at a sprint: 40 or more events, from the toddling flat-races to the ferocious earnestness of the 10-year-olds' relay, in under an hour and a half. Nor do they proceed totally unregarded along the hedge – it is just that news of them percolates gradually through more personal trials of strength, as cannon-fire is heard indistinctly at a ball.

How different when you are called out into the Sports Day sun, which is always hazy. The laughter of Randal-pops and the others sounds far away; you see the white lines in the grass track coming to a point ahead, you have the dry mouth and a cold foil of fear in the stomach, you feel the strange weight of the china eggs in their spoons, you catch the suddenly terrifying odours of sacking and shoe-whitener.

In the windrush of the race itself, isn't there sometimes, too, a taste of life as it may always have to be endured? That boy ahead whose shirt-back bulges with his own acceleration – for years and years he will be better than you; suntanned when you are white; bare-chested while you cross your arms across your vest; better than you, with your father looking on, for longer into the future than you can see.

'– and *what* do you people think you're doing?'

At the hedge, the effect of that voice is magical. The war-masks howling with the stumps of milk-teeth are transformed to upright and virtuous souls with hands behind their backs and eyes, below fringes, contritely downcast. This afternoon, with a free tea at risk, no teacher's powers of banishment will ever have been stronger.

Randal-pops, indicating his companion, remarks, 'See that girl with the long hair? He loves her.'

'Liar, I don't!'

'Yes you do' – and his faithlessness costs him a dead leg.

'– *he* loves Janet Usher.'

'I don't,' Randal-pops exclaims in anguish.

He receives a dead leg. Suddenly everyone is denouncing the alliances of their best friends, giving them dead legs if they protest. The voice that remarks 'Blues are one point ahead' is ignored in the thrust of knees, the stagger sideways of afflicted paramours. In matters of love, as in everything, the afternoon proceeds by way of certain original acts of violence or celebration, and 20 eager imitators.

'Polly Parrot loves . . .'

This refers to Paul Barrett, not the least of whose athletic achievements this day is the constant springing to avenge, by varied forms of propulsion into the hedge, this disrespectful use of his name.

If romance with the male eight-year-old is a matter of horrified denial, with a girl it is utter revulsion followed by computation. Barbara Tabora claims five. A girl they call Jill Maniac holds up 10 fingers and 10 again like a tic-tac man. Paul Barrett appears on several lists, as is the privilege of the hard-hearted. He returns from dealing with Randal-pops, and a sad-eyed girl holding his official programme crosses his path. In her voice there is the shadow of hopelessness as she says, 'Oh Paul, this just dropped out of your pocket.'

But strange are the ways of the female heart – the chemistry which compels such a girl as Karen Giles, so peerless at handstands against a wall, to favour an apparently insignificant individual who chugs about the edge of things like a train: which draws the intellectual beauty Caroline Sarah de Freitas away from a white-drill demigod like Paul Barrett to a swain even more unusual. He eschews any sporting dress whatever. He wears a fringe, a mark on his cheek and copious, grey breeches, and declines to give any name whatever.

'He can talk in French,' Caroline de Freitas says.

A union of minds.

'Go on, talk in French.'

'An pork,' her paramour responds. 'A door.'

She is radiant.

As the last of the dead legs return to circulation, somebody else experiments with a Chinese burn. A boy may hide his adoration but his fascination, he cannot. There is a Fancy Dress parade after the races. Therefore, an owl approaches Caroline de Freitas, with feathers reproduced on an upturned paper garbage-sack. For as long as his identity remains a mystery, her proud attention is upon him. With a finger poked from one eye-hole he can woo and tantalise her. She muses, 'What a pity I don't know who's under there because I wanted to buy him a drink . . .' Instantly the owl reveals himself: the spell has gone.

Perhaps the most self-conscious of present beauties is Lorinda Langley; in spectacles with flyaway rims, pierced ears, and wearing a ring that was given to her by an admirer not at Windlesham School. 'I hate all the boys here,' she says with no trace of coquetry. 'Because they call you nicknames. They call me Lammas and a girl called Janet Usher they call Usherbug and a girl called Joanna they call Bugsy.'

Without disturbing a hairslide she has won the skipping and three-legged race, that most severe test of enemy or friend. Its participants may never again race in a society so committed to the ideal of fair play or so full of inventive violations. And the fathers' race has been run: twice the normal distance in a thunder of stockinged feet. The fathers return to their miniature chairs, close to apoplexy in their desire to show no exertion.

The young visitors, too, have raced; some of them trailing walking-reins, all ferociously intent on the bags of dolly-mixtures that the winners receive. Every finish has a touch of Grand Prix in fact; a squad of teachers. They laud the winners, give the losers a clap, direct casualties to the first-aid table, pool their opinions in a dispute, quickly grab the pieces of school property involved in novelty items such as the bean-bag race, and check the most active from running and running on into infinity.

At last the relays are run. Even the hedge party pays attention now, for relay wins mean double points. The house-cries melt and mould over one another, and yet all through the preceding hours among the spectators they have been employed singly to add point to the destruction of a character, the denunciation of a lover, the administering of a dead leg:

'Blues Blues – always lose!'

'Reds Reds – wet their beds!'

A teacher says it has been a good and peaceful meeting. Out of its 120 participants, two only have cried – one sulked.

'Blues Blues – *never* lose!'

'Greens Greens – runner beans!'

'Yellows Yellows – big fat fellows!'

The teacher of course disallows the normal level of violence: the arm around a neck in a tourniquet, the Chinese burn which Randal-pops is even now perfecting, the sudden flights into Turkish rage without which no friendship is a true thing, the purple wounds of the knee, the pink ones of the elbow – all the grazes and black-soled feet which merge to make the eight-year-old summer.

1971

Fast Buck Abbey

After the midday meal, the monks go to the calefactory, or warming place. In ancient monasteries this would be the single room kept free of mortifying cold. The Buckfast Abbey version is a wide, light room, equipped with low-slung bright orange chairs, a Scandinavian style fireplace and all the daily papers. The monks, who have eaten in silence, stand round their Abbot, gossiping and drinking coffee from transparent espresso bar cups. 'I don't know what this country's coming to,' the Abbot says. 'We need a new clutch cable for the Ford. Can you believe that there isn't one to be had in the whole of Devon and Cornwall?' With a fastidious gesture, common in the community, he twitches straight the hood-collar of his black Benedictine habit.

The monks are expecting a wine shipment this very afternoon. At Buckfast, it is an event as important, in its way, as any in the liturgical calendar. A road tanker sent from France, containing 4,400 gallons of red wine, comes down the tilting South Devon roads, around narrow stone bridges; it passes beneath an ivy arch and enters the Abbey precincts. Here, it is awaited by Father Richard, Bursar to the community, a pale young monk with a skittish mouth, and suede desert boots protruding from the skirts of his habit. Father Richard, who has relatives in the licensed trade, supervises the transformation of vin ordinaire into Buckfast Tonic Wine. The tanker's contents flow into two thick vats, to await his ministrations. From two more vats, an equivalent quantity of tonic wine, already matured, is pumped back into the tanker to be taken away to London for bottling and distribution.

The monks of Buckfast Abbey innocently fulfil a marketing man's dream. Alcohol taken as medicine is a custom peculiarly British and obscurely ecclesiastical: what better recommendation for such a tonic than it should be manufactured by a community of Benedictines in the West Country, adding the odour of sanctity to phosphates and a dash of vanilla. Production in recent years has increased from the occasional hogshead to a statistic large enough to be kept secret by the Abbey's London distributors. The tonic wine business, their agent explained, is 'a jungle'. They wish to disclose nothing that might benefit the arch enemy, Sanatogen.

111

Tonic wine has been important in securing the Abbey's survival. As abbeys go, it is an upstart. It was founded in 1882 by a group of French monks, driven by government persecution from their original settlement near Dijon. The group found refuge in Devon, on the site of a Cistercian monastery, derelict since the time of Henry VIII. From these foundations grew the cloister, the grey cell blocks and the square, stripey church which, under the famous German Abbot Anscar Vonier, was to be the community's most notable feat of construction. Their initial money-making enterprise was honey, perfumed with Dartmoor heather. The Abbey hives stand to the south, in a neat shanty town. A boys' prep school for 120 pupils and a souvenir shop complete the quadrangle.

The fame of their industries has not released the Abbey's 46 inmates from a stern Benedictine life. They rise at 5.15 each morning, to make their first devotions at six. Mass is at eight, with further prayers before a silent – and self-service – lunch. Vespers are at six. Dinner is eaten again in silence, although the monks take turns in reading aloud to the others from a kiosk in the refectory, fitted with a microphone like a disc jockey's. Later they can watch television for an hour before Compline, the final prayers of the day, and retirement to their cells at 9.30.

Under their vows of poverty, they may own nothing as individuals. Father Benedict, the Prior, second in command after the Abbot, technically does not even own the cufflinks beneath his broad, black sleeves, that were a gift from his parents. The community provides a civilian suit for outside parish work, a monthly ration of 140 cigarettes, even the occasional transistor radio. Underwear and shoes are replenished from stock in the Bursar's office or on the Abbey's account at the local Co-op. At Christmas the Abbot makes a special dispensation to allow the monks to give presents to one another.

Allowance is made, none the less, for the special needs of monks with businesses to run. The present Abbot is against fasting, especially for the two monks who work on the Abbey farm. Scrupulous observance of prayer time might sometimes be impracticable for Brother Adam, the famous Abbey bee-keeper who has developed a strain of queen bee sought after by apiaries throughout the world. All monks have Saturday afternoons and Sundays off from work and three weeks' holiday a year.

Father Benedict joined the community after leaving school, and was sent to Oxford and teacher-training college. He is one of several monks teaching at the prep school in the Abbey grounds. He is not an intimidating figure. Thirty-odd small boys in grey and black jerseys turn cheerful, tonsured faces up to him in a classroom of lemon yellow.

'Sir! Sir! Have you marked the quiz yet?'

'Not yet,' Father Benedict says. 'What was the last question, now? "How many statues are there in the church?"'

'Sir, I put forty.'

'Rather a lot,' Father Benedict says, smiling.

'I put twenty, sir.'

'Nearly right.'

'Sir, I put nineteen.'

The church acts like a dynamo on the community's imagination. Their calling does not prohibit hero-worship: no other term can describe their awe for the memory of Anscar Vonier, the shock-headed Abbot under whose leadership the Abbey achieved the literally unbelievable. Six monks built the church, from a local architect's design, directed by a single trained stonemason, Brother Peter. How they ever succeeded in raising the heights and curves and columns of pale Bath stone will remain forever mysterious, eternal proof to the monks of the tangibility of miracles. Brother Stanislas, the elderly Cockney monk who shows visitors round the church, can remember when the floor was still earth, and when ashes packed the foundations. Today, the floor is a maze of coloured cartwheels.

Lately, the Vatican Council has called for extensive reconstruction. Behind the High Altar, to Brother Stanislas's disquiet, workmen are chipping holes in the great Brother Peter's handiwork. Rome has ordered that Mass must now be said with the priest facing the congregation, not turned, as formerly, towards the reredos, the gold altar-surround. The Abbot's idea is to separate the reredos from the altar table so that the priest can get between them.

In the church, the Abbot is inspecting lengths of coloured synthetic velvet. These will be hung in the archways behind the High Altar to shut out the mauve brilliance of a window in the contemporary chapel. A crimson drape is let down, followed by a gold drape. 'This really needs a woman's eye,' the Abbot murmurs.

Brother Stanislas is worried about the angels. Six have been taken down from their green-striped barber poles around the altar. Two can be reinstated on a pelmet in the arch: the rest queue up, spiky-winged, in the crypt below. Brother Stanislas thinks that the two angels on display do not match. 'One of 'em's sort of broader in front. It looks all cockeyed.'

Abbot Leo Smith is a fast-talking, rubicund man from whose lips 'Hell' or 'Take a pew' emerge with perfect naturalness. He joined the Buckfast community in 1934, in Abbot Vonier's time. After a spell in Rome, he spent 20 years with Brother Adam looking after the bees. Then he transferred to tonic wine. It was his proud boast that he could turn the wine tanker around, emptied and refilled, in only five hours. Last year he was voted into the Abbot's chair. Abbots rule for an eight-year term, but are seldom ousted.

The Abbot leads the way, past Father Richard's vats, into a room

113

that one would not expect to find in the Abbey precincts. It is a small lounge bar with tub-shaped seats, a collection of liqueur miniatures and a bottle-opener in the form of a fish. The bar is used to entertain visitors from the licensed trade. The unfailing astonishment of these visitors, who usually arrive with extra blankets and spirit-flasks, is greatly enjoyed by Abbot Smith.

He goes behind the mock stone bar and draws off two glasses of Buckfast Tonic Wine from an inverted glass dispenser. In colour and density, it resembles port. The flavour is decidedly medicinal. An after-taste lingers, of custard and something metallic. It is a taste, the Abbot says, which has to grow on you. It has sold especially well in Scotland. At 28 per cent proof, it is claimed to be a serious rival to whisky in some Clydeside pubs.

Abbot Smith must resign himself to the gradual shrinkage even of a community as celebrated as his. The monks are, for the most part, elderly men. In the past 10 years, four younger members – valuable highly-trained priests – have renounced their vows. One became a high official in the electricity industry; another is now secretary to a regional hospital board. All, the Abbot says drily, are doubtless married by now. Each year brings a few enquiries, mostly from unsuitable widowers or from school-leavers, attracted to the romance of monastic life. 'Monastic life,' the Abbot says, 'is just like any other sort of life. It's one damned thing after another.'

1977

The Liner that Never Sails

The Adelphi Hotel knew its proud days when mighty Cunarders put in to Liverpool and the emblazoned boat train ran direct from Euston to the Mersey's edge. Passengers about to embark were advised to spend one night at least in surroundings designed to initiate them gently into the grandeur of shipboard life. For the Adelphi did not resemble an hotel so much as an intermediate ocean liner. Its marbled foyer, set about with Art Deco lamps and brass-bound clocks, reproduced some great ship's central vestibule. Its Grand Lounge, both in massive height and sheer quantity of palms and orchestras, could compete with any salon on the *Imperator* or *Berengaria*. The very bedrooms had a nautical look with their recessed wardrobes and curtained-in cots, their doors opening outward, as at sea, into blue-carpeted corridors deeper and more silent than mid-Atlantic.

Today, such ships as visit Liverpool unload only containers. The Adelphi waits, at its berth in Ranelagh Place, for cabin trunks that will never come again. Grand hotels, alas, cannot dwindle away like the confidence which built them. There it still stands as you come out of Lime Street Station: the same sheer hull, towering above the cobbled streets and taxi-garages; the same iron and glass portico on the ramp built for slow-arriving limousines. Each time it seems a little emptier, a little sadder, a little more reduced by the sickness we choose to call 'these days'.

I write as one who has felt, however indirectly, the Adelphi's old comfort and protectiveness. I remember how often, after a day on some wind-blasted Merseyside picket-line, I have thankfully drawn its deep corridors around me, lying in one of its huge green-mosaic baths, then sinking to sleep in bedclothes that still bear the insignia of the London Midland Railway. I have missed many trains from Lime Street in order to have afternoon tea from a silver cake-stand in that sepulchral Grand Lounge, flanked by the two wide staircases where Roy Rogers, 'King of the Cowboys', once rode triumphantly down on his horse, Trigger. There was also that night, in the Adelphi's now-defunct Sefton Restaurant, when I heard the Beatles' one-time manager join with a Dutch cheese salesman, under the

115

Louis XIV ceiling, in an impromptu chorus of 'Brother, Can You Spare a Dime?'.

The deep melancholy, begun 15 years ago when the oceans ebbed from the Adelphi's foyer, is nowadays compounded by the deep embarrassment of its still being there, a monument to careless luxury, stranded on the mudflats of Britain's worst unemployment area. It is but a few hundred yards uphill, on the hotel's blind side, that Upper Parliament Street and Toxteth begin. Last summer's riots numbered the Adelphi high on a list of targets among Liverpool's old imperial buildings. The police, feeling it equally symbolic, checked the invasion almost within earshot of the hall-porters' desk.

For such an hotel in such a city, survival has an almost Russian irony – grand ballrooms and mirrored concourses and piles of unwanted card-tables, preserved in eternal twilight by the forces of social egalitarianism. For the Adelphi is, of course, owned and operated by the hotels and catering division of British Rail. Few enough praises are bestowed on British Transport Hotels, so let this be an unequivocal one. The Adelphi, together with other great old railway hotels throughout England and Scotland, is maintained by a policy of at least partly conscious conservation. No other hotel group would have kept it open this past dwindling decade, used less and less by business travellers; more and more – though never sufficiently – by those to whom its magnificence so poignantly recalls the age of *real* trains.

British Rail's hoteliers have striven for 'rationalisation'. The hotel staff has been reduced from 400 to about 140; its top two floors are now permanently closed. Its last surviving formal restaurant, The Sefton, gave up finally last year, deserting its sumptuous Louis room for a basement coffee shop. Trendiness hangs insecurely here and there like cheap sticking-plaster – a gaming casino, a 'racecourse bar'. The deepest, throbbing region far below the hotel's water-line, where to this day one can find the Roman blue mosaic swimming pool, discloses an occasional male figure in a bath towel, experiencing the Adelphi sauna and 'sporting club'.

Refinement persists, from long-accumulated habit. Each evening, while Toxteth burned and the police on Upper Parliament Street faced rioters like Zulu armies at Rorke's Drift, the Adelphi's dapper young cocktail barman set out plates of olives and nuts as usual. 'People aren't coming into town,' he said. 'You can't blame them, really.' At the porters' desk, which is also a postbox, Jim McLoughlin, the deputy head porter, fixes an expectant eye on each revolution of the door, prepared to revolve the newcomer back to the street again. In the men's cloakroom, a polished walnut shoeshine stand vainly offers its brass foot-rail to the next gentleman.

Once, there were half a dozen such stands, each holding aloft a newspaper-reading occupant. There were two dozen tailcoated porters, not to mention liftmen and 'carriage-attendants'. There were the squads of buttoned-in pageboys, moving through the Grand Lounge with bell and blackboard, or dashing forth with urgent maritime telegrams, across the clattersome junction where 'Green Goddess' trams rushed simultaneously from Mount Pleasant and Renshawe Street. So well-insulated were even the Adelphi's second floor bedrooms that the hotel's own fire alarm-bells remained inaudible.

It was to be, the Midland Railway had announced in 1914, 'the world's most palatial hotel', personifying 'everything that experience, science, art and hygienics can teach. Unstinted expenditure has been the order of the day . . . All the modern innovations of New York hotels of the highest grade here combine with solid English comfort, and that subtle air of refinement characteristic of a Parisian salon . . .'

The Midland Railway knew about palatialness and refinement. From its London showpiece, the 400-room Midland Grand, wrapped like a Polish monastery around St Pancras Station, it had implanted half a dozen scarcely less elaborate Midland hotels on the meridian of its own steel path through the manufacturing north. It reached Liverpool, and the coveted liner trade, in 1892, opening its first Midland Adelphi in an old warren of a place which had competed hitherto unsuccessfully with the North-Western Railway's grand hotel inside Lime Street Station. A third rival company, the Lancashire and Yorkshire, operated the black and gold Exchange Hotel at Liverpool Exchange Station, lower down towards the shipping piers.

The rebuilt Midland Adelphi, opened a few months before the start of the Great War, scorned such insignificant competitors. With its three first class restaurants, its Grand Lounge, its Athenian promenade and open-air Fountain Court, its Turkish bath, swimming pool, squash and tennis courts and shooting-gallery, its timbered cosiness above and many-candled brilliance below, its challenge was directed at palaces which floated. It became known at once among Liverpool people as 'the liner that never sails'. Most Liverpudlians dared approach no nearer than the seats along its frontal bastion, or the Mount Pleasant bus-stop, under its great Grill Room windows. Yet it was a source, not of class envy but of vicarious pride, like St George's Hall or the Royal Liver insurance building. Its slight damage by a landmine in the 1940 blitz was accounted as great a blow as the total destruction of Lewis's department store on the corner opposite.

'Benny' Bensburg, one of the Adelphi's last surviving banquet porters, leads the way across the huge, high, gilded, empty space of the old Grill Room. In 1914, the walls were silver sycamore, the hangings pink silk. Today, renamed the Formby Room, it is just

117

another unfillable vault, sporadically let for meetings of textile salesmen or probation officers. Most days, Benny is its only visitor, his off-duty raincoat over his porter's uniform, traversing the polished floor at a swimmer's economical pace, unfastening the double doors to reveal, beyond, the still-grander ghost of the hotel's main restaurant. From there, one came into the Fountain Court, a mosaic garden with real fountains, open to the sky.

Benny joined the Adelphi in 1939 as one of its eight scurrying page-boys. He was there the day Gracie Fields came to Liverpool, drawing multitudes even bigger than the Beatles. He was in the Grand Lounge when Roy Rogers rode Trigger up the left-hand staircase, waving a ten-gallon hat. He has seen the coming and going of Churchill and Bob Hope; the repeated return of Harold Wilson, MP for nearby Huyton, to his specially-bespoken Suite 100. Whom does Benny best remember? 'Guy Mitchell, the crooner chap. Lovely man, he was. We used to play games of darts with him in his room.'

There are still a few big, formal nights each year when a banquet porter comes into his own. There is the annual dinner of the Mersey-side Golf Captains, in their ceremonial red coats, and 'the Locusts', a corn trade fraternity whose top table displays two giant papier-mâché locusts with flashing light-bulb eyes. Each April on Grand National night, there is the 'Aintree Ball', frequently with Joe Loss and his orchestra. Alan Walker, the hotel's head pastrycook, makes a sugar model of horse and jockey in the winner's colours to be cheered across the ballroom's finish-line.

Mr Walker, for all his years among dough and butter, has stayed lean, long-legged and melancholy. He is just now off duty in the massive Adelphi kitchen, under the Grand Lounge, whose refrigeration-plant throbs like steam turbines through a heavy sea. He settles for a smoke in his private office, chef's hat aslant with unintended jauntiness, stretching his knees before him as cautiously as blue-checkered stilts.

Alan Walker, like so many Adelphi staff, reached the hotel via the kitchens of ocean liners. He sailed on the *Coronia, Parthia* and *Ruahine,* cruising the Mediterranean or to New Zealand, their passenger-lists crammed with sun-oiled millionaires. Mr Walker has kept a set of the first class restaurant menus. 'Two breakfasts, you could have. Onion soup, mid-morning. Lunch. Tea. Dinner. Supper. And deck-buffets. Nine meals a day you could eat on those cruises, if you wanted.'

There's little demand for Alan Walker's pastries and meringues now that the Adelphi's last formal sweets-trolley has vanished. Nor is it any longer the sign of a smart Liverpool wedding reception to be held in one of the hotel's great public rooms, though a card in the main lobby still offers a dozen different buffet plans with cakes at varying elevations. 'We had an Indian wedding here not long ago,' Mr Walker said. 'The bride was a maharajah's sister – from Litherland. They brought in all their own cooks to do the food. A four-tier wedding cake, they wanted.'

What survives of the old, splendid Adelphi does so in large part thanks to its present general manager, John Pearce. When Mr Pearce first took over, he found the Grand Lounge desecrated by tubular steel furniture and low-level spotlights; its glass-paned roof painted muddy crimson. The ceiling glass, unhappily, can never be reclaimed. But John Pearce immediately put back the Grand Lounge's traditional sofas and standard lamps. Then, in a basement, someone found the original gilt wall-lights.

Mr Pearce took me up to the disused fifth floor, whose narrow beds and communal bathrooms suggest accommodation for only valets, chauffeurs and maids. The third floor, connected by impossibly grand back-stairs, is where the big celebrities would stay. We peeped into suites of sheer oak, of deepest walnut, of gold-leaf white and pale chinoiserie. The air was heavy with old sunshine, trapped in leather chairs, and the smell of long-extinguished cigars.

I spent the night in a suite panelled with tan-coloured kid leather, its leather-impacted double doors running on to further suites in either direction. From that leather lounge, a visiting millionaire or maharajah could thus annexe virtually the entire floor. On the mantelpiece, a square-faced wooden clock gesticulated in vain at successive sailing-times. The sun dwindled behind Lewis's store and the Cammell-Laird shipyard cranes. I could barely hear even the police wagon which, in the small hours, screeched around Ranelagh Place and headed up Mount Pleasant towards the Toxteth front line.

Next day in the Adelphi ballroom, there was a Beatles fan club convention. The hotel whose threshold no Beatle ever dared cross welcomed their acolytes with hot soup and respectable bar-ladies – though not via the Ranelagh Place entrance. The sound of John Lennon's 'Imagine' came muffled through the Grand Lounge's firmly-locked mirror doors. It would be no part of the fans' pilgrimage to see the old Sefton Restaurant where, in the late fifties, Brian Epstein told his parents he had decided to give up drama school and stay in the family's record-retailing business.

Late that night, I sat in the Grand Lounge with Joe Flannery, a tall, mild man in dark glasses who, before he became Epstein's and the Beatles' confidant, used to be an Adelphi waiter, serving drinks and sandwiches in this very concourse. He pointed up to the secret place, above the lonely plaster Venus de Milo, where head waiters and supervisors and under managers would perpetually be watching.

Across the expanse of lamps and sofas there came a sudden, violent crash. An ink-haired punk, who had found his way through from the convention area but had been refused admittance to the organisers' private party, was venting his disappointment by kicking

119

over a tea-trolley laden with crockery. The cups and saucers smashed. The echo subsided. Nobody came to investigate.

1981

A Friend to the Last

All day, he had felt no pain: only absence of pain so unaccustomed, it was akin to shock. As he sat listening to the doctor, he would touch himself on the knee or the waist as if to reassure himself that the pain truly had fled. He was in his early 70s, blanched by illness, in slippers and pyjamas that had long since become his normal dress. No more pain, he said, but still those sweats . . . Some sentences were not finished, and could not be. Instead, the doctor's hand moved across to cover his.

This is a hospice – a centre caring for people with incurable cancer. It is the same hospice, in Oxford, where 25-year-old Jane Zorza died recently of a cancer that spreads with horrifying swiftness through young bodies. Last weekend, *The Guardian* published an article by Jane's parents, Rosemary and Victor Zorza, describing the peaceful, almost happy circumstances of her death. The Zorzas' moving testament has done much to draw attention to the work of hospices in Britain, and the difficulties with which many are forced to contend. Oxford's hospice, for example, is so under-financed that only 12 of its 25 beds are available to cancer-sufferers.

Sir Michael Sobell House, on the campus of Churchill Hospital, is known technically as a 'continuing care unit'. Its purpose is not, as in some hospices, merely to provide a peaceful setting where patients may fade into death, unresisting. Cancer patients are admitted initially for a short stay while their pain is brought under control. In many cases they can be rehabilitated sufficiently to resume a normal life, returning to the unit at intervals, as much for the sake of their families as for their own. The indirect suffering caused by cancer is of equal concern to Dr Robert Twycross, the consultant in charge. 'When we take on a patient,' he says, 'we take on the whole family as well.'

Twycross is fighting what he sees as a general inability among the medical profession to comprehend the nature of pain in advanced cancer. Many doctors, he says, scarcely begin to unravel the many strands of pain – from, perhaps, six different sources – which make up the lump of the central distress. Modern medicine, directed primarily towards cure, has come to regard the terminal patient as

121

a failure: that is often how the cancer sufferer will view himself or herself in the friendless days of the final confinement.

Sobell House is one of seven continuing care units built by the National Society for Cancer Relief, each in the grounds of a major hospital like the Churchill and run with full clinical support as part of the National Health Service. Hospices are also maintained by the Marie Curie Foundation, and by private institutions such as St Christopher's in Sydenham, which was the pioneer of this form of care. In all, throughout the British Isles some 800 hospice beds exist to serve a need which is, as yet, unfathomable.

For cancer continues to be the unnameable terror, likely to strike down one in five of us, yet shunned in speech lest even articulating it should somehow implant the malignancy. The pattern of the illness had been unchanged for centuries – first the term in a hospital, in surroundings attuned only to recovery; then the weeks of false convalescence; finally, the weeks at home, the days and nights of slow decline, of increasing agony, borne with resignation, for the doctors have said, 'There is nothing more we can do.'

This medical valediction angers Twycross, whose experience in hospice work has shown that there is *everything* to be done; not only for Jane Zorza but for anyone, young or old, the final months of life can be made hopeful and happy and secure.

At the Oxford unit, Twycross may spend the first week of a patient's stay in following each pain thread to its source, and in closing off the small circumstantial pains which, overshadowed by the chief affliction, have still helped in the body's decline. He is currently treating a woman of 71 who, before being admitted, had spent two months at home in bed, immobilised as much by aches as by serious pain. It has taken Twycross a fortnight to unravel the large and small discomforts twisting through her. Now, he says, she is 'ninety-five per cent pain-free' and able to walk again.

The hospice principle raises one perennial question. Should a person be told that death is inevitable? Is it not cruel to take away hope? Twycross's answer is that 'truth forms a spectrum' – frankness can often be gentler than obvious evasion. Jane Zorza was exceptional – intelligent, sophisticated, she could make the most of what time remained to her. For other people the experience is one of mental bewilderment. The question they ask is, 'Will it hurt?' – coming from a premonition of pain, but also of unutterable loneliness. The answer, communicated by Twycross and his staff is: 'Whatever happens, we'll be here to stand by you.'

The need for hospices is attested by waiting-lists at all seven of the Cancer Relief Society's units. A hospice bed is expensive to maintain, due mainly to the high staff-patient ratio. Since the Oxford unit opened, two years ago, the Health Service has been able to support only half of its available beds. Meanwhile Twycross is turning patients away.

The atmosphere is far from that of a hospital. There are no ordeals of efficiency and time-keeping, no clashing utensils or ceremonial staff rounds. If a doctor speaks to a patient, he does it sitting by the patient's bed or chair. Touch is encouraged, on the hand, the arm or shoulder. In Twycross's experience, this pressure is always gladly returned.

Ordinary routine is banished. In one small ward, Mrs Allen – who walked today for the first time in almost three months – is being visited by her husband, a British Leyland worker at Cowley. At last, after two months he will be able to go back to work again. She talks to him, rolled up in the bedsheet, conspiratorially, as if they have started to make plans.

Next door, John Pratley, a wide-eyed, elfin man of 65, has just had his supper brought. He had a brain tumour in 1968; it is marked by a groove cloven through his head. He comes to the unit for a week each month to allow a respite to his wife at home in Deddington. Today was memorable for him, too – he walked as far as the main hospital building. He delays the pleasure of his evening newspaper by licking his thumb repeatedly but still not turning over the page.

Miss Ursula Nott came to the unit from Parsons' Almshouses a week ago. As yet Twycross has not pursued all her pains to their source.

Neat as a grey nun, with folded hands, she sits looking out of her open door. 'I thought I was done for. I used to feel I couldn't even be bothered to get up in the morning. I had no friends left. One friend I had is crocked up with Parkinson's Disease. I've one sister – she's in a geriatric hospital in Coventry. She and I always wrote to each other twice a week ever since 1919. I still write to her, but she doesn't write back any more.

'When they brought me in here, I could have cried – the lady doctor, and the flowers they gave me, and the bedspread. They leave the door open: I can see what happens all the way down the hall. I feel I can be here, and just be myself. It's lovely. Oh, it's lovely!'

At the end of the five-bedded room, a man with a straight white moustache lies alone, in dignified distress. His name is Terence Monaghan. He came to the unit from lodgings in Oxford: this end bed is now his only home. To speak of the staff here causes a spasm to cross his face – not of pain but of admiration. 'Oh . . . wonderful. They never say a word wrong, and they throw in a joke now and then.'

His features compose themselves again to await the long evening. The unit becomes quiet, but for Twycross's voice, behind a drawn curtain. Miss Nott sits in her doorway, looking down the hall.

123

Through a half-open door, John Pratley sits on his bed with a nurse beside him, their two heads close in earnest conversation.

Twycross draws back the bed curtain, saying goodbye to the patient who called to him. He lowers her reluctant hand to the coverlet. The face that watches him go is hauntedly thin; but it, too, has managed to smile.

1978

The Fleas at the Mansion

The first international flea conference has been taking place this week in the middle of Miriam Rothschild's country estate in Northamptonshire. A hundred flea experts from 15 countries have assembled in a darkened room to present papers and exchange data about the object of their peculiar devotion. The delegates also included a tick and mite expert or two, as well as the world's foremost authority on the ovaries of the fruit fly.

Fleas, on the whole, have had a bad press. This is due largely to their ability to spread diseases such as typhus, myxomatosis and bubonic plague, the latter by means of infesting the equally unadmired plague rat. Plague remains endemic in countries like Vietnam and New Guinea, as well as smouldering quietly, often non-infectiously, on rats' backs in American national parks. The World Health Organisation received 700 reports of plague last year. Many more are likely to have gone unreported, or to have been suppressed by the governments concerned for the sake of political vanity.

Yet the flea has its grudging admirers. Naturalists who study it are impressed by its perfect integration with the blood-carrying world. Fleas have remained unchanged during the millions of years since their wings were taken from them. Specimens preserved in amber or in burial mounds are identical with 20th century fleas. Two thousand types of flea are known to exist, riding on all fur-bearing land animals but monkeys. One flea even contrives to dwell at the South Pole, where it exists for nine months a year frozen live into the ice.

The face of the flea, in scientific pamphlets and drawings, broods over this first international conference. A flea's face is striking rather than beautiful, resembling a Red Indian chief with long whiskers and old-fashioned motor goggles. It compensates for its plainness by performance. When a flea jumps, it is as if a man on his knees has leapt to the top of the Post Office tower, 30,000 times without tiring. Flea-accleration has been measured at 146G, or 20 times the rate at which a Moon rocket re-enters the earth's atmosphere.

The entry of Miriam Rothschild into the conference room proves, in its way, to be equally striking. She is a grey-haired, brown-skinned woman dressed in multi-coloured peasant clothes, yellow and black gumboots and seaman's socks. She is not merely a Rothschild but also a naturalist, in the forefront of flea-study. Live plague fleas, at this very moment, are breeding contentedly in her cellars.

Miriam Rothschild has organised the flea conference as well as lending her neo-Tudor mansion, Ashton Wold, near Oundle, for its four-day programme. The delegates are billetted in the village, and come up to the big house each day. In a room surrounded by portraits of ancestral Rothschilds, monographs and slide-shows have been presented on such varied topics as Rickettsia in Flea Tissue; Floating or Missing Genitalia in Male Fleas; Unusual Alaskan Fleas; Fleas in History; and The Wonderful One-host Flea, a poem.

The setting is not inappropriate. For the Rothschild family bred a formidable line of naturalists, outside banking hours. The Hon. Charles Rothschild, Miriam's father, in a short but crowded life, became a world authority on butterflies, irises and fleas. In Egypt he discovered the plague-carrying rat flea, which he named Xenopsylla Cheopis Rothschild, after the builder of the Pyramids.

His daughter has proved a worthy successor. It was Miriam Rothschild who discovered that the rabbit flea breeds in unison with its host. Part of the proof consisted of giving a contraceptive pill to a female rabbit, which also curtailed the breeding of the fleas in the rabbit's ears. She was the first to analyse the flea's miraculous jumping mechanism, with the help of a camera capable of recording 10,000 frames per second.

Like all flea people, she has a curious affection for the creatures. Study of them is helpful, not only in checking disease but also in the wider understanding of all biology. In the flea world, it is a compliment to name a new species after a fellow expert whom one admires. 'I've got a nice little worm named after me and a nice little flea named after me. Practically everyone at this conference has a flea named after them or a tick named after them.'

Miriam Rothschild climbed into her crumpled brown Rolls-Royce for the next stage of the programme. The car bumped along through part of a 500-acre nature reserve where tree stumps are not removed but left, so that insects may breed in them. This is not a big estate, she says – nothing in comparison with 'the locals', as Miriam Rothschild calls her neighbours Lord Fitzwilliam and the Duke of Gloucester, both of whom have contributed rabbit fleas to her collection. As the Rolls headed into the Fens, she admitted a further achievement. In 1940, she invented the first car seat-belt. Nobody would listen to her at the time.

Her father, the Hon. Charles Rothschild, was among the earliest conservationists. At the beginning of the century he could already see what a threat existed to the English countryside and, in particular, to the East Anglian Fens. He succeeded over the years in buying up the whole of Woodwalton Fen, near Ramsey, and in preserving it from agricultural use. So it still remains, officially protected, a tangled oasis of green plants and green water among the brown, level farmland. A thatched bungalow, built by Charles Rothschild for study purposes, stands on stilts which have gradually lengthened with the subsidence of the land.

Here the flea experts assembled for a packed lunch and a walk around the Fen. Miriam Rothschild held court inside the bungalow, which has its own interior slime-covered pond. The rest sat outside on the grass. Professor George Varley, the Oxford entomologist, remained standing with his tonic water bottle of home-brewed beer. The Eastern European delegates consumed their pears starting from the base. A cuckoo decoy honked suddenly, and there a guilty giggle.

The Fen warden, deferential and rosy-cheeked, servant to two Rothschilds, approached his tour group to ask what they would like to see on the Fen, which was looking its best that day. Cuckoo spit gleamed on the nettles and the hemlock in the dyke stood tall. A snipe cried suddenly from a near thicket. There was no dissent concerning what they wished to see.

'Fleas.'

'Fleas – please.'

Even a flea expert is susceptible to fun. At a supper party after the Wednesday session, one of the visitors admitted – or rather boasted – that he had never yet been bitten by a flea. A contest was immediately arranged between the visitor and Dr Norman Granz of the World Health Organisation, to see who would be bitten the most by some cat fleas that happened to be handy. Dr Granz was just the winner, six bites to five.

1978

The Meriden Triumph

The storms blew out, stilling the almond trees that stand between the factory and the road, leaving the air weighted with the breath of summer grass. At night the men on the gates saw huge caddis-flies come leaping under their hut, or fat moths that spun like whipped tops among the dominoes spread out for reshuffling. It was pleasant to be on picket-duty in the warm dark, beside the brazier with its crooked chimney, with the sparks and rustle from the fire.

Young Taffy – there are two Taffys, at least, among those occupying the factory – voiced the opinion of the domino-school tonight.

'Some people are going to make history and some aren't,' Taffy said. 'I think this'll go down in the history-books. It deserves to, like.'

If they are hijackers then they are very clean and neat hijackers. The Triumph factory has never looked as tidy as through the months of its blockade. Its ex-employees have painted it inside and out; they have swept the paths between the machines and scraped inches of mould from the vats in the chromium shop. They have taken inordinate care of the roof so that no single drop of rain shall fall on a single motorcycle. The thousand motorcycles stand pristine in the silence, plastic-covered, ticketed, lounging row on row. The production line waits petrified: halves of motorcycles, two-thirds of motorcycles, anticipating their turn, rear up and beg to be completed. It is as if work ceased only yesterday.

Two years ago, when people throughout the world were riding more motorcycles than they ever had before, the British motorcycle industry lay near to extinction. It was the fault of the Japanese, who conquered every market by the unfair advantages of efficiency, ingenuity and brightly-coloured plastic. The numerous British makes, illustrious so long for their glamour, solidity and speed, had declined into two undashing conglomerates. There was Norton Villiers at Wolverhampton. And there was BSA in Birmingham, which incorporated Triumph with its factory at Meriden outside Coventry, standing in an expanse of fields and pleasant woods.

In the summer of 1973, BSA-Triumph found itself in such severe financial difficulty that its shares were suspended on the Stock Exchange. The imminent collapse of this once patriotically affluent concern placed the crisis at last before the eyes of the Conservative Government of the day. Its remedy, evolved by Mr Chrisopher Chataway, was to procure a merger between BSA and the still profitable Norton company, and to appoint a Mr Dennis Poore, chairman of the Norton parent company, to effect what salvage he could. The surviving manufacturer was renamed Norton-Villiers-Triumph and it received £4.8m of public money to assist it to its feet.

Mr Poore is a businessman, and his businessman's eye fell almost immediately upon the Triumph works at Meriden. Indeed, Meriden, to Mr Poore, seemed to epitomise all that had gone wrong with the motorcycle industry. Its products were still famous – especially the Bonneville 750 'twin', with its sombre strength and hand-painted gold lines, perennially saleable in America. But the factory itself had been operating almost at half-capacity, it possessed an appalling record of strikes and had accumulated gigantic losses. One of the factories in Mr Poore's domain must close. He announced that Meriden should close, its 1,750 workers be made redundant and the manufacture of Bonnevilles, of Tridents and other Triumphs, be concentrated at the BSA factory in Birmingham.

Chuck Knight's father was a miner. When he used to come home from the pit at Arley his wife would have a bowl of custard ready for him to swallow, then vomit up again to free his lungs of the coal dust that was tormenting them. Before his death from silicosis, he forbade his four sons to follow him down the pit. Instead they went to Triumph: Chuck, his brothers and altogether so many of the population of Arley that in the Meriden canteen bread-and-butter pudding is traditionally referred to as 'Arley wedding cake'.

Chuck is a dreamer; the dream is silvery, fired on two cylinders. His house, one feels, was selected for its nearness to the Meriden works and for the copse at the back where Chuck taught his son and his five-year-old daughter to ride miniature motorcycles among the trees. 'My father *walked* beside me while I was learning, like I walk beside my little 'un. I proposed to my wife on a bike. First thing I said to her when I met her – it was in the Co-op Hall, Nuneaton – I said 'Do you like motorbikes, moto-cross and that kind of thing? I proposed to her on the back of a bike. It was a Triumph Thunderbird. I stopped the bike and put the ring on her finger.

'I think it's heartbreaking, you know. You like bikes, your work's surrounded with bikes, you've been with bikes all your life, and then someone just comes along and puts you out on the street and insults you. And insults the bikes too.'

Men like Chuck were the obstacle to Dennis Poore's 'rationalisation' plan. Chuck and his mates at Meriden occupied the factory, shutting in £1million worth of unfinished Bonnevilles. Initially their revolt took the form of a 'work-in', that curious antithesis to a strike, from which developed a proposal even more novel and unprecedented. A demand existed for Triumph motorcycles. The Meriden force was determined to continue making them at Meriden. Why could they not buy the factory from Mr Poore and produce Bonnevilles as a workers' co-operative?

On the day it all began, Frank, the gate security sergeant, was off duty, at home. An elderly but still big and powerful Yorkshireman, Frank is a motorcycle enthusiast himself; he was paddock-master at the Mallory Park circuit before his wife had her stroke. As the Co-operative was born, Frank was changing the glass in his bathroom window from clear to 'obscure', and unluckily he fell off the roof. 'I slid down that roof thinking "Ooh, me bloody knee!" and it was me back I injured: two vertebrae fractured in the lower lumbar region. I was off work fourteen weeks *and* I had to have a new glass put in the bathroom,' Frank said. 'It cost me six pounds eighty.'

Frank is still security sergeant at Meriden: still, by mutual concession, an employee of the dispossessed NVT management. An outsider inside, familiar yet disinterested, Frank has observed the year that followed from the windows of his gatehouse.

There was first the uproar; the reporters and 'Press conferences', the high-handed television lights, the questions in Parliament. There was the probability of arrest and the possibility of violence; of 'stewards' arriving to recapture the factory with quasi-official iron clubs. There were the sightseers and parasites, the *Workers Press* 'demanding' to join the picket-line. There was all the bitter opprobrium reserved for militants or disturbers of the peace. There was the affirmation of faith in a principle, and children and wives and outstanding bills at home, and, deep in one's stomach, the sensation of winter drawing near.

Winter arrived on its cue. They kept the gates all through the winter, day and night, in three shifts of four men each. In a jobless winter, when even those with jobs tended to despair, they maintained guard over the factory with its shiny, labelled ghosts, for the sake of which they postponed marriages, made love by appointment to their wives and watched as their savings were gnawed at by the rats of inflation. On Christmas Night the picket-hut, precariously decked with coloured lights, almost blew over. Worse than the nights, perhaps, were the days, after their notoriety had faded, when the trees were black and the brazier gave fitful warmth; when there seemed to be nothing in front of them but an ideal, and the strip of road that runs between Coventry and Birmingham.

'I try and keep a pound a week like, for enjoyment. But if the wife wants it, I have to hand it over.'

'Hard up, that's me. And falling out with the wife.'

130

'I'm at sea-level now. If I go any lower, I'll sink.'

'Social Security! Six pound a week! I can get more than that down in Arley, spud-picking. I give that to me mother for a game of bingo.'

'I've got a Barclaycard. That only gets you deeper in the mire, doesn't it?'

'I remember the old chap who was our picket-leader, he came to me at Christmas time and said: 'Taffy, we've won, we've won.' In tears he was. He's drifted away since.'

'That's what I say – nothing can worry yer much now after this. Nothing can disappoint yer at home, like, after what we've been through.'

A year to the day after the work-in, with 300 men left out of 1,750, they were almost there. The history of negotiations, broken off, resumed, challenged and endlessly revised, had coalesced, at last, into a single document whereby the Co-operative would buy the factory and two-thirds of the machinery from Mr Poore. The £5 million guaranteed to them by Tony Benn hung poised for the finalising of the document. They were almost there – that is to say, they were almost ready to begin. An empty feeling came now as they stood and watched the cars go by, or broke into sudden gesticulations against the sleepy wasps that haunted the forecourt.

A quiet factory is a curious place. In thoroughfares made for hundreds of men it seems unreal to see one man walking, and no silence is more pervasive than that of silent machinery. Gone, too, are the noises which divide the hours – the hooters, the bells, the transfer of many feet. At Meriden they have learned to measure time in the arrival and departure of Bill Lapworth's car.

Lapworth, as Divisional Secretary of the Transport and General Workers' Union, was called to the factory immediately after Mr Poore had pronounced sentence of closure. It was Lapworth who focused the waves of anger and shock into definite response; he, together with Leslie Huckfield MP for Nuneaton, must claim credit for bringing about the birth of the Co-operative. He has returned almost every day since.

Lapworth's influence has proved crucial in the Co-operative's battle with NVT. A dark, taciturn man, with a spark of mischievousness behind his squared spectacles, he admits to a fondness of strategy for its own sake. He convinced them that if they attempted to resist the closure on Mr Poore's terms they would have no hope; it was necessary to fall upon the flank. All along he urged them to establish their credibility as a unit: to announce the Co-operative first in the *Financial Times;* to stake their own redundancy money as an earnest of their desire to work; to confound their detractors on the Left and the Right by remaining immaculately apolitical. Trades unions, no less than employers, proved wary of the co-operative principle. It was Lapworth, with an adroitness which still slightly bemuses him, who procured for Meriden the support of his General Secretary Jack Jones. This considerable ally, together with the return of a Labour Government, finally secured the promise of public finance.

Those who remember Denis Johnson a few years ago are still apt to marvel at the change in him during the past months. He used to be so quiet; he was the last man one might have expected to fill out the contours of leadership. He used to be so meek. Now as chairman of the Co-operative's steering committee, composed from the eight unions involved, it is Denis Johnson, with Bill Lapworth, who represents them at the firing line; he, rather than Lapworth, who has acquired the gestures, and non-gestures, of command. He is fragile, nervous-looking and boyish in a white windcheater, still liable to be teased by the others for the size of his feet.

He sat at Frank the sergeant's desk and covered the telephone receiver with his hand. That single black, square-cut telephone has courted or kept at bay all the forces which they have unleashed in the world outside.

'– he's asking me if he can be sure of a job to come back to,' Johnson said to the others. 'I told him, "I don't even know if I'm sure of one myself." '

They calculate that they will be able to increase the work force to 800 when the factory re-opens. Men who were compelled to leave during the winter will come back and work for a flat weekly wage of £50.

'We're starting to go downhill,' Johnson said quietly. 'We can't afford to soft-pedal yet, but we're starting to go the other way.'

John Grattan, a former works electrician, completes the front rank. In so doing he, too, has astonished his companions; for, just as Johnson was considered too mild, so Grattan seemed too unruly to partake of leadership. He is a bearded, gingery Scot who at first glance seems given entirely to uttering four primal oaths and at second glance proves to be exactly that. Only the tin from which John Grattan rolls his cigarettes indicates any more emotional attachment. On his cigarette tin there is a *Triumph* sticker.

The pressure is never constant. Periods of intense activity die away; the leaders become men again waiting inside the gatehouse, watching men waiting outside. The document had left them now and was in the hands of their ally Geoffrey Robinson, managing director of Jaguar, who has largely drafted it in the form acceptable to NVT. They do the *Mirror* crossword. They read the brightly-covered motorcycle magazines, one of which is found to contain an item hostile to themselves.

132

'The Curse of Christ be on that reporter,' John Grattan said, 'and on his descendants and on his forefathers.'

He went outside. He reappeared a few minutes later riding one of the bikes from the experimental shop, his beard raised into the wind.

'You never used to see hardly anyone in this gatehouse before,' Frank the sergeant said. 'In fact we used to have a notice up saying "All enquiries to be made at window".'

Frank himself has worked continual day-long shifts on the gate during the past year. In September he had not been out of his uniform since the previous June. The re-opening under the Co-operative will mean his own redundancy.

'I thought I should see out my days here. I was due to retire in three years, and I finish paying for my house next month. Making glass bottles – that's how I started. A hundred and thirteen degrees it used to be in those furnaces. I could never get above eleven stone no matter how much I ate. Fourteen slices of bread a day I used to eat – fourteen full rounds and pound of tomatoes for my tea.'

In one respect the long wait has proved advantageous. It gave the Co-operative time to overcome the major technical objection to their manufacturing Bonnevilles for the American market. American safety regulations require the foot gear-change to be on the left, whereas in Britain they were traditionally fitted on the right. Under the old management some clumsy attempts at conversion had been made in the experimental shop, earning it from John Grattan the contemptuous name 'Slumberglade Hall'. That, they maintain, is typical of the way the factory was mismanaged before its closure. They found playing-cards and ping-pong balls all over the experimental shop. It was then given to Jim Barclay, a gentle, hirsute young Scot who formerly worked in production engineering, to develop a left-hand shift with the addition of rear disc-brakes. Chuck Knight tested the converted bike around the car-park until he was palsied with rain and cold, and the clock registered 1100 miles. Under the final agreement Mr Poore is to market the Bonnevilles which the Co-operative will produce. Mr Poore himself has ridden the test-bike and pronounced the conversion satisfactory.

Visitors were always numerous. Almost every day a passing motor-cyclist, bulbous in his trappings would swish across the forecourt to enquire about spares. Australians in overland buses came, begging to buy Bonnevilles to take home with them. A charabanc-load of teenage German trades unionists arrived unannounced, and were addressed in the canteen by Denis Johnson on the history of the Co-operative, with only the faintest tremor of the cigarette inside his hand. Two girls from the Belgrade Theatre, Coventry, were also to be observed on some opaque cultural business, bringing a kindling look into John Grattan's ginger eyebrows. Tony Benn came, and the Lord Mayor of Coventry, and Chuck Knight's mother. On one celebrated occasion a party of American Triumph dealers came up from London and were amazed to be received by other than the ferocious revolutionaries they had been led to expect. American dealers, in fact, have provided some of the greater boosts to morale. One in particular, Bob Myers, organised a petition of support and sent over the *Meriden* cheerleader emblem which adorns the breast of Chuck Knight's younger brother Tony. The Americans say that they could sell 50,000 Bonnevilles every year.

Up in the canteen this afternoon sits Dicky Price, a former Meriden man who, as the result of an appendicitis operation, has recently lost a leg.

'It's not very nice,' Dicky Price admitted. 'But it's not as bad as all that. The specialist said to me, "Mr Price, it's a state of mind." That's all it is. It's a state of mind.'

'Cheer-o Dick. Nice to see you looking so fit, cock.'

'It's done me good coming up here,' Dicky Price said. 'Normally at this time I'll say to the wife, "I'll have five minutes," but I don't feel a bit sleepy now.'

There are young men in leather jackets; there are older men who do not mind about clothes – age is, anyway, of no significance in the factory bond of 'mates'. Some speak in curses and some talk like schoolmasters; there is a man who brings a golf putter with him, a man who was born in Khartoum, a man who owns an Italian greyhound. Fortitude is not written in the face or physique, and assuredly not evident in the voice. There are talkative men; there are others who do not say very much. But in all their talk, one word is pronounced above all as explanation of their sacrifice and their survival. It is an unfamiliar, awkward word, being customarily found in the mouths of politicians rather than men. The word is 'Britain'. They desire to work and to make motorcycles for Britain. Why can it not be as simple as that?

Up in the gatehouse Co-operatives leaders have long since been disabused of such notions. Indeed, there is a disillusion to be felt at times among the leadership which may make the siege easier to withstand than the lifting of the siege. Towards Geoffrey Robinson, who perfected their charter, the feeling remains practically one of hero-worship. But there is hostility now towards some of their original supporters and towards a Press which, if sceptical, has hardly been unsympathetic. John Grattan especially takes pleasure in his private intelligence-system to observe the doings of a journalist about the neighbourhood. 'I can tell you what you'd to drink in the Queen's last night. A gin, you had. A Guinness. and in between drinks you'd a lemonade. Am I right?' He was perfectly right.

Above all, deep feelings are still cherished regarding Mr Poore. Their erstwhile overlord remains in their minds as a bloodless specu-

134

lator who desired the Triumph name, but disregarded the men responsible for that name. They recall the brusqueness of his announcement that September day, having informed the newspapers in advance, and his precipitate departure back to London. They suspect Mr Poore of employing psychological weapons during the long negotiation – of raising their hopes time and again only to confound them with some new objection. Bill Lapworth says that their resolution might, indeed, have been less strong had Mr Poore not behaved so intractably, had he at any moment seemed to be making any sort of concession. Since Mr Poore is not a frequent visitor at Meriden, a certain amount of malevolent fun is directed against his external manager Mr Palin, who has become known as 'The Pink Panther' for his loping and inquiring gait. The Co-operative's immediate future depends on its marketing alliance with Mr Poore. The alliance, on their part, hardly begins in circumstances of auspicious trust.

Mr Poore, for his part, naturally resists this characterisation as an ogre and tormentor. His office is in Love Lane, EC2; his manner, though peppery, seems not unsympathetic, though he clearly cherishes no romantic feeling towards any cut of motorcycle. Mr Poore cleaves to the point that he was assigned to rescue the whole of the industry; this was impossible with three factories, but it was possible with two. He claims that Meriden was doomed in any case, before his arrival: he has discovered evidence that the old Triumph management intended to shut the factory down.

As to the potential of the Co-operative – as to their ability to furnish NVT with the weekly 500 Bonnevilles mentioned by the agreement – Mr Poore is inclined to smile. He maintains that their scheme held no plausibility before the advent of Geoffrey Robinson. He enumerates the difficulties that remain: the old machinery; the hiring of management executives willing to be subservient to a workforce; the wrangle which must ensue regarding use of the Triumph name. Johnson, he says, is a good man, but the name of Grattan inspires no confidence in his face. He believes their great flaw is their unwillingness to accept that any of the trouble in the old factory had anything to do with themselves. His own brusqueness in closing the factory is attributed by Mr Poore to contumacious trades-unionists. Even the meeting at which he spoke the death-sentence, says Mr Poore, was convened under the threat of yet another strike.

The source of his irritation, however, is the disturbance that Meriden has wrought upon the remainder of an already enfeebled industry. The blockade is costing NVT already £1million in interest charges alone. A quarter of a million more was lost at Norton in Wolverhampton, where the recent dispute broke a work record unblemished for 30 years; at Birmingham, where the Triumph Trident is made, Mr Poore reports his employees to be likewise discontented and sardonic. His real business now is with the Government, which must provide more money to keep the other factories alive. Mr Poore is angry with the Government for its dilatoriness in this matter.

'Psychologically now I can see it would have been better to put a receiver in. If BSA-Triumph had gone bust and then we'd come along and built it up, like we did at Norton, everybody would have been delighted that we were saving something, instead of turning round and calling me some sort of hatchet-man. If I was a young man with a career in front of me, I'd be bloody annoyed – I'm nearly sixty; I can take a calmer view. I still think that in all this NVT have been treated disgracefully.'

In his gatehouse, Frank the security sergeant was preparing to go off duty. He telephoned his invalid wife, greeting her with a cordial, *'Buenos dias Senora'* He put back the receiver and sighed. 'A couple of hours on the box, then I start putting up my sandwiches for the next day.

'Spain – that's all I spend my money on,' Frank said. 'I'll be there again in a couple of weeks, God willing. This'll be the twentieth time I've been to Spain. And, you know, you never used to be able to get me to go abroad. I went fourteen times to the Isle of Man; I used to swear by the Isle of Man. Ooh, that sand you get in Spain!' Frank said. 'It's just like sand in an egg-timer – you seem to glide over it.'

NVT men had been inside the factory that day, determining the one-third of the machinery to be moved out for Mr Poore. Inventory had been taken of the bikes which would soon be restored to Mr Poore, in immaculate order, but a year late.

The man who came into the gatehouse with the work-sheet enquired, 'How's it going?'

'All right,' Denis Johnson said guardedly.

John Grattan rested his knees against the desk and tilted his reddish beard at the questioner.

'I've told the missis to put up new football-laces for the kids. And we're gettin' new carpeting in the rabbit-hutch.'

'Oh well,' Johnson said, laughing hesitantly. 'For a Scotsman I'd say that was very . . . extensive, wouldn't you?'

Then he murmured: 'Twelve months, and I'd do it all over again.'

'I fookin' wouldn't!' exclaimed John Grattan.

'I would,' Johnson said. 'Someone said they wanted to shut the factory – "John, put the chain on the gate. I'll get the people together." '

Down at the gate, a new picket had come on watch. The evening was quiet and rich with summer warmth. They sat on the crooked

136

bench, beside the unlighted brazier, and looked out at the strip of road that runs between Coventry and Birmingham.

1975

Girl Guides Sell Themselves

They are wide-eyed, open-faced, upright women with cheeks innocent of rouge, and wind-bright noses and grey hair, unfussily cut and often rumpled by their own enthusiastic fingers. They greet you with a left handshake, producing in the uninitiated a sensation similar to having collided with a lamp post. In a noisy room, if one of them lifts her arm, all the others fall immediately silent. It is one tradition that no ex-Girl Guide ever forgets.

The occasion is a conference organised by Guide Headquarters for its local public relations officers, to teach them better liaison with newspapers and the broadcasting media. Too many journalists, it is felt, stubbornly continue to associate Girl Guides and Brownies with knot-tying Brown Owls, sing-songs and having crushes. After this conference the media may well be unequal to Guide PROs newly armed with expertise in silk screen printing, TV and radio technique, photography, and a general pushiness exhorted by the Guides Chief Commissioner with the words: 'Ladies – go out and sell yourselves.'

One might ask whether the Guides have any need of such tactics, as theirs is already the largest youth organisation in Britain with an 870,000 membership that has been increasing every year since Baden Powell formed the movement, a helpmate to his Boy Scouts, in 1910. British Guides now outnumber Scouts by nearly 50 per cent, a fact that may well surprise 'BP' as he watches over the conference at Scout Headquarters from many a sketch and photograph and peppery little bronze statuette.

The Guide movement has modernised itself with none of the internal disagreements that trouble the Scouts. The old qualifying tests, in knitting or Morse, have been replaced by an eight-point programme which each Guide works through at her own speed and capability. Whereas all first-class Guides formerly had to learn to swim, it is now recognised that a girl has achieved more who conquers her fear of water sufficiently to wade up to her neck.

The uniform has lost its soldierly embellishments of metal stars and shoulder-cords, acquiring instead the bland, rather dated look of an airline stewardess. Belts and clasp knives may no longer be worn, except at camp. 'And we've dropped our long black stockings,'

138

a conference delegate said, going on to explain that they now wear nylon tights instead.

It remains palpably a uniform and as such a barrier to the older girls. When this is overcome, wonderful things may lie in store. Pam Gillard, from BBC Radio Humberside, a speaker at the conference on broadcasting technique, leads a unit of rangers – senior-Guides who learn flying with RAF instructors. The course also includes solo gliding and parachuting. 'A lot of girls get jobs afterwards with air traffic control,' Pam said, 'or else they marry men on the RAF station, which they like even better.'

Modern Guides' activities extend to potholing, car maintenance or foreign travel to one of the movement's several houses abroad. Pam Gillard describes how her life was changed by a trip to Canada, and the Algonquin national park. 'They put a whole lot of us who couldn't speak each other's language in a dangerous situation to see if we could cope. We had to paddle by canoe through country infested with rabid racoons.' The Japanese Guides, to whom racoon was a delicacy, tried to catch some for the cooking pot.

A notice board at the conference displays press cuttings of the sort of Girl Guide story which can achieve national coverage – 'Canal Kisses Shock Guide Leader'; 'Snowy Owl Must Go, Say Mothers'; 'Tough Guy Paul has joined the Brownies.' Such headlines are denied the Guides' community and charity work, or their rallies, so enormous that Westminster Abbey cannot hold them all.

The perennial question of wooing a jaded reporter was being discussed in a seminar yesterday morning.

'Do you write it all out beforehand?' asked a fair-haired lady in brogues, enunciating carefully. Or do you use the frontal approach? Do you ring a journalist up and say "Yoicks! I've got some super news!"?'

The Chief Commissioner, Mrs Owen Walker, a stately woman with pearl earrings and a bellowing laugh, urged Guide leaders everywhere to lessen prejudice by stressing their interests outside the Guide movement. She herself is a supporter of Nottingham Forest, and says she would travel 'any distance' to see a wrestling match. The Chief Commissioner admits, however, that she was never a model Girl Guide.

The old traditions die hard, especially among ex-Brownies, for whom life may never again have produced the equal of the Brownie Revels. In the cafeteria queue, they were remembering the mottos of their fairy patrols:

'We're the happy cheerful gnomes – helping people in their homes.'

'We're the elves – we think of others, not ourselves.'

'We're the pixies – helping people out of fixes.'

'Ah, but you can't be fairies any more,' a younger delegate said. 'It means something . . . different these days.'

'Oh dear,' her companion sighed, 'words are so *difficult* now, aren't they?'

The prevailing view is that no one will ever again be as brilliant at public relations as Baden Powell himself. In a glass case at BP House is a china mug produced in 1900 to celebrate his defence of Mafeking. Baden Powell's telegram is inscribed around the mug: 'All well. Four hours' bombardment. One dog killed – here he is on the handle.'

1978

QC Bowls Greig a Googly

It is doubtful if Tony Greig has ever faced a more testing adversary than Michael Kempster, that mild and velvety QC. The witness stand is half the trouble, contorting the cricketer's dangling frame into an uneasy, elevated crouch. His large hands pendant, he leans earnestly forward, sometimes tracing the syllables of a question with his lips. Cricketing metaphors have abounded lately in the High Court, but it is unavoidable to suggest that counsel for both sides are bowling to Tony Greig considerably under-arm.

An action before Mr Justice Slade marks the latest inroad by Kerry Packer, the Australian TV tycoon, into English cricket. Greig and two fellow players, John Snow and Mike Procter, are contesting the right of the cricket authorities to ban them from Test and county matches if they appear in Packer's so-called World Series Test in Australia this winter.

Mr Justice Slade must decide the matter upon which few Englishmen can pronounce without emotion. In signing with the Packer circus, are Greig and the others likely to damage a hallowed game whose mysticism depends largely on its remaining untouched by commerce? Or does the ban, imposed by the Test and County Cricket Board and the International Cricket Conference, constitute a 'restraint of trade' against already downtrodden members of the last unliberated professional sport?

Enough half-familiar faces have filled the public seats to provide endless prattle between overs. Snow and Procter, Greig's co-plaintiffs, sit close to Ritchie Benaud and far from their putative masters in the TCCB. Older heroes, their history told in tie-stripes, watch with spellbound revulsion behind the crooks of polished walking sticks.

The ogre is himself sporadically visible. Kerry Packer's style is to sit in court for long periods and then vanish with an abruptness that gives obvious disquiet to his opponents. Now he is back again, neatly folded, trainer-like, on a front bench among his solicitors. He has the narrow muzzle of a Beatrix Potter rabbit and eyes so wide, they seem to be studying the conduct of his protégés behind his back.

Alec Bedser's face, as wide and simple as the Vauxhall End, provides the best register of these supernatural events. Never in his

141

lifetime can Bedser have thought to see a captain of England, albeit a deposed one, not merely complaining about his stipend but even daring to challenge the Test selectors' inscrutable wisdom. And this while wearing an MCC tie.

Greig's halting voice and tortured vocabulary are peculiarly suited to totting up what he regards as long-standing wrongs. Modest are the emoluments he claims to have received as captain of Sussex and England. Sussex paid him £5,000 a season, for a life continuously on the move between matches. For each Test payment was fixed at £210 for five days' play. During his captaincy his views were never sought on the appropriateness of this payment.

Then there were the winter tours from November to March: the ceaseless travel, the play in gruelling heat, the MCC's strict paternalism. Wives were allowed to join their husbands on tour for only 21 conjugal nights. On the fateful tour of India, Sri Lanka and Australia, Greig almost lost Alan Knott as wicketkeeper because Knott wished to see his wife on nights other than those prescribed.

For that highly successful tour, Greig was paid £3,000 with a £300 captain's bonus – a sum 'absolutely, totally ridiculous' in view of the attendances. He felt fortunate compared with those who had not been selected and who, unpaid by their clubs in winter, took work in pubs or signed on to the dole.

Greig had approached Kerry Packer in Australia after the Centenary Test, in the hope of obtaining winter employment himself, on one of the tycoon's television stations. Instead he found himself offered leadership of the 'Supertest' squad, already under recruitment in Australia, whose matches would be televised on Packer's Channel 9 network.

Greig's allusions to Packer have been fond. He is indebted to Packer already for sending him on holiday to the West Indies. For the first time since he sacrificed a university degree to professional cricket, he can look forward to the future with confidence: beyond his three-year playing contract, worth £25,000 a year, he has been promised a desk job with Packer after he retires and a loan, if he needs one, to buy a house in Australia. He trusts Mr Packer's word.

Somewhat apologetically, Michael Kempster, for the defendant cricketing bodies, inquired if an English county cricketer could not make a large tax-free sum when his club awarded him a benefit year. He might, Greig answered, but at personal cost. In his benefit year, the player had to go around to pubs, soliciting donations. It was often 'a cap-in-hand situation'.

Was it not true that Amiss's benefit earned £35,000? And Underwood's £24,000?

Those were record figures, Greig replied.

Well then: how about Snow's £18,000?

'Can you tell me a figure higher than £35,000?'

142

Cross-examining counsel, on this occasion, did not exhibit the usual frigid rage at being questioned by a witness.

'You're not really supposed to ask *me,*' he said benignly, 'but I'm told that D'Oliveira's was £45,000.'

John Snow, Sussex and England fast bowler, described to his counsel a 12-year career in professional cricket, not all green turf and gracefulness: there was, for example, the winter of 1968 when, unselected for the MCC tour, he was forced to go on the dole. There was the dysentery he picked up on a tour of Pakistan, which came back again in Australia. His present salary from Sussex was £3,500; he had team-mates also forced to go on the dole in winter or beg an advance from the club against next summer's earnings.

At 35, Snow admitted, he was growing old for a fast bowler. He had received one benefit – a 'minor miracle,' since there was opposition to it within the club – which had earned him £18,000, for 12 years' play. The need to solicit money he had found 'debasing'.

Under Michael Kempster's genial cross-examination, Snow agreed that he was the author of a book called *Cricket Rebel.* And also of two books of verse, he pointed out. It was true, however, that he was of independent spirit, and had once taken to the field with advertising matter displayed on his clothes.

Where on his clothes?

'On my hat, my pads . . . and my backside, if I remember.'

'Your . . . ? Oh, yes.'

The witness-stand, so uncongenial to Tony Greig, fits Kerry Packer like one of his strange, round-shouldered suits. In no time at all, the oath administered, he is leaning back, telling the judge man to man how he rescued Australian golf a few years ago. It is as if an ogre has suddenly begun to read a bedtime story.

He is quiet, fluent, perfectly composed, a little vexed, a little wounded by the outcry that has always greeted his philanthropic gestures. One waits in vain for the bruising argot of his native land. The highest term of Packer approbation is revealed to be 'gentlemanly'. The cricket boards have been 'not gentlemanly' in their dealings with him over Channel 9 and the Supertest.

Great names rally to his aid with magical marginality. At different moments he invokes Bradman, Einstein and Caesar's wife. The last named is exemplar for his Supertest players, who have been warned to expect discipline. Their chief wishes them to be, like Caesar's wife, above suspicion.

And if he gets his way as a television tycoon and is allowed to show the existing Test exclusively on Channel 9, will he then, as some suggest, abandon the Supertest and the players contracted to him?

'If the Test and County Cricket Board say that, then all I can say is . . . they're being dishonest.'

143

As the court adjourned on Friday, English county cricket received the assurance that Kerry Packer intended it no harm. He required the services of his men only during the winter. 'In the English summer they can go and play in Brighton, in the water, if they want to . . .'

Kerry Packer watches the ball.

1977

The Misery of Merseyside

On weekday afternoons, all around Kirkby estate, there is a moment when you see men coming out of their houses simultaneously, as for the beginning of a shift. They are young men, although long married, in platform shoes, afforded two or three years ago, and pastel-coloured trousers, no longer worn for best. In each case, their journey leads no further than the garden gate. Small children in pedal cars bear them company; their front doors, left open, show hallways endlessly redecorated, the sole respite from having nothing to occupy their hands. Four o'clock is the nadir of a jobless man's day, after he has slept to distraction, after television grows unbearable, shut curtains press in, yet the atrophying idleness still cannot stifle a memory of what would be happening now at work.

Kirkby has been christened the Belfast of Merseyside. In Bolton Avenue, a pub called The Mainbrace carries on trade behind a palisade of boards and tin. Bricks continue to shatter the remaining lounge bar window. Muggings happen frequently in the passage to the toilets. The muggers are children, 10 years old, or less – these are the terrorists in Kirkby. They start fires in empty Council flats, they smash every window, they climb over the roof to rip out the tiles. They have laid waste whole squares of the estate. Maisonette blocks, built not so long ago, stand roofless and smoke-stained on grassland bombarded with junk. The children have learned to pull down even brick walls with their hands. Official demolition goes on, pitifully in arrears.

There are 70,000 people living in Kirkby. Twenty per cent of them are unemployed. During the Depression – an era commonly believed to have ended in the 1930s – the level of unemployment nationally was 23 per cent.

Sheila King is among the luckier ones. Her husband Joe was unemployed for six months only. An insulation engineer, he left his job at Christmas because Sheila was afraid to stay in their flat alone. The flat is the last inhabited one in its block; the last with windows not broken in silhouettes of madness. Damp from the damaged water tank on the roof crusts its ceilings; damp from empty flats below rises via the bed-linen.

Now Sheila is alone again; Joe couldn't stand the idleness. A skilled man like him can find work, but it is in Stafford, two hours away by road: he leaves home every morning at 5.45 a.m. That is how you cling to work on Merseyside. Sheila stays in all day, Hoovering her lounge, with its cherished red velvet suite, crowding her small balcony with washing, above the place where gardens used to be. She has tried to repair the oozing kitchen walls with cheerful yellow paper. Joe has fitted bolts outside every door along the hall. 'It's like a prison; I'm a prisoner,' Sheila says, still smiling at the notion because she is only 23 years old.

When British Leyland shut down their Triumph sports car plant at Speke last May, 2,000 more workers paid the price of what is seen as Merseyside's insatiable appetite for sabotage. This appetite is indiscriminate, we are told; it is ultimately suicidal. It has brought about, in less than a year, the closure of factories along Merseyside manufacturing Leyland cars, Lucas lamps and GEC cookers, and produced a national shortage of Bird's Eye frozen pies. We cannot but believe testimony given by such household names. They say they are weary of combating a work force that will not work, that is greedy and contumacious beyond reason. So, rapidly, they pull out of a region whose cursedness for manufacturing purposes is the talk of industrial Europe. By August, as much as 13 per cent of Merseyside's labour force – 100,000 people – will be without jobs. Even as national unemployment climbs towards two million, few elsewhere in Britain think Merseyside's problem can possibly be other than of simple, bloody hara-kiri.

To arrive in Liverpool by rail is to feel the region's ostracism at once. Lime Street Station, under pigeons and welcome placards, reveals its purpose as the marshalling-point for offensives against the South. The carriage windows bear remnants of stickers that read 'TR7 not dole', commemorating the efforts of Leyland's Speke workforce to keep the Triumph plant open. Another train full of trade unionists, a thousand at once, bound for Parliament to lobby their eight MPs. London defeats them always, with drizzle and polite interest. A petition is handed over; Eric Heffer explains, 'We're on the wrong side of Britain for the EEC'. Placards collect vaguely on the pavement opposite Westminster Abbey.

Yet in Central Liverpool, few signs of despair are visible. The wide piazzas, the black colonnades of an imperial province, laid out to celebrate so many approving visits by George V, slope downhill into consumerism as frantic as anywhere in Britain. Nothing has happened on Merseyside yet to frighten Marks and Spencer away. In tall, safe windows, the jumpers gesticulate; shoes for a carefree summer lie heaped in baskets; on a jeweller's board, gold rings by the hundred await the wedding harvest. Pale green buses drift through the insurance district; up again to the Pier Head, that broad river front graced by classical maritime buildings, where hundreds of clerks, sunning themselves on parallel seats, suggest, if anything, excess of employment. The river demurs – so empty that the cranes on Birkenhead side seem to stand still from sheer embarrassment.

Merseyside is not Liverpool alone. The fact is insisted on by those struggling to dispel the curse. Birkenhead, its long, tired streets; respectable Wallasey; New Brighton, which gloried once in a tower higher than Blackpool's – these cross-river, unharmonious adjuncts define the limits of the Mersey no longer. Local government reorganisation, in 1974, bestowed the name on a 'metropolitan county', hurling its boundaries south to annexe the stand-offish Wirral; east into Lancashire, engulfing St Helens and Newton-le-Willows; north, through Bootle and Crosby, across the Birkdale fairways to rope in even Southport's spacious sands. This is the 'new Merseyside', its muddy name diluted among 250 square miles, many districts of which can be flatteringly depicted in tourist guides. Great change has occurred theoretically, through repainted signboards and council lorries.

The Government shades Merseyside dark red, signifying heavy transfusions. It is listed as a Special Development Area, much as backward children are frequently called 'special': a place needing perpetual life support. That support arrives in what is called 'footloose industry', which the Government steers towards Merseyside on alluring financial terms. A factory setting up here is reimbursed for 22 per cent of its building and machinery costs. In purpose-built premises, of which an abundance waits in hope, up to five years are offered rent-free. These emoluments – so liberal as to put some prospective newcomers on their guard – prolong the charity felt by Government to be Merseyside's due.

It began in the postwar years, in reparation for Hitler's bombs; it continued through the fifties and sixties, when Ford's were lured to Halewood and Triumph Motors, to Speke. It has produced a concentration of factories and refineries, and the weary roads between, conceivable only if you imagine two southern car plants like Cowley and Luton, together with Corby and perhaps Swindon, all dumped down at once beside Southampton Docks.

The future that never was lies along the East Lancs Road. The signs planted in smooth verges point off to Knowsley Industrial Estate – a signwriter's trick, for this is Kirkby again. It is Kirkby where, for mile after mile, new factories sprawl bleakly among the huts of an old munition dump.

147

Lee Martin does not look at her work. She looks straight ahead, down the long room, lit by ghostly blue insecticide lights, where rows of women rip up boiled chickens, like dissatisfied embroideresses, flinging each carcase into deep tubs while the good meat drifts on to its destiny in a Bird's Eye frozen pie. The women are permitted no rings but plain wedding bands, no earrings but 'sleepers'; their hair, under white mobcaps, is restrained in normal shape by nets without elastic. Pale nets are issued to blonde women, dark ones to brunettes.

A woman on top bonus can dismantle a chicken in 60 seconds flat, never ceasing to talk to her neighbour above the roar of radio music. All must scrub their hands, before each 'service' of chickens, 11 times per shift. At the far end, where chicken fragments are sorted meticulously into white meat and dark, Lee Martin stands, looking tranquilly into space while her chickeny fingers sift and heap. She is searching for the tiniest bones which the strippers may overlook. She has worked 12 years in the chicken room – here and in the previous place, where one wall was painted red for Liverpool supporters, the other wall blue, for Everton.

The Kirkby Bird's Eye factory suffered one of the longest recent strikes on Merseyside. For four months, until last April, the workforce of 1,200 were out in sympathy with 110 maintenance engineers who had stopped work over a pay claim. Among those unable to cross the picket line were builders engaged on a £7 million expansion plan for the factory. Bird's Eye, as a result, were forced to revise their scheme to concentrate pie and cooked meat production at Kirkby. The strike's sole consequence was 465 new redundancies.

Today, the pie lines are moving again, up their spiral to the refrigerator that glazes their pale pastry to a rock-firm frost. George Tickell, the general manager, hopes devoutly that the bitterness is past. He has appointed a community relations manager, Tommy Hawkins, whom the chicken women like; in best managerial style, he draws a diagram of balloons encircling such words as 'Consultation' and 'Relationships'. George Tickell is young, like a retired pop singer; his balloons are well-meant; the fact remains that, on Merseyside, a firm that fights its employees generally wins.

A couple of hundred yards away, calmer habits prevail. On the forecourt at Murray (Scientific) Ltd, Mr Ferguson is leaving for the afternoon. Mr Ferguson is a man in his 70s, the son of a Mersey ship-repairer. He worked with his father in that trade when men would gather at dawn on 'the stand', each hoping for the mercy of even half a day's work at 4s 6d. His face is gaunt and tanned, a deep groove worn in each cheek by hardship and ill-health. His voice is quiet, although a mention of Everton Football Club – of Dixie Dean, flickering down the field in championships long past – can still bring a kindling in Mr Ferguson's pale eyes. Latterly, he became works manager for Murray (Scientific) Ltd. Six years ago, one Friday, he retired: the following Monday, he was back at work as usual.

One can understand Mr Ferguson's attachment. The factory inside is clean and snug, full of warm concentration and cosy blue flames. It builds and repairs pressure dials, temperature gauges and other instruments that give sensible warning. With 60 employees, holding among them one token union card, its labour relations are Utopian. It has a reputation for filling orders within hours, sending cars across country to ships at Hull, even Tilbury, on one occasion receiving an order from Hamburg one Monday afternoon and delivering it in Rotterdam the next Wednesday night.

Roy Rossiter, the present works manager, does his best to supervise without hurt to Mr Ferguson's feelings. He leads the way from hut to hut, where men work cloistered with quiet gas and thin capillary wire, and unemployment is a rumour, heard through acquaintances or brothers-in-law. Anyone here can be called on to work all night, sweep a floor or take a car to the docks. At Christmas, they leave their telephone numbers, for emergencies. They have free tea and a subsidised football team. At the back, someone has put a bird house on the telegraph pole. They have dug an earth plot, here in the midst of Kirkby, and planted roses.

Not only such small firms escape the Merseyside curse. Great companies escape it daily, testifying by their utter silence to the possibility of being multinational from here. Esso, Shell, BP, Bowater, Dunlop, Kodak, Rio Tinto Zinc – the silted-up skylines, the depots and dumps and faint silver silos – all flourish along Merseyside to their inscrutable satisfaction, among car parks reaching to infinity. At Bromborough there is Unilever, which – save for the rankling unpleasantness at its Bird's Eye satellite – functions along Merseyside in almost bucolic tranquility, if that be possible in so vast a heap of chemicals and soap. Unilever shows no inclination to retreat from its 14 companies employing 12,000 people, its private dock and power station, and its model township, Port Sunlight, commemorating the industrial vision of William Hesketh Lever, that consummate soap-maker, who stares down dreamily from his boardroom portrait in an aptly well-washed white evening waist-coat.

In each large firm, the view of Merseyside labour is enthusiastic beyond diplomacy and caution. Not that the Merseysider is thought to be acquiescent, or to relish authority. It is to his enthusiasm that managers pay tribute – to his quick-wittedness and bruising honesty; to the good humour which has made Liverpool football supporters a wonder of the world; to the loyalty to principle and his fellow workers which can transcend mere union allegiance, and which

149

makes so dangerous that oft tried management phrase, 'A small group of troublemakers among you . . .'

The strike mania proves to be largely mythical. Figures kept by the Merseyside Development Office show that of 25,000 companies in their register, 75 per cent are permanently strike-free. In the strike table of British cities, Liverpool stands, well behind Glasgow and Coventry, at sixth place. Even last winter, when Bird's Eye, Leyland and the dockers were together on strike – when all of Merseyside seemed to be gesticulating at TV cameras – they still represented only 1 per cent of the total workforce.

Where the blight occurs is in industries universally strike prone, in greater quantity here than anywhere else in Britain, and forcibly grafted into a region psychologically unequipped to accommodate them. Leyland's Speke No. 2 plant was such a case, transferred north with Government aid during the 1960s and slowly laid waste – in the management's view – by absenteeism and sloth. When Michael Edwardes was appointed chairman of Leyland, and its putative saviour, almost his first act was to announce closure of Speke No. 2 and the transfer of its production south to Coventry.

The men's doom was sealed while they were already on strike, complaining of the procedural irregularities in negotiations with the Speke management. As pickets, they attracted little favourable publicity, yet on their side lay the only spark of creativity. They protested their loyalty to the plant and to its final product, the Triumph TR7 sports car, for which Leyland's own enthusiasm had long since waned. The sourest part was a memory of having once been called 'the pearl' in British Leyland with a strike record of only one day out of every 1,000 days lost by the group as a whole.

Leyland, fearful of a sit-in, promised 'generous' redundancy payments. The workforce found them less than generous – indeed, a mass meeting voted acceptance by only a tiny majority. 'You're being asked to sell your job,' a skilled engineer said bitterly afterwards. 'That's what it amounts to. Now they can just pull out with all the machinery they got cheap, with Government certificates, and go and set up where they wanted to be all along. They're getting that place for a couple of bob. It cost them nothing to open it up and it's costing them nothing to close it down.'

In Liverpool people feel despised. Among the abundant official literature is a pamphlet, put out spontaneously by some local businessmen to remind themselves of Liverpool's fame as a city, its architectural endowments, the many famous people Liverpool has produced. These are listed at random: William Gladstone . . . Frankie Vaughan . . . so many other stars, in showbiz and professional sport. Might some of them not be called on to rally to Merseyside's defence? So ran the talk at a Docks & Harbour Company lunch, among brisk, unsentimental marketing men. 'Did you hear what Arthur Askey said the other week on *Celebrity Squares*? "Quicker than a Liverpool docker going on strike." Not fair, was it? Not necessary.'

The city's demoralisation is inescapable. Rising from the Mersey tunnel exit, behind that palatial river front, one feels one has strayed behind the opera scenery, into some sad, steep, windy lumber room. From Scotland Road, where a yellow Tetley pub is wrapped round every corner, the East Lancs traffic flings itself upon a skyline without character or cohesion. One would say that bombs had fallen recently here, missing the two cathedrals. Destruction or evolution, the job is manifestly incomplete.

For a decade, Liverpool has waited in sad abeyance, made manifest by an inner city motorway scheme abandoned for lack of funds. You can trace its intended route from the top of a new concrete office tower – girders of spare land in loose connection, lying through districts long robbed of their streets and little shops. Heavy slum clearance has bequeathed nothing but the sites of slums, made eternal by car parks and graffitists, drifting hungrily around some lonely waterworks or church.

The South Docks are all closed. Docks exist now only north of the Pier Head, past the Belfast and Isle of Man ferries, past the 18th century Stanley warehouse, down a long road gateposted with blackened castle keeps. The impression is of shipless berths, but this is an illusion. Where five vessels would once have docked, at Sandon or West Huskisson, tying up for a week or more, their cargo can now be brought by a single container ship, unbricked of its 20,000 tons by one 20-man gang in a night.

The Liverpool docker, so long notorious, has lately grown tractable and serene. He has also improved at his job. Last spring, he unloaded 4,240 tonnes of Canadian timber from the container ship Marheike in three and a half days instead of the expected five. Once, in 'The Pen' he would wait, corralled with his fellows for cruelly-inequitable selection. Today he enjoys security of employment that anyone would envy, for himself and his sons yet unborn. Liverpool can disown the stigma of a strikebound port. Working days lost by industrial disputes have decreased from 27 per man in 1972 to one and a half per man in 1976. In 1977, the first serious relapse for five years – still raising the amount of strike days per man to only two and three-quarters – attracted the usual club comedians' jokes.

Five years ago, the Mersey Docks & Harbour Board emerged from its cathedral at the Pier Head, metamorphosed into a limited company responsible for cargo-handling throughout the port. Since then, it has produced a £4.5 million profit by a policy of feverish entrepreneurism, scouring the word for likely loads – for those West

151

African logs, those Egyptian potatoes, those 18,000 tons of Indonesian tapioca being lifted from their transporter amid milk-white clouds of flour. Five miles from the Pier Head, where Liverpool fades to a dim Atlantis, the Royal Seaforth Dock and container terminals cover 500 acres of reclaimed land. Big ships bask in a wide lagoon, encircled by broken rocks. They have only to turn the corner into open sea.

Liverpool after dark regains itself a little. This is still, despite its tatters, a place of soul and wit and unique sensibility where eight theatres can survive, together with a world-class symphony orchestra, where the pub named The Philharmonic, panelled by shipwrights, draws half pints in an oceanic grandeur, the very urinals carved from rose-coloured marble. It is a place where youth can still rejoice, where studentship remains enviable, where anti-apartheid posters hang in a wine bar window through which can be observed the strictest of courtship rites. Girls arrive together, in fours and fives, to talk and drink – hard – for an hour. Proceeding to the disco, they dance for two hours more, each solemnly around her handbag on the floor. Fiancés, even husbands, sprawl dourly in their own enclave, awaiting the hour of coalescence.

Liverpool politics form one further derelict area. Nor is this for want of politicians. They shout in, often formless, debate. They indulge in coups, in putschs and night surprises. Their activities are headlined in the *Liverpool Echo,* on front pages quickly turned over. No one questions any more the omissions of the past decade – why, for instance, nothing was done to capitalise on the Beatle craze, which might have made Liverpool as rich as Nashville, Tennessee. An extrovert city suffers this worm of reticence, unerringly selling itself short.

Eight Liverpool MPs, appear strangely lightweight in Parliament. The region, as a political theme, can claim nothing like the potency of Tyneside. 'Sure, over there they had T. Dan Smith', a Liberal City Councillor said bitterly. 'But at least he gave Newcastle its Civic Centre, its motorway. Liverpool got nothing.'

The Councillor was young, only 26, with a sweater tied round his waist, but deputy leader of the Liberal group on a City Council where Labour then barely held sway. He was elected four years ago, in a Liberal renaissance brought about chiefly by University students, who impudently carried off a block of 'safe' Labour seats. A freak result, as Labour and Tories condescendingly agreed, even after the Liberals finished second in the May elections – even after Labour, powerless on its small majority but abhorring proportional representation, had conceded the city to the Liberals. At the age of 26, David

Alton* became chairman of the Housing Committee. Mike Storey, chairman of the Education Committee, is a 27-year-old school-teacher. These may be grounds for hope.

Merseyside County – of which Liverpool is only one-fifth – has appointed a new Chief Executive. His name is Ray O'Brien. He is a terse, young, brawny Classics scholar, with a rugby-player's head who seems to be running at his task with a will. The county-run Merseyside Development Office is now to be expanded, from purely industrial activity into marketing and tourism. A £3 million budget exists to perk up local business, service industrial land, offer backing, in finance or credit, to worthy but unconventional business projects. A scheme is in hand at last to make use of the South Docks for a leisure centre, housing and the Maritime Museum that has been talked about in Liverpool since 1884.

People are optimistic – a quality sometimes akin to valour. It will be sorely tested now, as the slump enters high season. Closures at Speke, GEC and Western Ship-repairers, Birkenhead, gave 6,000 new redundancies to the spring. In August, some 18,000 young people will join the unemployment register, the fact that they are 'only' school leavers bestowing a mysterious comfort on the Government. From that midsummer peak, it is hoped, the total jobless will decline a little, settling at around 80,000. The plateau pushes higher every year.

Optimism is their only recourse across the river at Cammell Laird, at four o'clock, when the welder shuts down his bright blue arc, deep clangs and hammers cease, when the high cranes show each its gnat-like operator, scaling down. A shipyard day is strangely foreshortened, ending lamely, on a scale too large for cheerfulness. From siege towers on their scaffolding, from the lamp-strung keelside redoubts, an army 5,000 strong, in white or yellow helmets, in caps and tammies, in torch-users' Bedouin hoods, drifts off to dispersal near the walls of a Victorian abattoir. At this hour also, the shipyard apprentices leave their training school. Boys by the hundred in unsmirched overalls come leaping over well-kept grass. For these, most of all, tomorrow must be presumed to exist.

The Mersey here forms a wide bend where a ship after launch can swing at ease, unchecked by dragchains. In the 1860s, they launched the *Alabama,* the Confederate raider which almost took us to war with America. There were ocean liners like the *Mauritania;* warships like *Ark Royal.* There was the submarine *Thetis,* doomed to founder on her trials in Liverpool Bay. A perky little shipyard manager

* He has been the Liberal MP for the Liverpool constituency of Mossley Hill since 1979.

recalls the horror they all felt, for Cammell Laird men were among the 99 lost. But they salvaged her, refitted her, re-launched her under a luckier name. Later on came *Polaris*, in a long, black, closely-guarded shed.

The present – for what is now a nationalised concern – looked promising enough last spring, when two newly-built ships stood fitting out in the wet basin, their shallow draught exposing fat red under-bows. Three more were under construction on the slipway, in sections of unequal length. Cammell Laird have been provident in evolving a standard type of petroleum products-carrier. These five, however, represent orders given in 1973, at the height of a ship-building boom. When the last in the present series is launched, the order book for merchant ships will be empty. And 40 million tons of unwanted shipping already rots at anchor throughout the world.

There remains some work to be begun. The yard's long Navy connection has brought a contract for three missile-carrying destroyers. One is built; another soon will be, dispensing along the way with 150 shipfitters. A third destroyer has been laid down this summer, in the new covered construction hall that represents a £32 million Government investment. Meanwhile, the market could always revive. The Japanese yards are worried now, having been undercut by the Koreans. The Government may step in again, with a policy of 'scrap and build'. The Cammell Laird workforce awaits a future less certain than the flick of a coin. Their managing director, for all his optimism, can put it no higher. Something may turn up.

Yet only a mile or so down-river there is a new shipyard, the first to have opened on the Mersey for 100 years. The owners are McTay Limited, a construction and engineering group with 600 employees, operating five sites around its head office at Bromborough as well as subsidiaries in the North-East and Scotland. A company, indeed, which has grown at an almost fretful rate, acquiring reputation enough to attract one of the few major new investors in Merseyside. Last year it merged with John Mowlem & Co, a construction group numbering among current projects the City of London's National Westminster tower.

Jim McBurney is sensible of the compliment. He, with a fellow shipyard plater, set up McTay's first works 18 years ago, in a cattle auction shed at Hooton. He is Glaswegian by birth, with a sideways-talking toughness that cannot conceal his passion for every depart-ment of the company's work.

McTay's shipyard is on a stretch of the Mersey called 'The Maga-zines', after a gunpowder hulk which once lay at anchor there. McBurney – chiding himself for sentiment – has dredged up old ship's timbers to decorate the foreshore. High on the stocks rests the first of two pilot boats to be built for the Pakistan Navy. From here they often see the 1,000-ton grain barge they completed in 16 weeks, seven ahead of schedule. In the late afternoon, a duster flicks and flashes busily around an upstairs office window. The cleaners do refreshments for every launch: it is always a bit of an occasion.

A Faroese trawler, recently launched from McTay's yard, lies finishing now in Unilever's private Bromborough Dock. McBurney, a trawlerman himself once, seems almost in love with the still-unfitted hull. He shows pride that it should be here, on Lever land, amid monuments to the strength of Lever. The name is inspiration to him; a shot-blasting furnace, like music in the distance.

'Confidence – that's what the Victorians had. That's the only thing you need. I think the temperament of the people round here is bouncy. All they need is a bit of confidence.'

Kirkby is always there. Kirkby can defeat anyone's confidence.

Philip, folding his cuffs back, strides over the rubble that used to be Whitefields Square. He is 22, clean-cut and blond; although six months unemployed, he can still find a fresh white shirt. His last job was 'balcony lad' at the Pilkington glassworks in St Helens. They put him on early shift, starting at 7 a.m. The first bus from Kirkby did not leave until seven. For as long as he could, he hitched to work along the East Lancs Road. They sacked him, in the end, for being late.

William Hesketh Drive was named in Lord Lever's honour. The name-plate looks as if fingers have been tearing at it.

Outside a well-barricaded chemist's, Ian is sitting on the wall. He is 20, fresh-faced, with clean hair, neat jeans, a modestly-tattooed wrist. He was sacked a few weeks ago from a traineeship with a local laundry. They told him he had no aptitude. He has had one other job – about two years ago, he thinks – packing kitchenware in Skelmersdale. He draws dole of £13 per week. 'I give Ma eight pounds; three pounds goes on the Catalogue' – HP payments. He stays in bed until two each afternoon, then watches television until his younger girlfriend comes out of school. He hoards his weekly £2 to take her out once a fortnight, when Liverpool are playing away. They hope to be married soon.

In Bolton Avenue, Kevin stands watching the children, the dogs. He gave up his garage job six months ago. 'Scab firm it was, in Upper Parliament Street. I was on forty-five a week, and I had to catch two buses to get there. On the dole I get forty. What's the point?'

A gaunt man emerged from the next door house, to stand with his hands in his pockets. His last job, he calculated, was in 1969. Nothing he can find in lorry-driving will pay him more than £50 a week. His dole is £45. 'You're working for buttons. What's the point?'

Sunny days bring their own threat. Around Whitefields Square the flats the children have stripped stand gaping at the sky. The houses opposite are still well-kept and neat. Children are kicking a football around the road. A woman waits by one gate, comforting a neighbour afraid for her windows. She is more afraid of what the children will scream at her. She is a delicate-looking girl, not long out of her teens.

'She's only just come out of hospital after losing her baby,' the neighbour said. 'In fact, last week she'd stopped breathing.' The girl's eyes filled with tears. 'Now, don't be crying. Don't let them make you cry,' the neighbour said, staring hard at a boy as he swaggered past the gate. 'There he goes! There's the chief fire-raiser around here!'

At a street corner, Richard sits on his bicycle, holding the hedge for balance. His bike is his pride, a BSA *Tour de France*, £94 in the Catalogue. He bought it for £12 from a well-off friend, saving up £2 a week. Here in Kirkby, he will not let it out from between his knees. He cycles round, sometimes stops, keeping close to cover. He is nervous of going out since a teenage gang attacked him at a pub in South Dene.

He is 23. Since leaving school at 15, he has had two jobs. The second, in Bootle, ended a year ago. He couldn't get there in time on the bus. He is married with two children. 'We lost a baby last year. My wife's just had another little girl. My last job, I was getting thirty-four pounds a week. I get thirty-three a week dole. What's the point?

'I'm not brainy. I only know about making things and fixing things, like my Dad taught me. My mates are brainy, and they're on the dole.

'It's borin', that's all. It's so borin'! You lie in bed some days, thinking you'll never get up again. You think it's the end, lying there. Then you think, "Oh well. I'll go and have another look".'

1978

A Garden Full of Wallabies

For most of the residents of Regent's Park Zoo, it is as if the recent cold weather never happened. Ching-Ching, that eternally unsusceptible female panda, lies snug in her metal-lined boudoir, cuddling a spray of bamboo leaves like the lover she never had. In the small mammal house, no finger of frost reached through to shrivel the large tree shrew's specially-cultivated toadstools.

Emergency calls to David Jones, the assistant director, have mostly come from zoos outside London, for whom Regent's Park traditionally provides an unpaid animal counselling-service. 'There was some inquiry from the north this morning about a squirrel. And a reptile, losing weight. And someone else in a panic, saying "Our giraffe's done the splits and what can we do about it?"'

David Jones, an outwardly unromantic Welshman, is also the zoo's chief veterinary officer. He works from the animal hospital, close to an operating theatre where zebra undergo abdominal investigations and South American degu mice are occasionally assisted to give birth by Caesarian section. Beyond lies the corridor, symbolically twilit, in which a cheetah, a black buck and a deeply sceptical-looking wart hog wait to play their part in the zoo's researches into artificial insemination.

Such serious scientific work remains the zoo's pre-eminent purpose. It is a learned society which happens to be London's third-largest tourist attraction. As such it fails to qualify for the kind of financial support unquestioningly given to the world's other great zoos. The government has thus far maintained it should be subsidised as a purely metropolitan attraction by the Greater London Council. The GLC says it is a national institution, and should be aided by the government. The zoo, meanwhile, has no significant income other than its gate-receipts. A million and a quarter visitors in the last financial year still proved an insufficient bulwark against inflation and recession. With a current deficit of £550,000, the zoo faces the prospect of being unable to cover even basic running-costs.

An effort to boost Christmas trade by cutting admission-prices unluckily coincided with weather that reduced the 35-acre site, with its iron bird-gazebos and artificial crags, to the stillness of a Hollywood scenery-store. Even in warmer weather last week, most of the

157

animals still clung to their heated withdrawing-rooms. Nothing took the air but pelicans, a clattersome grey vulture and, in his end box, a polar bear, bowing this way and that to non-existent applause.

David Jones led the way through the 'hoof stock' pavilion, where huge, woolly, busty camels stood in shop-fronts like German tarts, and zebra trotted in unison to nowhere, and giraffes peered around airborne screens with mildly remonstrating eyes. The coats of massed giraffes have an aroma like liqueur honey.

Two okapi, their hind quarters striped like half-sucked humbugs, epitomise to David Jones the unfairness of regarding zoology as a pure profit-and-loss enterprise. The pair come from an okapi herd bred in co-operation by zoos all over Europe. 'That one was born in Bristol. That one was born in Paris. Now if an American zoo-director came in at this moment, he'd make us an offer for those okapi running into hundreds of thousands of pounds. The answer would be no, of course, because to us they're beyond price.

'Beautiful, aren't they? Ten pounds a day each, they cost us to feed. The best hotel in London couldn't give you the sort of grub we give those okapi.'

As things stand, there can be no thought of improving the animal sites which Jones admits 'we're not very proud of' – the old decorative bird-of-prey aviary, or the now cramped and outdated First World War bear-pits. The crags above leak directly into the Aquarium: merely running repairs are estimated at £300,000.

The zoo has owed its past expansion chiefly to private donations, deftly extracted by its president, Lord Zuckerman, from the likes of the late Charles Clore. Such philanthropy, alas, is now as outdated as buns for elephants, though 'Lord Z' remains an indefatigible campaigner, both for running-costs and also the £600,000 which the Zoological Society aims to spend annually on scientific research.

Even Clore's main bequest, the small mammal house, a technological marvel 15 years ago, now presents problems of maintenance. 'It was designed for a lot more staff than we've got now. If we were being really cost-effective, we wouldn't bother to give each animal its authentic habitat. We'd have what other zoos do – just plastic and sterile surfaces. But why should we? It's nice to let the tree shrew have his favourite toadstools.'

A zoo vet's job, David Jones says, is rather less dangerous than a domestic vet's. 'Personally, I'd rather deal with any of this lot than with an unpredictable Alsatian dog. You soon learn which end of which animal you've got to watch out for. Now, take her' – he indicated the female of a pair of white rhino forming peaceful, armoured bookends over a bale of straw. 'If she's lying down and you're treating her, you can be sure she's going to take at least five seconds to get on her feet. Rhino are no trouble, anyway. You can tickle their tummies and they'll roll over like a great big pig.'

158

White rhino are, of course, not white. The word comes from the Dutch *widj* – wide-lipped. 'That female was one of twenty sent over by the Natal Parks Board. We put her into Whipsnade but the strange thing was, she became completely agrophobic. She was the only rhino I can ever remember who's tried to attack a train.'

Ching-Ching, the triumphantly barren panda, is an object of reverence to David Jones merely for the weight of medicines and surgical skill expended on her love life. On the rafters over her contented form, one can still see brackets for the electronic cameras that watched so long without result. In the next pen, Chia-Chia, the male, fresh from an unproductive visit to Washington's female panda, sits up stern and straight as a Taiwanese millionaire, fastidiously crunching off single bamboo-stems.

A quiet day at Regent's Park, without a single post-mortem, still did not mean a quiet day for David Jones. That morning, there had been a gathering to mark the centenary of A. A. Milne, whose Winnie-the-Pooh was inspired by a black bear in residence during the Great War. So casual were safety-regulations in those days that children were allowed to go into its pen and feed it honey.

There were also reports from field expeditions sponsored or staffed by the Zoological Society – among mountain gorillas in Luanda or scimitar-horned oryx in the Sahara. The zoo currently has a large team studying the ecological implications of the new Jonglei Canal in Southern Sudan. Only that afternoon had come news of a government purge, and the locking-up of several local politicians sympathetic to the project.

At night, David Jones does not exactly leave work behind. His house is at Whipsnade, inside the zoo perimeter. 'I'm about a hundred yards from the tigers and the emus. My garden's full of wallabies. On clear nights, when the moon's full, I can hear the wolves mating.'

1981

PART THREE

Away

The City of Dreadful Night

The Walled City of Kowloon knows when a stranger is near. From the watchman in Sai Tau market the word passes, between hissing, glistening noodle stalls, instantly to the centre of the fortification. Swift boys hasten it, flap-slippered, through doorways, across stairways, around cracks and crevices; The Grass Sandal whispers it to The Red Bamboo Pole, who communicates it reverently to The Golden Paw. As it passes, doors close which had stood open, shutters close upon the doors, the very walls seem to glide to a new position with joss-sticks glowing innocently outside. Secrets dwindle and are dissipated, up through the washing-lines into fissures of night.

The intruder may be a harmless customer for the City's child whores, dogmeat or medicines. It may be a missionary, to whom equally little attention need be paid. Only if the visitors are police, plainclothesmen from Kowloon CID, does The Walled City consent to show its innermost forms of life. The oozing streets suddenly throng with the clienteles of gambling dives and heroin dens. All watch as the policemen stroll by, nonchalant in drip-dry raincoats. The raids are purely symbolic: they have no power to do anything but inconvenience. This is a city no one wants but the men who rattle mah-jong counters all night, and the men who lie in tiers, row on row in the opium trance they call 'chasing the dragon'.

To reach The Walled City you must first leave the other stronghold, the island of Hong Kong, upon whose serene heights they have nearly abolished Chineseness, save for the eyes above the white gloves which offer cocktails to diplomats in the evening. You cross by the Star Ferry to the Kowloon mainland. There you pass not into Britain nor China, but to some indeterminate hinterland where nations stand mesmerised and cabinets of gold watches glitter savagely up and down the boulevard. You pass along Nathan Road, among blocks of flats. The thrill of restless trade is felt by these flats since jets from the airport pass over, nearly touching them, and pass screaming through the gaps between the streets.

The Chinese advent is sudden. The houses plunge low, dusty, dishevelled with laundry. Whole pigs sit up on hooks, begging with

163

the red bibs of their slit breasts; the waxy ducks hang suspended like bats among bunches of fresh, edible grass. Beyond the food stalls is an almost continuous row of unlicensed dentists' parlours, furnished with ancient drills and potted ferns and showcases, like jewellers', in which teeth are daintily silhouetted on the points of fans, or stuffed with silver and gold into the jaws of enthusing skulls. When you reach this wall of teeth, you have reached The Walled City of Kowloon. Nor will your approach have gone unnoticed.

The City is the last indigestible anomaly in the paradox of our Hong Kong 'colony'. It was illegally seized by Britain from China in 1898, and thus forms no part of the lease covering Hong Kong island and the inland 'New Territories'. As Communist Chinese property, it is unadministrable, but sacrosanct. Britain will have nothing to do with it, for fear of upsetting Peking, and the consequences that might befall this last golden niche of Empire. So a city of six acres and 27,000 inhabitants is claimed by nobody.

It has passed, instead, to those who rejoice in chaos: the property developers. Above Sai Tau village it rises, a drunken clutch of primitive apartment blocks. The flats, unhampered by building regulations either British or Chinese, are finished without sanitation, without water, enjoying only that daylight which they can seize before new flats arise alongside. Bound by the limits of the old walls they can expand nowhere but inwards; slowly the thoroughfares are throttled with raw concrete as the quick, new walls arise, nearly touching, towards the disputed sun.

Somewhere inside, a woman kneels on the ground. She is folding plastic flowers and plastic leaves into posies. Life by day throughout The Walled City is occupied largely with the manufacture of fripperies; busy fingers alone holding at bay the preliminaries of death. There is the rapid clack of unlicensed looms. There is the sound of building, with which the sound of destruction may sometimes be confused. Overhead runs the stolen electricity and stolen water, received by some fortunate apartments through pipework thrust and knotted together like foul barley-sugar. More sand is brought in from the street by yoked and dusty men. More sand. More cement. The streets contract a little further.

To be so entombed is not without its grotesque advantages. Despite the horrendous possibility there has been neither fire nor epidemic in The Walled City; germs cannot live, as people can, upon its air. Curiously acquiescent grows a life piled on another life without sky above. There is not territorial anxiety to disrupt the spirit, since each footstep of earth must endlessly be re-used; no barrier, in the discoloured darkness, between sleeping and waking.

The woman folding plastic flowers is called Mrs Chow. Her neck, her almond mouth, are made for coquetry and kisses; her home, in the nameless alley, is not even a room but a transition, a ragged

164

vestibule wherein youth and decline are simultaneous. In the dish between her knees, the blooms rustle scarlet and buttercup-yellow. A second child lies quietly, suspended in bedclothes from the ceiling. He is three years old and has not yet learned to walk. Meningitis? Mrs Chow knows only that the doctors tell her it is not worth curing him simply to return him here. Watching the shadows of his world, he sways a little.

Jimmy Sweetman, City Commissioner for Kowloon, wears a shirt of patterned black and white outside his trousers. His person, indeed, presents so marked a constrast to his dapper young Cantonese subordinate Mr Neoh, that one wonders if self-determination for the Hong Kong Chinese is not somewhat belated. The Commissioner arose to his post by way of a commission in the Gurkhas and a tour with the 'Indian Tea Association' during which – this is intimated by winks, nudges, the phrase 'off the record' – he assisted in the flight of the Dalai Lama. One of Jimmy Sweetman's kidneys was shot out in Surabaya; the remaining one, in the transactions of his office, is considerably occupied.

Jimmy Sweetman holds responsibility for such vestigial and peripheral government as The Walled City may unofficially receive. He is frequently and vocally contemptuous of this sidelong policy. He believes, as others do, that even the Chinese find advantage in Hong Kong's pandemonium of money, and so are unlikely to try to repossess it on ideological grounds. It was he, furthermore, who last put the matter to the test. In 1963 he proposed that part of The Walled City be demolished to make way for a new road. Then, even more than now, the displaced people could easily have been redistributed in what Anthony Neoh, with his files and folders, refers to as 'an urban exercise'. Instead, at the prompting of the Kai Fong, the local residents' association, a deputation from The Walled City went to Peking and a protest was issued from China to Britain. Gone are the days when all Chinese protests were ignored on principle. Jimmy Sweetman was told that his proposals were 'not opportune'.

'It never is opportune. If we're friends with China, they say, "Oh, not now, don't do anything to rock the boat." If we're not friends with China: "No, not now old boy, better not do anything – might make it worse." Oh, they can *protest* in Peking. But it's when they word their protest, "You will be responsible for the serious consequences of your action," that you've got to worry. If they just *protest*,' said the City Commissioner, 'it's all bull.'

Seven years ago a girl named Jackie Pullinger arrived in Hong Kong by ship and on impulse disembarked with her holdall, her guitar and her oboe. She was a very English girl with a sensible complexion and hair, parted in the middle, which her fingers pinched as she talked; she possessed that habit of grimacing slightly in the expression of feeling which is peculiar to girls who have attended private boarding-schools with names like The Manor House.

Tonight the dormitories of The Manor House are very far off as Jackie Pullinger sits at dinner in her flat in Sai Tau. The room is on the roof, swept by the gusts of night and smells from skylights lower down. With her at the table sit five Chinese boys and a smiling, abrupt old lady named Mrs Chang; Jackie feeds as they all do, employing the white sticks for levers rather than pincers. Outside, a Boeing 707 comes in to land at Hong Kong airport. It passes so near the house, they can see faces in its windows.

'Watch him eat the head,' Jackie says.

The boy named Ah Wing deftly separates the countenance of the fish, rolls it around in his cheek, then spits the remnants out on the broken plastic with which the table is covered.

'I can't get keen on the eyes,' Jackie says.

Jackie Pullinger is a Christian and a missionary, though each term is too fraught with social unease aptly to describe the business of her life. Christianity for her consists largely in not questioning how, from the punctual objectives of an English country-life, from yachting and skiing and going to dances, she came to be roaming through The Walled City of Kowloon at night, clapping her hands to warn off rats, which can grow as big as young cats.

Six boys now live with her in the flat in Lung Kong Street. Mrs Chang comes in and cooks for them, or not, according to how she feels. They found Mrs Chang when her only son was sent to prison and she had retired to her room in The Walled City to die. Her geniality now, and her appetite, serve as equal tributes to the power of God and Brand's Essence.

For the boys, too, life has been modified. Their world was formerly the labyrinth of *dongs;* the opium-dens, the heroin-dens; a life of witnessing bestiality and going to sleep beside it which has left no mark yet on their impassive adolescence. Their allegiance is secured when they are inducted into the *triads,* the secret brotherhoods. To the elder brother who adopts him a boy owes obedience to death. So, in equal fascination of fear and affection, the word will pass into the hierarchy of secret officials, from The Grass Sandal to The Golden Paw, that strangers have come to The Walled City.

'I remember you saying it was frightfully important to preach in the right sort of skirt,' Jackie remarks to schoolfriend Mary, who renders her clerical assistance, Mary is a secretary from Hong Kong side, with hair spun upwards into a lustrous *bouffant,* curled outwards to the tightest conceivable bounces. She is chaffing Ah Ping, lieutenant of Jackie's protégés, an agile young blue-denim jet who already enjoys some reputation as a street-fighter. Her Cantonese is fluent, if a little horsey.

Mary is also responsible for the newsletter the two girls send to England about their missionary work.

'Somebody rang up from Sutton – *rang up* from Sutton – and asked if she could send us a Chinese New Testament,' Jackie remembers.

'And we had this letter from a sweet woman saying she'd love to be out working with us in the field, but she'd been called to look after a saint of eighty-five, so she must have been at least seventy-five herself. Remember she said, "Do you speak Chinese or Jap?" '

Some mail from 'UK' as they call it, had arrived that afternoon.

'Oh!' Mary exclaimed, pouncing. 'Here's a letter from Jilly Joynson-Hicks!'

At night in The Walled City the flat-dwellers retire upwards, shutting their metal grilles after them. A noise of machinery continues; but now it is not a loom, it is the steady, anxious racket of *mah-jong:* wagers ceaselessly offered behind veils throughout the concrete; wagers instantly taken up. The darkness of day yields to darkness softer and stranger; a faint starlight, falling down through the cracks in the buildings, softly illumines the piles of fresh rubbish or the rat which lies cosily in its unlamented death. Doors stand open which were not there before.

Jackie Pullinger has rented space in one of the streets. A room below a petrified fan, an adjoining room with some dusty prayer books and an old piano-accordion, she had made into a 'youth club'. At first the boys took against it and threw rubbish inside. Afterwards, somebody she did not know visited her to inform her that such a thing would not happen again. He would say no more, nor reveal to whom she was indebted for this undertaking. The cloak of the *triads* had descended upon The Father and The Son; which is a kind of miracle.

In the ante-room she sits all evening, dressed as if to give the labradors a run. The boys come to her and she listens, her lips jovial in the Cantonese monosyllables, pinching her hair as she replies. Ah Ping's reputation is such that a girl has offered to live with him – should Ah Ping accept the offer? Through the doorway, salvation and shelter are expressed by the game of ping-pong. The boys hold the bats like fountain-pens; their tight eyes, focused for shady death, follow the bouncing of the ball. Occasionally the ball bounces out into the alley. Further down, a squat woman sits, trousered and significant, upon a tiny camp-stool. The woman's face turns, with measured dispassion, towards the door of the 'youth club'. The siege has not yet been lifted.

Another youth enters and introduces himself enthusiastically as

167

Jonathan. On the Chinese face pleasure and grief are fortunately indistinguishable. A heroin-addict, he has been living with a bar-girl who begged him to lose the habit. The girl came from a good home, and eventually it reclaimed her. He determined to lose his addiction; eventually he succeeded. Now, not from grief or want, but in her good home, the girl had died. 'It's hard,' Jackie murmurs, 'oh, it's hard.'

Jonathan springs up and flourishes a rusty toy pistol. To be found with it would mean his instant arrest.

'We'll keep him with us tonight,' Jackie says.

High in her room, Mrs Chang divides her attention between the blue television screen, on which a plump movie-queen is giving out lottery prizes, and the photograph which hangs near it. He is a cleanly youth displayed therein, frontways and in profile. So she will always cherish her dead son, his hair cut, shirt fresh, unbroken by his own reality, gravely reclining in a photographer's rattan chair.

In the bakery where Ah Ping helps, the baker and his girl work into the night. They kneel together wrapping up rice-cakes and chicken-cakes, made with pork and sugar, by which tomorrow they may earn another day. He was a heroin-addict, but is reclaimed. She remains a heroin-addict; she is pregnant. Over the filthy oven, over the mangled bedclothes, the rice-cakes and chicken-cakes, love reaches still; and contrives to touch.

The ball flies, *pock-pock,* in the room belonging to Jesus. In the ante-room, a baby is now present. The father has been two years on the run from a penal settlement. His girl has left him to care for the baby with the aid of his sisters; all this, descending on a boy's turnip head, makes him long to be restored to custody. But the baby is wonderfully kept, wrapped up in a scarlet cloak. Love may short-circuit, but it cannot be suffocated. If dusty prayer books and dusty words truly foster it, this must be the act of the God who is beyond Christianity. The ball bounces – *pock.*

Someone picks out 'Proud Mary' on the strings of Jackie's guitar. She pinches her hair, then bows her head. Jonathan plunges his head low and desperately repeats The Lord's Prayer rendered into his language, rocking the baby with its scarlet cloak tightly in his arms.

1974

To Philly on the Formica Queen

There is still a boat train from Waterloo, attended by porters in caps with sea-blue facings, packing the luggage van with bags 'not wanted on voyage'. Through the grimy compartment windows, celebration drinks are already much in evidence. It is just as transatlantic travel used to be, but for the long, shuffling queue of self-help trolleys, the tartan trousers of the American passengers and a recurrent rumour that, owing to 'industrial action' by Southampton dockers – to say nothing of military action by Her Majesty's forces in the South Atlantic – the *QE2* may not sail on schedule.

The seats on the boat train are squashily comfortable dark green with white antimacassars. Across the aisle, a Scottish lady, seasoned voyager from her cropped grey hair to her zip-up boots, has already struck up a friendship with an American businessman. 'When I first crossed, it was on the old *Queen Mary,*' she tells him. 'Eighty pounds one way. Third Class. Now they call it "Transatlantic Class".'

By Clapham Junction, they have discovered a common interest in golf.

'I'm much more demonic in match play,' the Scottish lady says confidingly. 'Not that wretched business of counting every stroke. But how *interesting* that we're both keen golfers . . .' The American looks uneasily out toward Arding and Hobbs.

The *QE2* at first sight seems disappointingly small, looping towards us round the edge of the dock railway. The white above her stern looks stained, even rusty. And *why* did they do away with majestic red funnels in favour of that single odd little withered-up thing, like a tooth missing its crown?

Going aboard the world's last great ocean liner has, inevitably, been made to resemble going aboard an aircraft. You must pass through a check-in desk before crossing that most exciting covered gangway. At the entrance to the Midships Lobby, you are met by a photographer with a flash camera and a bevy of smiling men in pale blue blazers, white flannels and white shoes. Behind them, in the circle of lime green banquettes, a jazz band is playing 'Hello Dolly'.

Embarkation happens at astonishing speed. To dock the *QE2* in

169

Southampton for a single day costs something like £100,000. The ship earns money for Cunard only while she is at sea. It was just this morning that she docked after a two-week Mediterranean cruise, unloading 1,700 other passengers barely in time to begin loading the present 1,300. Even on her return from her 90-day world cruise, she remains in port only overnight. There is, in fact, no vessel better suited for commandeering as a troopship.

Her present intake, however, sorely lacks the discipline of those who will march aboard with kitbags in two weeks' time. Today beyond the Midships Lobby, pandemonium reigns. The only Cunard official in sight is a bearded young man, not in blazer and white flannels but in regulation buttoned tunic and an old-fashioned peaked cap.

'Excuse me . . .' someone ventures. 'Does "B" stand for Boat Deck?'

'No knowledge, squire,' the seafarer replies thickly.

The crossing is not to New York this time but to Philadelphia, an inaugural run celebrating the city's 300th anniversary. The passenger-list is largely made up of Philadelphians, returning from an exploration of their ancestral roots in Bedfordshire or Hertfordshire. A civic welcome awaits the *QE2* when she first sails up the Delaware, to be chartered by Philadelphia city council for three days' municipal junketings.

First nights at sea are traditionally informal and subdued. A certain sadness seems to accompany this conclusive severance from land. Our *QE2* radio station strives to invigorate us. 'This is your Embarkation Station, featuring the best in rock with Rick Spinks . . .'

Time, before dinner, for a rapid tour of the ship that outlived all her transatlantic rivals, even the exquisite *France*. Launched in 1969, she is now a stunning sixties period piece. The First Class Queen's Room, with its white leather pedestal chairs, pot plants and pelmet lighting, could be transferred intact to the V & A. Most of the ship's interior is made from a substance called Marinite. The creak, as she rolls, is not of timber, but of Formica.

At dinner in the Columbia Restaurant, our waiters introduce themselves. 'I'm Gary – this is Paul.' Gary comes from Liverpool; Paul is a portly southerner. Neither looks over 18. The other occupant of the table is an elderly, rather deaf lady named Miss van Strawbenzee. 'I'm Gary,' Gary says to her. 'This is Paul.'

'No – no soup, thank you,' the old lady says, at which Paul collapses against Gary and pretends to burst into tears.

England, and the thought we may soon be at war, fade together into the night. In the scarlet 'Transatlantic Class' Double-Up Room, Bobby Crush thumps his piano and shakes his freshly-washed hair.

170

Other bands are playing, below in the Queen's Room and astern in the Q4 Club. You stand at a certain point on the central stairway and hear four bands playing at once.

It was Cunard's great wheeze in the mid-seventies to bolster their flagship's dwindling transatlantic passenger trade with a programme of 'one class' winter cruises, ranging from two weeks to the now famous 90-day round-the-world blockbuster. Her cruises are what have kept the *QE2* afloat and, in latter years, richly profitable. The world cruise, starting in January, is booked solid for months ahead. Always, the first stateroom to go is the super de luxe 'penthouse' at £130,000.

Frank and Margaret Chapman, sipping their first mid-morning *bouillon* in the Double-Up Room, make an average of three *QE2* voyages each year. 'We've been on all the big boats,' Mr Chapman, a nut-brown Yorkshireman, says. '*Franconia* . . , *Carmania* . . . *Empress of Britain*. We've been around the world twelve times.'

For Mr and Mrs Chapman, as for many elderly people, the *QE2* is the last way of seeing the world in any safety. 'I advise people not to go ashore in certain ports,' Mr Chapman says. 'Like Rio. Beautiful it used to be. Last time we were there, a man had to have eighteen stitches in his bottom where they'd cut his trousers to get at his wallet.'

'They'll take anything off you, them natives,' Mrs Chapman said. 'We were in Barbados with a man named Norman and his wife . . .'

'He were a bookbinder from Buxton,' Mr Chapman put in.

' . . . some native in Barbados stole his swimming-trunks off him,' Mrs Chapman continued. 'A year later, we were back in the same place with the same people. This woman grabbed my arm and said, "Eh – look! That chap's wearing my Norman's swimming-trunks!" She went straight up to this dark fellow and said, "You stole those trunks off my husband last year! Take 'em off!" And the fellow did!'

The daily shipboard entertainment schedule bears the age of most *QE2* passengers in mind. Cabaret artists (Peter Gordeno; Bobby Crush; the Derek Butterworth Orchestra; Ray and Jackie, 'the Fabulous Toaduffs') are all strictly middle-of-the-ocean. By day, the emphasis is on 'life enrichment'. Classes in needlework, backgammon, ballroom dancing, duplicate bridge and elementary Yoga happen all day all over the gently-creaking, public rooms. And lectures: on 'Masterpieces of 18th-Century Decorative Art' by Clarence E. Conger, 'Speedreading' by Al Clemens, 'How to Get Invited to the White House' by James C. Humes. Add to all these the traditional maritime pursuits of deck tennis, shuffleboard, trap-

171

shooting, betting on the vessel's daily mileage and doing communal jigsaw puzzles, and it would be hard to find a spare second in the day. Many, none the less, contrive to spend hours at a time immobile on the same bar-stool.

World cruising has added to the ship's company a 14-strong 'entertainments staff', responsible now for pushing the passengers through these labyrinthine amusements in five short days across the Atlantic. All but two of the entertainments staff are men, in tight blue safari jackets, white trousers and shoes, under strict orders to smile at anyone who speaks to them and dance with anyone who requests it. The world cruise, especially, is preponderant with lonely single women.

John Gow, the Cruise Director, holds a daily entertainments strategy meeting in his cabin with his 14 staff. Every spare surface seems occupied by white trousers in filmy dry-cleaner's bags. John Gow is a hunted-looking man with great bunches of tension in each epauletted shoulder and a nervous way of kicking his white shoes to and fro as if trapped in some eternal quickstep.

'Geoffrey . . . can you do the Scrabble at eleven? Cheryl . . . the Tote with Larry and Gordon. Duggie . . . the Yoga. And there's the Under-20 Get-together. Let's hope more turn up than yesterday. Four . . . or was it five?'

'No-one's down to run the Kids' Fun and Games,' someone points out.

'They can do it themselves,' John Gow says. 'There's only four kids on board anyway.'

Ten years ago on the *QE2*, small rope barriers everywhere proclaimed the class divide. Today – outside the reataurants – there is almost democracy. The Captain's time-honoured First Class cocktail party is followed by one for Transatlantic Class at which the sweet champagne and canapés are identical and the mutations of male evening dress hardly less extreme. Our skipper this crossing is the *QE2*'s 'Relief Master', Captain Alex Hutcheson. A tall Scot with a twinkle in his eye – as, presumably, all *QE2* commanders must be – he is the model of a modern liner captain, very good on the hand-mike, endlessly willing to link arms with unintroduced females, never blinking as Instamatics flash in his face.

At dinner in the Columbia Restaurant, Miss van Strawbenzee gives a vivid account of being operated on for a cyst in the year 1903. ' . . . of course, I couldn't drink anything. The thirst was terrible. I asked the nurse for a drink and do you know what they said? "O, Baby, we can't give you a drink. We can't catch the cow to milk it." '

Our waiters, Paul and Gary, attend us with gestures grown increasingly satirical. Paul, in particular, has a way of offering a menu as if it is a bunch of fives. Both speak to Miss van Strawbenzee like deckhands hailing the foretop. A large, white-haired man, two tables away, also under the ministration of Paul and Gary, has begun to show marked restiveness. 'Couple of right Fangios, aren't they?' the man says, little realising how perilously the gravy-boat is wobbling above his head.

Paul and Gary and the other waiters, in fairness, face a lengthy sprint for each order to the servery of a kitchen which constant remodelling has made only a little less hideously inconvenient. The *QE2* was the first ship to have restaurants set high above water-level. The kitchen came up with the restaurants but the store-rooms, of course, could not. They remain below, separated from the kitchen by seven decks.

John Bainbridge, the *QE2*'s Executive Chef, first went to see 45 years ago on the four-funnel *Aquitania*. He has worked in the kitchens of ships whose First Class passengers expected to order any dish they fancied, any hour of the day or night. 'Churchill now . . . he was mad for game. He'd have a bit of pheasant at four in the morning. With the Queen Mother, it always used to be guinea-fowl . . .'

The world cruise is the supreme test of John Bainbridge's ingenuity. To stimulate jaded palates over the full 90 days, speciality chefs come on board in successive ports. 'Last time, we had a Chinese chef, an Indian chef, a Mexican. All beautiful stuff – and, do you know, some of the passengers wouldn't touch any of it! *Health* food was what they kept asking for. One woman sent me a long list every day. Special flour, special bean curd. You never saw such a ruddy performance . . .'

' . . . there's another *very* well-off woman,' George, the steward, says, 'who comes on board, goes straight into her stateroom and never comes out again the whole cruise. You'll only see her when we're in port. Then she'll order a hire-car, go off in it and come back with masses and masses of flowers. She'll spend the whole of the next week shut away in her stateroom again, just arranging and rearranging all the flowers.

'I'll tell you what some of these very well-off woman have said to me. Coming on a world cruise with us is the only chance they ever get to wear their jewellery. I've seen them walking down these passages with – I promise you – *millions* in diamonds on them. At home, they'd have to keep it all locked away in banks. But on the ship they feel absolutely safe. Nobody's going to mug them here. It's about the last place on earth a nervous, rich old lady *can* feel safe . . .'

' . . . some of them are *really* ancient,' the girl in the flower shop says. 'It's sad, really. You see their families dump them on board, hoping they'll never see them again. And quite often, they don't. How many deaths did we have on the last cruise?' she asked her colleague. 'Eight? Or was it twelve?'

'Remember that poor old man in Sydney?' the second flower girl said.

'He came on board in Sydney and died that very same night. It's all too much for some of them.'

'Another old man, in one of the real expensive cabins, had gangrene in one of his legs. He'd already got it when he came on board. Eventually, one of the stewards smelled it. They had to amputate his leg here on the ship.'

One of the flower shop girls goes to serve a male passenger with a single white orchid.

'He's going to throw it over the side,' the other girl whispers. 'His wife died at sea a year ago and today we're passing the place where her ashes are scattered.'

Our fourth day at sea is mildly choppy. Early morning joggers round the Boat Deck run a genuine risk of being tweaked overboard by a wet and tearing wind. Captain Hutcheson's social engagements are cancelled to allow him to remain constantly on the bridge. With a faint bump, far below, the ship's stabilizers begin to operate.

With America now imminent, our waiters, Paul and Gary, stand by their hotplate, deaf to cries of 'Hey – Fangio!' from the white-haired man, deep in computation of their end-of-crossing tips. Tipping remains a hallowed maritime tradition, not confined to stewards and waiters but running through all levels and departments of the ship. Waiters, in their turn, have to tip the 'glory-hole steward' who makes their beds, draws their clean linen for them and wakes them in time to go back on duty.

The QE2's 1,300 workers are compensated for their long hours by four crew-only bars. These are nicknamed, with sailors' love of slang, 'The Dhobi Arms', 'The Shotaway', 'The British Legion', and – for female crew only – 'Cruft's Dog Show'. There is also the more select Petty Officers' Club whose entrance displays the Queen's portrait with a panoply of military and Metropolitan Police flags.

Under the Queen's portrait sits a young crewman, very drunk and full of bitterness at the way, he believes, the floating Queen has been overworked. ' . . . she's been treated like a hotel, not a ship,' he mumbles. 'It's been thirteen years. I've seen the engine-room . . . I know. The poor bloody ship's knackered.'

Our five-hour passage up the Delaware is an elaborately-staged regatta. Hundreds of small boats put out to join us astern, bucking madly on the big ship's gentle wake. Dozens of light planes and helicopters circle recklessly overhead. On the afterdeck, a nine-piece

174

showband plays 'Hello Dolly'. We pass under a bridge with a sign that reads WELCOME QE2 – WORLD'S LARGEST TWIN-SPAN. The nine-piece packs up its instruments to be replaced by a 12-piece one, playing 'Watermelon Man'.

Our coming is 'top story' on the Philadelphia radio stations now babbling from every cabin tannoy. Second story is that one of the small planes has crashed. Third story is the sudden explosion of a small boat in the flotilla. Fourth story is that Britain and Argentina have opened fire on each other in the South Atlantic.

To dock at Philadelphia, the *QE2* must execute a giant three-point turn. We see, for the first time, the vast crowd awaiting us on shore round a flag-hung dais, and, that more modern American welcome, a demonstration in support of the IRA.

Two hours after docking, we still have not been permitted to disembark. The public rooms become, suddenly and disconcertingly, like airport transit-lounges. It is a chance, anyway, to meet one of the shipboard celebrities, Lady Teignmouth. She proves to be young and sporty, in a button-up denim skirt. 'I've got a bottle of vodka in my cabin,' she says, 'if anyone can find some glasses.'

In the lime green Midships Lobby, the un-disembarked crowd is becoming openly fretful. To make things worse, Philadelphians in evening dress are already coming aboard for tonight's $300-per-ticket gala ball. Finally there is a spontaneous mutiny. Pushing past the single guard, we surge out, ungratefully glad to be at liberty.

We are still waiting three hours later on the dockside for Cunard's promised transit bus to New York. We watch blearily as, across the arc-lit terminal the last of the cars the *QE2* has carried are brought up from the emptied hold.

Among the car-owners stands an Australian boy in shorts and anorak, a knapsack on his back. He, presently, regains possession of the drop-handled racing bike on which he plans to ride around the world. The *QE2*, it is worth remembering, carries bicycles free of charge.

1982

The Prince and the Pauper

A plump, middle-aged man with an Oxbridge accent and chain-smoker's fingers, sits in a noisy bungalow in New Delhi, complaining about the high cost of everything. His Highness Karni Singh, Maharajah of Bikaner, points at the bomber jacket he is forced to wear because – even in this land of unnumbered tailors – suits are becoming so expensive. Since Indira Gandhi came to power two years ago, His Highness has lost all the accoutrements of a maharajah but his ancestral palaces, his loyal Rajasthani subjects, and his legs. Even as he smokes, rolls his eyes and deplores the bomber jacket, one cannot help noticing those legs. The are regally short, for folding beneath him when – as still happens – one of his people seeks an audience. Encased in ballooning white, His Highness' legs, at least, evoke old times of majestic ease when jewels were so commonplace that fresh linen became the luxury.

'There is no income left in my hands.' Karni Singh continues. 'It is already confiscated twice over by Mrs Gandhi in taxes. Today, this morning, I stand to lose this house of mine – in 1948 [India's Independence Year] who would have thought that a man could lose his house? My wealth tax and income tax are double my income. By the time I even offer you a cigarette, I have to sell something to pay for it.' So His Highness does not offer us a cigarette.

The princes were the tool by which Britain subdued India: their abolition was thus a concomitant of self-rule. Nor was it surprising that Indira Gandhi, in her quest to be the single and prevailing dynastic figure in the subcontinent should have abolished their pensions also, depriving Karni Singh, for example, of an annual purse of 10 lakhs of rupees (about £50,000.) The entire sum paid equalled scarcely a million rupees a year, little enough, as Mrs Gandhi's opponents point out, compared with the amounts embezzled by her own administrators. No matter. It was symbolically the end of that race of creatures who used gold as if it was lemonade-powder; who wore the Koh-i-Noor diamond for a saddle-ornament; who lived cossetted in silver and marble and sweetmeats, and silk so fine it could be drawn through a wedding-ring. 'Now,' Mrs Gandhi said triumphantly as she removed the princes' last perquisites, 'they will have to be *men*.'

Viewed against his countrymen en masse, Karni Singh is not poor. You cannot hear from his verandah their ceaseless shuffle. He eats. He sits on musty palace brocades; he is the All-Asia clay-pigeon shooting champion; the Maharani goes shopping in a Fiat. Such a predicament seems slight especially after dark, when the world sleeps out in gutters. Poverty in India we can comprehend – but penury? Now the government intends to limit property ownership to a value of five lakhs (about £25,000). To stamp out profit, all recent land-sales will be cancelled. Such shreds of a realm as remain to the Maharajah therefore have no value as real estate. Beggars at least suffer no irony. He is losing his bungalow, yet still owns palaces and a hill station.

'If I sell this house, I can pay taxes for two more years. In six years, my capital should have disappeared. I don't want to leave this house. I built it myself, it's my creation, I love it, but if that helps to solve the poverty, take all my houses. But a man is entitled to live on his income, howsoever small it may be. I have already sold off eighty per cent of the jewellery I own to pay taxes. My grand-father had a golden throne. I sold that off last year to pay the wealth-tax. Now we find ourselves flat-footed. Absolutely lost.'

Mrs Gandhi's view of princes as jewelled parasites ignores the record of such as Karni Singh's grandfather Ganga Singh. Solemn, proud and incorruptible, he ascended the throne of Bikaner at the age of seven and ruled for 56 years to the great benefit of agriculture in Rajasthan. He brought the Gang Canal to the desert, and 1,000 miles of railway, even if it did terminate in his personal locomotive sheds. He was ADC to George V in France and present at the Imperial War Conference. 'King George used to call him "Bikaner" and they used to exchange cards, and all that.'

Nor was he prodigal of habit, although his hospitality to Viceroys undoubtedly caused the water to run through his state, and 37 ele-phants passed by in procession for his Golden Jubilee. 'He was not fabulously rich', Karni Singh says, 'as one would conceive a prince to be. In my forty-nine years I have not seen any flaunting of jewel-lery by men – hardly ever. You might have seen a good palace, good guns, good cars, that was all. If they wore jewellery it was just gold buttons or diamond buttons. That was all.'

Mrs Gandhi notwithstanding, there are still those who consider the plump, hard-up man to be god-like, who esteem him greater than their Prime Minister and who revere no less the last two gener-ations of his family, 'Late His Highness' and 'Late, Late His High-ness'. On Karni Singh's birthday, they come and offer *nazana,* a gift of one or two rupees, bowing backwards out of his presence. His two reluctant palaces, his hill station at Mount Abu, his establishments in Delhi and Bombay, all still occupy a staff of 100, though he is constantly obliged to dismiss loyal old men from the private armies and the gun-rooms of the past. There is also a private secretary and a youth in pointed shoes who, to the Maharajah's faint regret, is a Communist.

Being princely, he cannot stoop to employ the many subterfuges by which Indian business – and, for that matter, Indian politics – survive the tax-system. He will not use the black market. A few treasures have been safeguarded by the turning of the palaces into museum trusts. All Maharajahs are reputed to have fortunes concealed in Swiss banks. Lately Karni Singh discovered a sum which he had deposited in Switzerland and forgotten. He declared it at once to the revenue authorities. 'The government,' he says, drawing himself up, 'cannot make me stoop to steal or tell a lie or dishonour my pledge or my word.'

India informs you it is not a dream by the sound of spitting. Bikaner palace awakens empty – card-rooms, billiard-rooms, assembly-rooms stretching all emptier than the mind is willing to imagine – but somebody is afflicted by catarrh terribly near at hand. Not a dream. The bedroom is still there with its bell-pulls and mahogany. Beyond the windowless wall the cloister is still there; the bust of Victoria facing that of Edward VII; and the courtyard within, framing the sky in pink, floating gently on the lake of marble where a ragged figure already crawls with dustpan and brush.

Karni Singh could not join us on our visit to his palace. He is still in Delhi, worrying over his tax-returns. His face seems as dead as all of them, all the plump proud faces of his line in photographs down the corridors, where bats flit along at night. The photographs are windows into beautiful days, of levees, garden parties, military parades. Lancers ride past in complacent review. The Viceroy's lady, peering to inspect the new waters of the Gang Canal, uncovers, for all time, a length of silver-stockinged leg. And for Karni Singh, his father Sadhul Singh, his grandfather Ganga Singh, under ancient sunlight or arc-light the kills are enshrined – dead heaps that were tiger, bongo, leopard, and other beautiful, strong beasts shot for the pleasure of little men with moustaches and no necks.

From far off, an indefinite object is approaching the palace. It crosses the horizon of lawns with no grass, it skirts the edge of lakes with no water, it passes beside the mansion entitled 'Motor Garage' and, under the Moghul cowl of the main arch, the access of Kings, delivers itself as time's final affront, a motor-scooter.

The rider is Manvendra Singh – to his intimates, Kinu. He belongs to the Rathores, the same Rajput clan as the line of Karni Singh but is a princeling, he hastens to say, in his own right. The princeling wears a red shirt, a woollen outer garment striped like a bullseye, a small but truculent cap. He has a broad, chewy smile. 'Sorry I am late,' he says as he kicks the scooter back on its stand. 'Last night was Saturday. I had a free-for-all.'

We drive with Kinu towards the Temple of the Sacred Rats. The desert in winter is more pleasant than the town, cool, empty but for the sleek red goats which burst out of its banks, across the road. In the distance the vultures sit conferring like solicitors.

'The first day I entered college,' Kinu continues, 'I hit a wrestler over the head with a spade. I was afterwards prosecuted – assault with a sharp weapon. To avoid prosecution it is necessary to have a knowledge of the law. I have, taken over the whole year, one fight per fortnight. I know how to box, and when I hit someone, I put my whole box behind him. God help him,' he added piously, 'because nobody else will. He will see the curtains.'

Karni Ma, an incarnation of the mother-goddess Durga, lived here in the desert 500 years ago when the first of the maharajahs installed himself at Bikaner. At her death she promised her followers that they should remain close to her, their souls represented by rats, or *kabas*, to distinguish them from the unholy creatures which every year eat 38 per cent of India's grain. The line of Bikaner, has a special connection with Karni Ma, for she told the Karni Singh's Rao Bikaji that his descendants would rule for only five centuries. The end of that period and of the princely states exactly coincided.

The holy rats are not large and seem rather too bruised to be sacred. They are not even very hungry as they pursue their urgent errands over each other's backs and create a clatter like high heels in the dish of grain provided for them at the altar. Two Sikhs in dressing-gowns have been there since early morning in the hope of seeing the *kabi,* the sacred white rat. An old man wearing a brand-new US Army greatcoat, who had already left the temple, returns down the hurrying path, gently lowers his shopping-bag to the ground, and a rat runs out of it. The old man's whiskers touch his breastbone, his eyes are red with wonder as he proffers a two-rupee note to Karni Ma for this omen.

The high priest rises from the outer portal where he was asleep. He is a poet, formerly employed at the palace as tutor to Karni Singh. He points upward through the wire netting to the pinnacle on which an eagle always comes and perches when a royal personage is within. Karni Singh came there to pray on the eve of his last international clay-pigeon shooting match. His grandfather once camped out in the square for successive days, praying for the arrival of a delayed monsoon. As the high priest talks, people approach barefoot among the tails, touch their foreheads with the orange *sendoor* paste and leave presents of money or sweets for the rats. Should one of them ever be accidentally killed it must be paid for by a weight of silver equal, not to the rat but to the person whose soul it represents.

We left the temple as the rats' formal meal-time was announced with incense and gongs. Down the road, we passed the UN compound, where resources are currently been concentrated on a programme of rat-extermination.

We drove on to Bikaner town. 'Over there,' Kinu said, 'Is the largest sweets-shop in Bikaner. Each time I pass it, I curse the silly people inside. Some of us fellows raided a sweets-shop where the proprietor had a large refrigerator. He ran after me along the rail-road-line in the lights of the engine, then he fell down. That is where some of us cornered the silly Collector. The Police came, and the Armoured Constabulary and the Army, too, came. I had three serge-ants' helmets.'

What are the objectives of a princeling of Bikaner? He reflected. 'I would like to hi-jack a plane,' he replied. 'A MiG. I would like to raid a wine-shop. "I do not have your wine", I would tell them, "I have pissed it all away".'

The fort above the midden was first the stronghold of the Bikaners and, afterwards, their summer palace. It is a crushing of many castles one above another, towers and courts and ramps stepped for ascending elephants to courts higher up, and inside, the colours make an orgy of sight; colours so dense that stone, leather, wood, marble become one surface of such monotonous richness that the precious things are the drops of sun which fall through the lattice-work. But the colour is finally not as awesome as the cunning. Each chamber of the labyrinth, each shower of red, of green, of gold and red, is accessible by two passages, one of them secret; each stairhead is wide enough to admit only one person; each silver bed is so small that a sleeping man can instantly put both feet on the ground if attacked.

The fort is commanded by Lieut. Col. Sohan Singh of the old Dungar Lancers. 'Nobody could attack,' the Colonel said, 'And nobody still can. They will get a broken head if they do.'

The Colonel has white hair like wax, parted in the centre, and an iron grip. He points to the gallery round the Karamahal, the grandest of the courts, with Kings and Viceroys vivid in his eyes.

'They used to get well drunk – drunk like anything. Kummel, you know, from Russia. Monsieur Clemenceau the French Prime Minister was here, and they had dishes from France and wines like anything. And the tribesmen used to get well drunk and come, while they sat up there, and dance for them like anything. On swords. Lances. Drops of sugar which they did not break. You could never get what we had again,' the Colonel said. 'Not in a dream.'

'I will make it clear,' Karni Singh said, in his New Delhi bungalow. 'I am not a believer in rulership today. I am no ruler, neither is my son going to be one. My son will often turn and say "I don't want to do so-and-so". I often feel I don't want to do something, too, but I jolly well have to do it. You see anyone from the former ruling families and you see a Minister of the government today, and see how they pass through a crowd. You don't have to tell who's who. As a ruler your first trait is humility. You are respectful to the very poorest. You must make that man feel happy so that when we've quit meeting each other, that man will think of you for another couple of days.'

The people of Bikaner, over whom his ancestors had power of life and death, have returned him as a member of the Lok Sabbha, the Lower House of Parliament, for the last 20 years. No one in opposition to Mrs Gandhi's ruling Congress Party has a rewarding time exactly but Karni Singh detects an added gusto in the regime's destruction of his private member's bills for such reactionary and imperial causes as education, unemployment benefit and the adoption of Rajasthani as an official language. 'This is a democracy.' He gave a melancholy smile. 'You just have to go home and try to think of a new bill to introduce.

'Only yesterday I was speaking in Parliament of the fraud committed against the students of a medical college which was started without being properly recognised, and now two hundred students cannot proceed with their examinations. I said "I see a very dismal future for these boys". And a Congress member on my left said quietly, "The only dismal future lies before the princes".' His Highness fingered his bomber jacket and smiled wanly.

'I don't think that we are in for a very pleasant old age.'

1972

181

Kind Hearts and Kotex

Some years ago, Agnes Ash, publisher of the *Palm Beach Daily News,* decided to turn her experiences along Florida's Gold Coast into a play. For a collaborator she approached Helen Bernstein, who contributes a regular column to the *Daily News* – or 'Shiny Sheet' – and is, moreover, noted for pithy one-liners about Palm Beach, its impossible glamour and unique social order, its superabundance and shortcomings. There was, for instance, the time Mrs Ash telephoned Mrs Bernstein to complain about the local shortage of reliable doctors, as distinct from socialites with medical diplomas. 'Helen,' she said, 'if you ever got sick in Palm Beach, who would you call?' Mrs Bernstein thought for a moment, then replied, 'The airport.'

The line, to this day, sends Agnes Ash into peals of her frequent, gurgling laughter. She and Mrs Bernstein are lunching together at Club Colette, a restaurant recently acquired by a noted new Palm Beacher, Aldo Gucci. The very butter dish bears Gucci's logo, although the butter pats so far have escaped it. The head waiter weaves Gucci logo shapes of adoration round Helen Bernstein, a dour, shy woman who has no need to earn her living from journalism. Her husband, Joe Bernstein, put up the New York Telephone building in midtown Manhattan. Her aunt, Kate Wollman, gave the skating rink to Central Park.

For all that, she takes her Shiny Sheet column seriously, and was eager to work with Agnes on the Palm Beach play. 'I even went to courses in playwriting at NYU,' she recalls wryly. 'All I learned was that I couldn't write a play. I didn't know how to get the characters on stage and once I'd got them on, I didn't know how to get them off again.'

Agnes Ash, in any case, realised that superior dramatic skills would be needed to portray what she and Helen Bernstein constantly see and overhear around their town. She mentions a vignette she once observed at the height of the winter season, when Palm Beach glitter briefly dissolved, as it sometimes does, to reveal undercurrents of barely expressible pain and loneliness.

'I was at a lunch, sitting at the same table as Rose Kennedy. She was the star that night: everyone at the table was obviously trying to think of something to please or entertain Rose. Finally, a friend

182

of mine hit on the perfect line. "I see Gloria Swanson's ailing and may die," my friend said. Everybody knew, of course, that Gloria Swanson and Joe Kennedy had had a longtime affair. It was saying the right thing to Rose without actually saying it: "Hey, your husband had an affair with a movie actress, but she's sick now. *You* came through."

'After that, everyone round the table started doing the same – mentioning women with whom their husbands, or their friends', had had affairs, and how those other women were ailing, or in financial difficulties. You could feel the same spirit in all these wives who'd been hurt or neglected in the past. "We've paid our dues. *We're* the survivors."

'Every day, you get scenes like that,' Agnes Ash says. 'Palm Beach is a play no one would *believe*.'

To commemorate its 90th anniversary, in March this year, the Shiny Sheet published a shiny supplement filled with pictures from its archive, spanning half a century of everyday Palm Beach life. There was Winston Churchill, wheelchair-borne, with cigar and jaunty yachtsman's cap. There was the Duke of Windsor, smiling bleakly from his exile in high fashion. There was Barbara Hutton, then Countess Haugvitz-Reventlow, nursing a poodle – and, evidently, a grievance – as she watched tennis at the Everglades Club. There, buttonholed en route to dinners, teas, or costume balls, were Bea Lillie, Irving Berlin, Douglas Fairbanks Jr, Aristotle Onassis, the young John F. Kennedy. There, in understandable pride of place, was the breakfast-food heiress and queen of Palm Beach, Marjorie Merriweather Post, whose name grew more glitteringly polysyllabic with each successive marriage, and whose 108-room mansion, Mar-a-Lago, conceived by a Ziegfeld set designer in an amalgam of sixteen different architectural styles, remains the consummate Palm Beach winter hidey-hole.

The famous faces collectively bore witness to the success of a publication which almost no one refers to as the *Palm Beach Daily News,* any more than one would refer to a Palm Beach hostess by her formal name. In Palm Beach society, there is only 'Muffy' or 'Ancky' or 'Deedy' or 'Dysie' or 'Brownie'. And, no less essential to the Florida season, there is the Shiny Sheet. The name comes from the paper on which it is printed – white, glossy, 'book quality' stock that can be handled without the usual newspaper-reading experience of grimy fingers and inkstained clothes. 'We love you Shiny Sheet . . .' ran a typical birthday tribute. ' . . . You keep our linens clean and neat.' Each morning the folded missive, eerily pale, as crisp as if pre-starched by attentive housemaids, throws weightier

Florida journals like the West Palm Beach *Post,* even the lordly *Miami Herald,* into grey, proletarian eclipse.

On one level, the Shiny Sheet is a conventional daily, conscientiously serving a resort area of 10,000 permanent inhabitants with necessary but unexciting small-town news. The tone changes dramatically each September when the rich return from their northern summer haunts or their European travels to reconstitute the true Palm Beach community. Then, as well as police and town council news, the Shiny Sheet reflects wealth and pleasure-seeking conducted with grave ceremony such as barely exists nowadays even on the Côte d'Azur. At mid Palm Beach season, the time of the Red Cross Ball, the Hospital Ball, and Debutante of the Year Ball, a Shiny Sheet staff photographer can expect to wear out three tuxedos on the unremitting social treadmill. The front page, the back page, and two or three inside become a panorama of parties, a landscape of lunches, a seething picture gallery of more people in evening dress than one thought remained on earth.

Social life in Palm Beach is, indeed, of such intensity from September to April that the Shiny Sheet, for all its 10,000 daily circulation, cannot alone satisfy the desire of prominent Palm Beachers to see themselves displayed in print. The town, each season, supports four other independently owned publications, dedicated to gossip and printed on paper of competitive glossy whiteness. There is a daily, *The Palm Beacher;* there are two weeklies, the *Palm Beach Social Pictorial* and the *Palm Beach Chronicle,* and a biweekly, the *Palm Beach Mirror.* The Shiny Sheet company also puts out a monthly magazine, *Palm Beach Life.* Each, when it appears, will have covered the same functions and photographed the same faces. The steady average 4,000 circulation of each suggests that Palm Beachers on the party circuit regularly buy all five.

The gap between the Shiny Sheet and its rivals has widened since 1977, when Agnes Ash became publisher after a career with *The New York Times* and *Women's Wear Daily.* The Shiny Sheet's balance between cocktail gossip and real journalism is the balance Mrs Ash herself manages to strike in the Palm Beach community – an insider who never forgets she is primarily a thoroughgoing reporter. Two years ago, the Shiny Sheet received heavy criticism for its coverage of the Pulitzer divorce case, which rent Palm Beach open with allegations of lesbianism, incest, and cocaine use among the under-fifties. Agnes Ash is proud that her paper broke the story, and does not regret having published a single, steamy column inch.

The gurgling laugh is much in evidence as she sits with the Shiny Sheet's editor, 29-year-old Ellen Koteff, running through the names that shine brightest and oftenest in the Palm Beach society press. Great Palm Beach names have always tended to be synonymous with products crucial to American home life.

'There's Sue Whitmore,' Mrs Ash said.
' . . . Listerine,' Ellen Koteff added.
'She owns the company that makes it,' Mrs Ash said. 'Yeah . . .'
The publisher gurgled again. 'Every time Sue gives a party, she's
made a buck from all of us before we even leave home.'
'Zuita Askton. Her family invented the Q-Tip.'
'Victor Farris. He invented the plastic milk carton. And there's
Meade Johnson.'
' . . . Johnson and Johnson,' Ellen Koteff said. 'And there's Jacqui
and Jim Kimberly.'
'He's the Kimberly in Kimberly-Clark,' Mrs Ash said.
' . . . They make toilet paper.'
' . . . and Kotex.'
'*Paper products*,' both agreed diplomatically.
'Jim is honorary consul to Jordan,' Agnes Ash said. 'King Hussein
often stayed at their house, though I don't think he has since he
married that third wife. I remember seeing Jacqui in a beautiful
velvet cape that King Hussein had given her. I said, "Jacqui – aren't
you going to leave your cape at the check room?" She said. "I'm
certainly not." It was trimmed with eighteen-carat gold.'
' . . . and there's Liz Whitney Tippett,' Ellen Koteff said.
'She was tested for the part of Scarlett O'Hara in *Gone With the
Wind*,' Agnes Ash said. 'They thought she'd be perfect for the part,
until they heard her voice. Liz used to be a great horsewoman. Once,
when a horse was being troublesome and threw her, she got up,
went over to it, and punched it on the nose.
'Now she says she's leaving Palm Beach. She complains it's not
lively enough for her. She's in a wheelchair, so I don't know what
she can want!'

No other town made of money wears it jewellery with such discretion. There is a plain, pastel-coloured front elevation of blocks in
mid-twenties mock-Spanish, mock-Tudor, or mock-Palladian style;
a leafy back elevation, scooped out to accommodate boutiques and
art galleries down tiled passageways for which the correct term is a
'via'. Worth Avenue, the principal shopping via, proffers the names
of Bonwit Teller, Brooks Brothers, and Hermés with a quietude
marred only by the Gucci building, which, in certain lights, could
be mistaken for the Town Hall. Understatement becomes almost
deafening along the via nicknamed Mansion Row and containing
the foremost readers, and stars, of Agnes Ash's Shiny Sheet. Each
mansion is masked by a high front hedge, beautifully planed into
continuous green-gold ramparts; the millions make no sound but the
snip of gardeners' shears.
Across the island waterway named Lake Worth, the uninhibited

185

satellite named West Palm Beach displays all that is abhorred on this side of the water. Palm Beach positively prides itself on all it does not allow its inhabitants to do. In Palm Beach, you cannot buy a car, rent a tuxedo, find a fast-food stand, or be admitted to a hospital. Casual visitors are tolerated only so long as they observe the labyrinthine rules of local etiquette. The Breakers Hotel – centrifuge of Palm Beach society – issues its guests with a special guide to dress protocol, specifying, for instance, that one may not appear at breakfast in 'a collarless shirt', wear swimsuits in the front hall or golf shoes in the drugstore, or be seen anywhere in the frescoed lobbies after 7 p.m. without a jacket.

With the ubiquitous black tie and Rolls-Royce Silver Cloud go certain predictable habits of thought. Palm Beach is seamlessly Republican, a condition personified by the towering figure of ex-ambassador Earl E.T. Smith, and by the Conservation Society's refusal to designate John F. Kennedy's former home as a place of historic interest. Habits of thought prevail unchallenged at the two most exclusive Palm Beach clubs, the Everglades and the Bath and Tennis, both still firm in preferring an exclusively non-Jewish membership. It seemed a reference to more than the town's lack of high-rise office buildings when a local businessman commented that Palm Beach was 'basically a no-growth area'.

The society papers – apart from the Shiny Sheet – remain silent on all such tactless topics. Though each paper is different in format – the *Pictorial* starchy, the *Chronicle* jazzy, the *Mirror* wacky – all maintain the same resolute editorial policy of saying nothing that could remotely offend any possible subscriber. The six-day-a-week *Palm Beacher,* in particular, was loud in its refusal to print a word about the Pulitzer divorce, and bitterly upbraided the Shiny Sheet for covering the sensational trial with such enthusiasm. ' . . . in *another paper*,' the *Palm Beacher* said loftily, ' . . . we have read the term "lesbianism" 127 times, "incest" 63 times and "ménage à trois" 48 times . . . Compliments are coming from our readers . . . "Thanks for not printing such vulgar rubbish." '

Palm Beach, like Hollywood, shows a veneer of amoral flashness, but on the inside has always been deeply conventional and shockable. Its founding father, Henry Morrison Flagler, was a devout Presbyterian, uncompromised by having set up the Standard Oil Company with John D. Rockefeller. It was for health first, then stimulating social intercourse, that Henry Flagler brought the railroad south through the swamps from Jacksonville in the 1880s, and built the chain of sumptuous Italianate hotels that culminated in the Palm Beach Breakers. Flagler controlled the Shiny Sheet – bought from its founder, 'Bobo' Dean – when the paper titillated readers with such regular features as 'Gossip Overheard in the Corridors of Palm

Beach Hotels', 'Pointers About Pretty Women and Gallant Young Men', and 'Spicy News Picked Up Between Lake and Ocean'.

Henry Flagler's spirit lives on in the Palm Beach principle – that pleasure must always be seasoned by conspicuous virtue. Or, as one local society editor put it, 'philanthropy is the name of the game'. All the glittering midwinter affairs, the lunches, brunches, dinners, and balls, are functions for charity. The 'Top Five' in the Shiny Sheet's social calendar, bringing forth Palm Beach society at its apogee, are the balls organized in aid of the American Cancer Society, the Red Cross, the Good Samaritan Hospital, the Heart Fund, and the Palm Beach Preservation Foundation. Admittedly – here in what Helen Bernstein, with a droll upward glance, calls 'The Great Waiting Room' – those good causes tend to be medical research programmes in which Palm Beachers have a more than academic interest. Admittedly, too, there is an odd dissociation of ideas at work when socialites ask one another eagerly, 'Are you going to the Cancer Ball?' The fact remains that hundreds of thousands of dollars, collected by whatever ostentatious means, annually make their way from Palm Beach to worthy and deserving ends.

Anyone who wishes to penetrate Palm Beach society must subscribe lavishly to this charitable endeavour. According to Jesse Newman, president of the town's Chamber of Trade, the investment need not be so large. 'Let's reckon on thirty-five to forty balls each season. Suppose you buy a table at each one, for a thousand to two thousand dollars each. You're bound to be noticed. You get your picture in all the society papers. People will start asking you to make up numbers at *their* tables. For fifty thousand dollars . . . not such a great sum . . .' Mr Newman threw out his hands like champagne foam, ' . . . you can be the toast of Palm Beach.'

The prospect must be an alluring one, especially, to the many accidentally wealthy women who join each winter's migration to Palm Beach, hoping that its hot days and warm, frondy nights may provide a cure for widowhood. They are the women one sees, in bright white slacks and chiffon scarves and the neck braces their poor driving has bequeathed them, daily adrift along Worth Avenue with cheque books, small dogs, and too-bright, hopeful smiles. They are the reason why it is a positive advantage in Palm Beach for a doctor or lawyer to stay single, and why the town has such a half-submerged history of con-tricksters and predatory gigolos. 'Most of the cases we never even hear about,' Jesse Newman says. 'The women who get robbed or conned are too embarrassed to report what's been done to them.' At the Heart Ball, clustered round a $2,000 table, hoping to see oneself in tomorrow's Shiny Sheet, there is, at least, safety in numbers.

'New money' always betrays itself at functions covered by the Palm Beach society press. New money clutches at Shannon Donnelly, the Shiny Sheet's society editor, bargaining for column inches with an embarrassed, and unavailing, hundred-dollar bill. New money leaks only into the corners of those daily photomontages where true, old Palm Beach money – the twenty-year maturing of fortunes from mouthwash or plastic milk cartons – smiles its gracious, confident philanthropic smile.

We observe the Shiny Sheet during a busy, newsy late March week. A water shortage has gripped Palm Beach, causing local hostesses to form lines at the Publix supermarket for supplies of Evian water in which to bathe. There are reports of hair being washed in swimming pools and of poodles having to submit to shampooing in the ocean. At the 568-room Breakers Hotel, each time a guest uses the lavatory, a porter is sent upstairs with a bucket of water to flush it.

At the Shiny Sheet's office on Royal Poinciana Way, Shannon Donnelly surveys a week's calendar slightly thinner than at the peak time of December and January, but crowded enough with the Chamber of Trade Ball at the Breakers, the Preservation Ball at Mar-a-Lago, an art show opening, a luncheon for Planned Parenthood, and a Red Cross auction. Shannon is a brisk girl who took on the society editor's job chiefly because it allows her to spend the mornings with her baby son. Her style is two-fistedly forthright. 'Over Worth Avenue way, *Helga Wagner* – she of the blonde hair and flashing teeth, etc. etc. – threw an opening night party to celebrate her new boutique . . . Seen at the festivities were the likes of new couture designer *Lorina Gabrielli, Baron Arndt von Krupp, Caths* and *Gene DeMatteo, Pam Wynn, Rutilla* and *Arthur Burck, Bonnie Walker* and so on.'

All the Shiny Sheet's young reporting staff get the chance to vary routine newspaper chores with celebrity interviews that many a bigger-time journalist might envy. 'Everyone who's rich and famous comes through Palm Beach sooner or later,' Ellen Koteff, the editor, says. 'And because they're relaxed, they're always much more accessible here than they would be in New York.' So 23-year-old Angel Hernandez, the municipal specialist, has one assignment this week to write about beach erosion and another to interview Andy Warhol.

Karyn Monget, the elegant, multilingual fashion editor, is trying to confirm an interview with Joseph Brooks, head of Lord and Taylor, the New York department store. Mr Brooks is famously punctilious about his appearance and does not want to be photographed too soon after his daily tennis game. Karyn's other problem is how to write up, in any sensible form, her recent, long sought-after interview with Norman Parkinson. The venerable photographer greeted her, disconcertingly, drinking piña colada and wearing a hat with an artificial parrot attached to it. 'I asked him which era he thought was the most exciting in fashion, and he said "The present". Then, a few minutes later, he started saying how *boring* everything was in fashion nowadays . . .' The willowy girl shakes her head in perplexity.

At House of Kahn, the estate jewellers in – where else? – House of Kahn Via, they are preparing to auction treasures that once belonged to the Hollywood star Dolores Del Rio. Agnes Ash, stopping by to see her friend Adele Kahn, greets a lady in a violet dress and crocheted knee socks who is inspecting some $175,000 impulse buys in diamonds.

'It's Mrs Bronstein!' Agnes Ash says. 'In the paper, we called you Evel Knievel!'

Mrs Bronstein earned the nickname by driving her car over Lake Worth across the Southern Boulevard Bridge just as its two halves were being raised, and leaping the gap.

'That's me,' she agrees placidly.

Andy Warhol is in town for the opening of Baby Jane Holzer's ice cream parlour on Worth Avenue. The spare little figure, under the heavy grey cockade, is more youthful then anything in his life would have seemed to allow. People do not talk directly to him, but, rather, take short trips around him as if viewing some interesting obelisk. Civilisation may search for definitions of Andy Warhol but Shannon Donnelly, the Shiny Sheet's social editor, does not, firmly typing in her night's copy that he is an 'esoteric artist'.

The news is not all diamonds and ice cream. Four years ago, the Palm Beach town council became embroiled in financial scandal after $2 million of local taxpayers' money was discovered to have made its way, via New York, Texas, and Mexico, to a mysterious bank account in the Cayman Islands. So insistent was the Shiny Sheet's pursuit of the story that the incumbent town council petulantly withdrew all civic advertising from its pages. Under a new town council – led by Mayor 'Deedy' Marix – the ban has at last been lifted. Ellen Koteff remembers a queasy moment at the height of her investigations into the scandal, when Agnes Ash cautioned her about the methods some people can use to throw a persistent reporter off the scent. 'Mrs Ash told me always to be sure and lock my car, in case anyone interfered with it or tried to plant some drugs on me.' Palm Beach, did they say, or Dodge City?

Mrs Ash spends her morning at the beauty parlour, writing her next month's article for the Shiny Sheet's glossy stablemate, *Palm Beach Life*. Punctual as ever, she hands it to Ava van der Water, the managing editor, who is leaving shortly to take up a job in public relations.

It will be a relief for Ava no longer to be the target of PR people trying to scrounge editorial space for products aimed specifically at the Palm Beach consumer.

'I knew I'd reached breaking point,' she says, 'when someone called me and asked me to run a piece on transparent plastic toilet seats filled with gold coins.'

The glittering names can be observed outdoors each weekend at Palm Beach Polo and Country Club, watching the sport that so suits this environment being played by a mixture of royalty and hired mercenaries under the sponsorship of international jewellery firms. Today's polo game, a semi-final in the Cartier International Open, features a team from Dallas versus one billed as 'Palm Beach-Piaget'. The ponies close in thickets of legs; the white ball flies off with a costly click, wafted over ten other polo fields and a 1650 estate whose residents include TV host Merv Griffin and Zsa Zsa Gabor. Dallas's team features two high-rated brothers named el Effendi from Pakistan. Their forenames, respectively, are Wicky and Podger. No frisson disturbs the cut-glass British voice of David Andrews, the club's resident match commentator. 'Wicky el Effendi breaks away . . . Oh! Nice set-up there by Podger.'

Jim Kimberly, paper magnate, Palm Beach playboy, and honorary consul to the Hashemite Kingdom of Jordan, sits in the main grandstand in Gucci shoes and yellow plastic baseball cap, watching a game he first saw played in an indoor version in the Midwest half a century ago. His 77 years are belied by his racy young wife, Jacqui, and his narrow red Ferrari.

'I've seen polo played with Model T Fords,' Jim Kimberly says. 'They were fitted with hoops over the top so that when they rolled over, they'd roll right back upright again.'

A $250-per-ticket ball at the Polo Club, sponsored by Cartier in aid of the American Cancer Society, sees Agnes Ash in her alternative role as correspondent for *Women's Wear Daily*. In grey cocktail dress and pendant necklace, cradling a large notebook, she strikes her habitual skilful note of detached insider; accepted, not assimilated. All five Palm Beach society papers have photographers there, working through a crowd believed to contain Zsa Zsa Gabor, Andy Warhol, the ex-king of Tunisia, Britain's Duke of Marlborough, and both parties in the Pulitzer divorce. An elderly man, peeping into his old-fashioned Rolleiflex, is hardly less a celebrity. Bert Morgan, dean of Palm Beach photographers, in his heyday knew where the Duke of Windsor could be found, even when the duchess had temporarily lost sight of him. Bert Morgan came to America from England by sea in 1912. 'I wanted to sail on the *Titanic*,' he recalls. 'But the ship was all sold out.'

In the centre of the marquee, Cartier jewellery worth $11 million is displayed on the necks and shoulders of white shop-window dummies, bald and eyeless, arranged in a tableau that, ever and again, fretfully stretches up an arm or crooks a leg. The dummies are dancers from the Ballet Florida, in all-enveloping white body stockings. As dinner is announced, each blind, white, sparkling figure is helped down from the podium and led away by an attentive sheriff's deputy.

And there is Zsa Zsa, whose very name renders Palm Beach life into onomatopoeia; blonder and pinker than one could ever have hoped. Young men stand close, smoking caddish cigars, as the 'darlings' blow among them like chinchilla fluff.

'Darling – of *course* I know Bunny Esterhazy . . .'

Of course.

'Palm Beach is a place where you can laugh a lot,' Zsa Zsa's friend, Helen Bernstein, says. 'My problem is, I see the miserable side of it, too. A good friend of mine, in her seventies, would like to be accepted by the in crowd, but she can never quite manage it. She's always just on the edges – always trying to make up for it by being seen around with very young men. She's an intelligent woman; she knows the problem. "Helen . . . " she said to me once, "it's just that I'm so *scared* to stay home alone in the evenings".'

1984

The 'No Comment' Island

The lone policeman who spends the summer on Sark does his duty in a manner approved of throughout the island. Each morning, he stations himself on the Maseline harbour, waiting for the hydrofoil to approach from Guernsey, round Point Robert. The harbour, though tall and primitive, is comparatively modern; it seems designed partly to repel boarders. Drunk or unsuitable day-trippers are greeted by the policeman at the top of a slippery staircase and invited not to come ashore. Back they go in an empty boat to the less fastidious world beyond the lighthouse.

Some 80,000 visitors each year pass through this tactful selection process. Their reward is to discover themselves to be pioneers. Farm tractors, noisily deputising for the forbidden motor car, haul them uphill in long, shallow carts, knee to knee and smiling in disbelief, past walkers venturing downhill with the heavy-footed caution of astronauts. Voices carry with eerie resonance along empty lanes, where hired bicycles stop at crossroads to compare notes. A kind of nervous laughter, disbelieving the pure quiet, drifts up from the cow parsley in valleys to the ever-visible sea.

Sark has become famous against all its wishes. The noisiest day-trippers are abhorred less than the journalists who have flocked to create parodies in many languages of the island's feudal statehood. A society without cars, divorce and income tax exerts its fascination through every realm of capitalism. Prolonged media attention has tended to harden that oblique manner which is the characteristic of all native Sarkese. Men turn away as you pass, intent on scything a verge. The very dogs, roaming at will, seem to pass by haughtily as if to say 'No comment'.

Yet they need the outside world, as even the Greffier admits. This is not an heraldic beast, but a rosy-faced stipendary official named Hilary Carré. His surname is an ancient one on Sark, his civic office unchanged since Elizabeth I created the fiefdom in 1545. The Greffier is Sark's chief administrator, clerk and treasurer to its very own government, the Court of Chief Pleas, which meets three times annually, with pomp, in the schoolhouse.

His Greff – the island's city hall – is an extension in someone's garden. He sits beside an ancient safe, writing on a passport envelope, his irritation with journalists breaking into vivid reminiscence. He remembers when sledges, not tractors, were used for transport or as brakes behind horses descending Harbour Hill. His father was postman for Little Sark, the peninsula to the north, crossing La Coupée, the causeway, when it was only a grass embankment. It took German prisoner-of-war labour to make La Coupée safe with concrete. The Greffier remembers the last days of Occupation, when the starving German garrison littered the roads, reduced to eating nettles and wild parsnips.

What is there now for the island but tourism? Agriculture? The Greffier smiles sardonically. Sark and its government were founded originally on forty tenant farms. Nowadays, only two of 'The Forty' remain under full cultivation. The rest have been bought by tax exiles, who care only for the houses. The fields, hanging like counterpanes from the cliff-edge, are rented out, to graze unlovely carriage-horses, or sewn with spent cartridges from clay pigeon shoots.

The immigrants are everywhere conspicuous. A tax-exile's wife, returning from Guernsey as if it were Harrods, sits on the boat speaking with a plum in her mouth that the sea wind cannot dislodge. A small, neat governess cart trots the lane, conveying the slim, neat, upper-class proprietress of the Victoria tea-room. A party of military-looking men sit at lunch in the Dixcart Hotel, their moustaches bent in homage to the flushed Sark lobster. The tourist carriages are driven mostly by mainland hippies who live rough in farmer Paul Carré's barn, not bathing until the season's end.

So many have settled here, bringing nothing but bank-balances. Sark is wise to them now. They have more than enough lurking millionaires. For two years past, there has been a ban on all new building. Now, permission is given only to islanders or to foreigners in residence for ten years. The effect has been to surround Sark with a barrier of property inflation remarkable even in the Channel Islands. As much as £20,000 has been paid for a wooden one-storey house with a French name and a face turned shyly from the road.

Sark people, on the whole, do not sell their houses. The community has come apparently unscathed through its career in the world's scandal sheets. The Sark language, the gestures, songs, folklore, remain intact, if hidden for the summer season. Though families of seventeen are no longer common, the population, at 500, is the same as a century ago. Young people, leaving school at 14, show little inclination to defect to the mainland. Each tractor that passes seems to have a boy on it, waiting to climb into the driver's seat.

There are menaces to the island, however – less obvious ones than exaggerated journalism. The beaches are polluted. You can see petrol scum shining like silk on the sea. A coastline so untouched brings thoughts of other coastlines, obliterated in an oil-rush which

193

could shift here just as capriciously. As could a worse demon. Sark, only a mile or two from France, is popular with French yachtsmen. Warnings against rabies are posted at all landing-places.

In summer, the gardens of La Seigneurie are open to visitors. A charge of 10p each is 'requested' to assist upkeep of the Gothic pigeon-house, the old watch tower, the chapels and walled gardens. In these grounds during the Nazi occupation, German officers walked with the Dame of Sark, doing battle with the weapons of mandarin politeness. A German anti-tank gun now stands with the Elizabethan cannon, pointing down the lawn to face the next invaders.

The Seigneur opens his kitchen door, accompanied by a poodle with its head in a bucket. He is a sunburned, shy man called Michael Beaumont, the grandson of the late Dame of Sark. Before he succeeded her, two years ago, he was an aeronautical engineer. His poodle has been fitted with a bucket to stop it from biting its injured paw.

The Seigneur keeps house these days on a somewhat reduced scale. His grandmother bequeathed him land and responsibilities, but not much capital. His tithe from the farmers – one-tenth of their harvest – is now paid in cash, less valuable than crops. He and his wife do most of the gardening, and rather dread the arrival of dignitaries for lunch.

Changes on Sark, apparently coinciding with the new Seigneur's rule, are mildly disowned by him. The granting of women's rights, which recently ended wifely servitude, was a process initiated in Dame Sybille's time but subject to lengthy digestion by the Court of Chief Pleas. Seigneur Beaumont has no wish to accelerate this process of rumination. Not even to provide a civic rubbish incinerator? Ah, says the Seigneur, but it would not end there. An incinerator would require two men, at least, to run it. The bureaucratic implication, in Sark terms, is daunting.

Even in high season, the island is sometimes granted its wish to be alone. A mist comes down, shutting in the cliffs, cutting off the tourist boats from Guernsey. The carriage horses, and their lank-haired attendants wrapped in blankets, stand glumly at the top of Harbour Hill as the fog warnings boom and bleat across the curtained sea.

Word of insurrection travels swiftly. A party of young men were recently at large, their boisterous coming telegraphed ahead of them from pub to pub. Eventually the Sark policeman collected them in a trailer and conducted them to their launch. He was wearing a Guernsey sweater, and unrecognisable. The invaders thanked him profusely, offering him tips. They thought he had rescued them from the police.

1978

The Beauty that Dies from Within

As Mr Ryanto, the family planning officer, climbs the muddy slope, a starving cockerel runs out of his path. The colours expended on it – like that splashed over all Indonesia – suggest, quite simply, that Nature is roaring drunk. Here in the Melati sub-district of Jakarta, life is entirely mud, remodelled or multiplied by the morning rains; yet even the mud is beautiful, vermilion, truffle-soft. Over ridges and precipices of mud, along trunks and troughs of mud, no stain adheres to Mr Ryanto's person. He carries privilege with him as a charm.

All eyes in Melati follow the neat figure in fawn clothes who wears a wristwatch, carries a briefcase stamped 'Z. Ryanto' and represents yet another of the government agencies whose acronymic menace rule all lives. Mr Ryanto is considered wondrous looking, with his shiny hair, his gold teeth and all the pricks and pockmarks in his cheeks. In Indonesia, a perfect complexion denotes poverty. The poor have unmarked faces, for they are dying from within.

Each dwelling in the mud has an exterior portion, screened with chicken-wire, and chairs arranged as if the priority over survival has been to provide for casual guests. On the wall hangs a coloured calendar of the type distributed by foreign business corporations. These calendars decorate every house throughout the *kampong*, the illimitable warren of Jakarta's slums. In rags, in rotting leaves and mud, it is nice to know the day of the month.

The householder has lost a baby only hours before – his third. How did the baby die? In answer Mr Ryanto presses the sides of his stomach. The father listens intently with elegant legs crossed like a man in a lounge-bar. Against the wire screen cluster the children who live in the mud. With them, too, Nature has been spendthrift. Faces against muddy arms they cling to the wire, trembling eyes against muddy fists, barefoot yet with beauty spots. The man has eight children more. What is the destruction of just another lovely face?

Indonesia is a place, above all, where people should find it easy to breathe and stretch their limbs. The republic is colossal: the breast-

195

work of islands, and seas which flow through them, curving below Asia like an open paddock. The islands are almost insolently fertile. Through jungle corridors the roads rush, while there is time, past carpets of tea, of adolescent rubber trees, past fruit heaped gold-green, electric-yellow, past water meadows like polished dining-table tops; pepper, macassar, cloves, timber, oil, wealth for which empires have contended, and still contend, pour nonchalantly from the intoxicated earth. It is Nature's ill humour that people, in such exhausting profusion, should contrive to go hungry. So, from the unnumbered islands, they come to a single, tormented island: Java. From Sumatra, Sulawesi, Kalimantan and a thousand promised lands, ceaselessly they come into Jakarta.

It looks pleasant enough from the sky. A meadow of crinkly red-tile roofs, baking in the sun or covered with silken humidity, the capital city of Indonesia offers a prospect as clean and bland as a Dutch kitchen-floor. Between those prim red roofs, five million people live where space exists for two million, and more arrive each day from the thankless beauty outside. Ten years from now, when Jakarta can accommodate seven million, nine million will live here, or try to live.

Ichsan is one. A little boy with a black moustache, Ichsan could find no means to feed his wife and two children on the green breast of central Java. He came with the others to Jakarta on the illegal trucks. Since then, he has seldom felt the sun on his shoulders.

Ichsan rides a *betjak*. Rattling, sliding through the *kampong* lanes, honking their advent by means of loose cords, the rickshaw tricycles connect slum with slum; the city's whole plight is depicted in their brightly painted tin. There are too many *betjaks*. Each stateless, hungry immigrant tries to become a *betjak* boy as a first means of survival. They mass together, blue and red, silver the flies glittering on the cabs; from each cab lolling one sleepy bare leg.

Though Ichsan is a night-worker, the hazards of his life are still considerable. The Indonesian national pastime is to form a sub-committee, then to abbreviate the initial letters of its name. Above the *betjak*-driver's unworldly head BAPPENAS and BUTSI, PPNI, YTKI and the multitudinous other bodies devised for his discipline, circle like official harpies. He may be challenged at any moment to produce his authority to reside in Jakarta, or the receipt for the cash deposit which must be lodged with the municipal authority. Returning, on exhausted legs, to his hut, he may find it beaten flat by the police. He will be taken by truck and dumped outside the city boundaries; compelled to begin the game of survival again.

Even should Ichsan survive these misfortunes, life can never be easy. The energetic Governor of Jakarta, Ali Sadikin, has banished the *betjaks* in daylight hours from Jalan Thamrin, the road with the skyscrapers along it. Formerly Ichsan might earn 1600 rupiahs (£1.60) each night: now he will be lucky if it is 500. Of this he pays 150 for the hire of the *betjak,* 250 for food, and 100 rupiahs a day he saves: 10 pence a day, if he has been lucky, Ichsan saves to send to his wife and his children.

'Riding the *betjak,* what do you think about? Your family in Indramayu?' No.

'The President?' No.

'About God?' A dreamy assent.

'Then what do you think about?'

'Making money.'

In Jalan Thamrin is proclaimed the city's coming renaissance. Here, like orderly gravestones, stand the savings-banks and bijou foreign embassies; here, with ominous rapidity, arise the new international hotels. Along Jalan Thamrin now the traffic may go, unhampered by anything whatever. Of all human activity in Jakarta, few sights are more affecting than that of some citizen attempting to cross over this prestigious artery. The chains of cars lash out of the mountainous horizon, endlessly shrieking, circling endlessly, their design spanning four decades of colonial occupation. It is as if, by eliminating people here, someone hopes to redress the burden of the slums.

This is Jakarta's purported salvation; and who shall blame Indonesians for believing it to be so? Worse dictators have ruled here than the motor car. Even great *Bapak* Sukarno could not persuade the Asian travel-agents, as they have now been persuaded, to hold their convocation in Jakarta this summer. So the thinking runs among those who still dare to think of *Bapak*. Seven years after his overthrow he is commemorated, as he lived, impractically. The monuments which he caused to be erected arise on white pillars from the trees: great athletes, nudes and leprechauns, gesturing at the clouds which were the repository of President Sukarno's dreams.

For seven years, General Suharto, not Big Daddy Sukarno, has ruled Indonesia. This feat he has accomplished chiefly by exhibiting the contrary of everything in his predecessor; so that, whereas Sukarno was hot-tempered, warm-hearted, garrulous, greedy, lecherous, brilliant, fanciful and inspiring, Suharto is none of these things. He personifies to a remarkable degree the Javanese distaste for any form of ostentation. In official photographs he invariably has his back to the camera. So, modestly he arose to his present eminence; mildly he contains the plots of his opponents. To have deposed Sukarno without a revolution, to have countenanced the slaughter of perhaps a million so-called Communists; what else has been at work but an infinite and eerie species of tact?

197

Suharto has brought *growth* – that encouraging and ambiguous word. Where Sukarno remained indifferent to the benedictions of IBM or the Bank of America, the new administration welcomes foreign investment with a red light district's avidity; their great placards sparkle in the sky above the students from the suspended university. It is in commerce, above all, that the tact of President Suharto rings its curious chord. The most susceptible foreign investor might be pardoned for forgetting that Indonesia is directed almost entirely by military men; by generals, chunky with gold, whose satisfaction with themselves is only too manifest. Generals take gracefully to business. The Army has large commercial holdings, both official and clandestine. Even кopкamтiв, chief in the bestiary of official abbreviations, the Inquisition dedicated to annihilating Communism and supposed Communism, deals also with the licensing of nightclubs.

But ordinary street life in our cities does not depend to so lively an extent upon the survival of potentates. Whatever the dilapidation of personal liberty in Indonesia, the Jakarta municipality has palpably benefited. New health centres in the *kampong* have cut the death-rate by a quarter, though sewage still flows languidly among the palms. In place of fatuous monoliths, bus-services have been improved – the buses which one must board at a run, since they never stop but occasionally go backwards. The roads are constantly under repair, if never actually repaired, by the fastidious ballet of the maintenance gangs. Civil servants, that somnolent inner nation, are more frequently stirred into activity, in certain forms.

'The people are beginning to respect us,' said Herman Soesilo, the Chief Medical Officer. 'Now they will even agree to pay their taxes.'

Herman Soesilo dresses in a heavenly white doctor's smock and white platform-heel shoes.

'But surely most of them still refuse to pay their taxes?'

'Not so many. We make them pay.' Herman Soesilo grinned. 'Only, sometimes it is easier to pay the tax-collector than to pay the Government.'

'Is there still corruption in the Civil Service?'

'The trouble is, we still can't pay them enough. Myself, in America this job would earn three to four thousand dollars a month. Here,' said Herman Soesilo, 'I make only two hundred. Yes, two hundred!'

The Chief Medical Officer glanced to his wrist, at a glittering thick gold watch which must have accounted for two years, at least, of his salary.

Concerning Jakarta's overpopulation, the Government is commendably frank. It employs diverse counter-measures, with varying degrees of finesse, but admits that none significantly diminishes the bubonic inner mass. Enlarging the city boundaries, or sealing it tight like an egg, have proved equally unsatisfactory. Each year, too, a few thousand families are persuaded to migrate to the outer islands, and given land with a cash settlement to remain there. In West Irian (western New Guinea) two people may enjoy the space in which, in Jakarta, 7,000 people must exist.

The weight of President Suharto's second Five-Year Plan is placed entirely behind family planning as the single hope for Jakarta and for Java. Birth-control came late to Indonesia, thanks to its racial amalgam of Muslims, Catholics and Dutch Protestants, but its implementation has been swift; Indonesian dialect now readily admits of a *kondom* and a *pil*.

Today, the family planning agency is visiting a kampong-dweller named Mr Daam. Mr Daam's house is near a vegetable-market, in a tunnel of dank stone and wood still spouting from the morning rain. Unemployed, he has 10 children; five more have died; the youngest, on his knee, has been carelessly dealt its measure of physical perfection. Mr Daam is also a grandfather, yet he himself looks no more than a child, with a boy's grey head, a boy's bare legs. No one ages or was ever young. Babies carry babies on their hips. The old women watching from the doorways look like girls who put their hair up for a dance that never came.

Still Mr Daam cannot understand. The two lady field-workers, with handbags on their knees, take out the contraceptives, *kondom*, *pil*, and flourish them beneath his nostrils; he smiles. Still bemused by these tablets of silver foil which – if officialdom is to be believed – can rescue him from the mud, the dust, the brown river where he washes, the stink of human waste, and the rotting yellow *durean* fruit.

This is where *Pak* Kasur can help. *Pak* Kasur is a *dalang* – a puppet master. When Mr Daam sits with his children, his daughter's children, his friend's children, before the puppet-stage glowing in a breathless Jakarta night, however oblique the message, Mr Daam is certain to understand.

There are two forms of Indonesian puppet. The *wayang kulit*, leather puppets in shadow-play, belong to the east of Java. In the western region around Jakarta *wayang golek* are more commonly found; figures slender as grasshoppers, their heads clasped in jewelled helmets, gesturing fastidiously by means of wands attached to their wrists. Their 140 different voices are accompanied by an orchestra of gongs and pots, so subtly beaten with thumbs, with muffled sticks, that the music seems to orginate in the mind.

Pak Kasur is like a puppet himself, his smile so broad it might be mounted on hinges, his arms swaying as in obedience to the wands of the *wayang golek*.

199

'My name, really it is Suryono – Son of Light, because I am born very early in the morning my mother say: six o'clock. But I am Boy Scout!' He saluted gravely with two fingers. '*Ka,* in Indonesian it means brother, but the children cannot say *Ka* Suryono, so they call me *Ka*-Sur. And *kasur* it means – mattress! In Holland they call me *Faderje Bultzak.* In German they call me *Onkel Matrasse.* In England they call me Father Mattress. The President, too, he calls me Father Mattress!'

Pak Kasur fell under suspicion in the anti-Communist purges following Sukarno's downfall, but was in the fortunate minority that survived. He now runs a small, bright-painted primary school where he is reluctant to charge fees to the children of teachers or journalists – two of Indonesia's more persecuted professions. With the Government he is more than rehabilitated for the service which he does their family-planning campaign.

Among the jewelled *wayang* in *Pak* Kasur's puppet show, there is a doctor and a nurse. The plot has a family planning theme. 'Lady comes, and on her forehead is *pilis* – spices put on to stop headache after baby has been born. Doctor say, "Ah, you have baby! How many is that?" She say, "Oh, just twelve." "But that is no good!" Doctor say. She say "You must see my husband." For some, wife is the only recreation. That is too frank? 'I am not expert. But I am Boy Scout!' He saluted. 'In village they will walk twenty kilometres to see *Pak* Kasur. Our Minister of Interior Affairs, Mr Amir Machmud, he order from me nine hundred sets of these puppets – nine thousand puppets I must make. I have no factory. I have no fire – only sun!'

There are flaws, however, in the best-laid Five-Year Plans. Riots occurred in Jakarta during January, brief but furious, like the rains. Because they coincided with a visit by the Japanese premier Mr Tanaka, the riots were widely believed to be anti-Japanese; a protest against the increasing concessions being granted to Indonesia's wartime conquerers. The Government itself preferred to believe it was so. Swiftly, entrepreneurs became soldiers again. Ten Jakarta newspapers were abolished, an order went forth from KOPKAMTIB that anyone found damaging an item of Japanese merchandise would be 'shot to death on the spot'.

It was conveniently ignored that the rioters also stoned neon signs and attacked the very steam-baths in which their rulers and betters were accustomed to spend off-duty hours.

The Five-Year Plan continues as ordained; like all long-term projects, perhaps a little careless of the moment. The streaming light is unabated along Jalan Thamrin: the generals' sons on their Hondas and Suzukis, haughty as only Eastern privilege can be. In the plaza of the Hotel Indonesia, dozens of military jeeps intimate some great Society occasion. Bats fly squeaking among the louvred fronts of the smart new savings banks. In the dark of the pedestrian overpass a naked boy sits. The bones in his body are perfectly carved, Nature's model for a neck and breast, though she has neglected prosaic details. The boy has no arms. Above the thundering lamps he turns his face in endless supplication towards the few thin Asian stars.

The *betjaks* cannot come into the city centre until 10 o'clock. At 10 o'clock exactly the *betjaks* are everywhere, gliding on the sacred avenues, going the wrong way around traffic islands, a quadrille of silent, pumping knees. Like all crowded cities, Jakarta at night seems empty. The air is sparse and cindery as millions breathe in at once, preparing to survive the darkness.

The *betjaks* come bearing prostitutes, their wigs back-combed; their smiles, like searching lanterns, turning this way and that.

'Hello Sir. What you want?'

'Pom Pom? One by one, okay?'

'I give blue-job?'

'This one good,' the *betjak*-drivers promise. 'Clean.'

The seated girl draws her garments up to her chin.

'She is from Kuala Lumpur,' the *betjak* drivers murmur reverently.

Another carriage drifts from the fog. A creature steps down from it, more exquisite than any of the colloquy. In a slow, soft, courteous voice she says:

'I imitation girl.'

Behind flaring cigarette-stalls stretch the corridors of dark. It is never quiet, though millions are asleep, because millions more cannot sleep or, if they do, cannot rest. In their open parlours, under oil-lamps, they sit, the audience of their own despair. From slum to slum the rice-seller passes, striking his gong. He stops, ladles from his jars a cup of rice, scatters a few pink flakes on it. He takes back the cup, flexes the yoke on his shoulders and moves away, striking his curious gong. The hissing lamps shine on coloured calendars given away by the foreign companies; on a girl in a cornfield, a girl smiling happily, or a neat design of pretty Japanese flowers.

1974

A Day Out in Kiev

I was standing on the Paton Bridge, one of the several causeways which cross the Dnieper into Kiev. I had been admiring the view over the broad waterway with its several islands, the forests banked softly beyond, and the gold domes of St Sophia like bulrushes, gleaming in the sun. It is said that one ought not to linger around bridges in the Soviet Union, but the grey-coated militiamen, stationed at either end of the bridge, had offered no objection. It is somehow fascinating to watch even heavy traffic in Russia – the lorries, the pale green taxis marked with a T, the numerous motor-cycle combinations. In a land where enterprise has been abolished, one wonders where all of them can be going in such a hurry.

It was then that I noticed a street-washing machine making its way across the bridge, along the side of the footway behind me. I was familiar with this large municipal object which is often seen at work in the Kiev streets. It resembles in size and slowness an English dust-cart, with the addition of a thick hose at the side which emits a vertical column of white water upon the road, the pavement, parked cars, and any people which it happens to encounter on its course. In Russia they do not yet embrace the principle of pedestrian right-of-way. A Russian considers himself fortunate that cars stay out of the subways.

I began to walk, quite rapidly, across the bridge, away from the street-washing machine. As I walked, I could hear it growing gradually in volume behind me, the throaty chug of its dynamo, the rhythmic *woof* as section after section of the footway received its discharge from the hose. I could not get around it owing to the presence of a rail, low-slung but emphatic, beyond which the lorries and sidecars lashed up and down. To walk in front of the street-washing machine seemed preferable to walking behind it, for the shoes I was wearing had been bought in Russia.

So I walked, now a little more rapidly, in front of the street-washing machine, across the Paton Bridge towards Kiev, across the wide river shaded by white sand-flats, fished by earnest white dots, parted by the barges and cut by the nippy hydrofoil; all shining faintly silver in the tentative sun.

The Hotel Dniepro stands in the cobbled, newly-washed square near the amusement park. One can be comfortable in a Russian hotel, so long as one is willing to absorb an entirely new set of rules. There is a total lack of public rooms and of the casual comfortable seats so promiscuously offered by capitalist establishments. The foyer rings with echoes rebounding from the concrete of which it is largely composed; the only decoration is vast, insular deposits of American wet-look luggage. Old women in headscarves move with mops across the concrete or the carpet. You obtain your room-key, not from the reception-desk but from a lady on your own floor, seated gravely at a bureau beneath an ornamental lamp. The lady at the bureau draws open a tray of keys, attached to large, transparent ping-pong balls with the room-number floating within; she hands you your ping-pong ball with a murmured '*Pozhalsto*'. Late at night, in smaller hotels, she will hand you your key lying prone on a little bed made up beside the desk.

In the dining-room, the tablecloths are adorned with the flags of several nations. Ours has an American flag. The Americans next to us have been given a Greek flag. Lunch, in Russia, is the major meal of the day, which may account for the heavy incidence of '*Nyet*' at offical counters during the afternoon. Soup is served as the second course. Our Intourist courier, Rita, arrives at the table, bringing with her a large tomato, acquired in Samarkand. She is a chubby girl with humorous eyes, full lips, poor skin, a red shirt and sky-blue dungarees cut, in the Russian manner, rather loosely at the back. Her blonde hair presents one with a constant dilemma. Is it worn up, but trying to get down, or down but trying to get up?

After lunch, I must go shopping. The zip-fastener of my boot broke in Samarkand; the blue-enamelled splendour of that city was slowly poisoned by the soreness in my right index finger as I strove to haul the parted zip back to its origin. As soon as I had zipped it up, it began to unzip itself from the bottom. In that gentle but inexorable fissure, my entire personality felt undermined. I further had a quirk of fancy to possess a pair of Russian Army boots. The brain, in the isolation of travel, can often grow feverish.

At the military department store, I discover Russian Army boots to be unsuitable. They are grey in colour and smell pungently of tar. At the entrance to the ordinary shoe-department (behind the headscarf department), a lady with her hair up – or down – supervises the queue: I am allowed to go in only when someone at the other end has gone out. Russian shoes can range in price from £15 to £30 while ladies' fur-lined boots may be had for as little as £50. I try on a pair of ladies' boots, then a pair of child's. They are laced together, and one is not allowed to undo the laces. I discover quite a nice black lace-up brogue by itself on a plinth. I try it on. I think it will do, I ask the assistant in sign language if she will fetch me the other shoe in the pair. She shakes her head and answers '*Nyet*'. A number of saleswomen convey to me in sign language that one shoe is all they have in that line. In desperation, I seize another pair – £19 – and go to the cash counter.

Tonight, Eve Arnold, the photographer, and I have resolved to escape from the 'international' menu at the Hotel Dniepro; the fried meat, cold chips and clotted carrot. We obtain a reservation at the *Vitryak*, a Ukrainian restaurant at the edge of the city, to which our Intourist guide accompanies us. We are seated at a wooden table in a white-washed room, at one end of which a band with elaborate rock and roll instruments is playing a sentimental tango. Our welcome at the *Vitryak* is slighty qualified, for reasons of bureaucracy. We have paid for the meal in advance, but neglected to bring the receipt with us. A long argument begins as we sit at our unprepared wooden table. Though it is only eight o'clock, the room is smoke-filled.

Our dinner, eventually, consists of fried meat, cold chips and carrots which stick together; a bottle of wine and a bottle of vodka; a little caviar inside a butter-pat. The restaurant is very noisy. At one end, near the band, there is a wedding party.

We ourselves are approached by a thick-set man, wearing a very slim tie, who bows elaborately to Rita, our Intourist guide. Because of her painted eyes and her sky-blue dungarees, he has mistaken her for a foreigner. He has, further, mistaken me for her husband. He places his hands together and bows to me. He leads her out in front of the band where, to her ill-concealed disgust, they foxtrot the night away.

He returns to us after the last dance, carrying a small saucer. On the saucer, in a shallow pool of water, is a crayfish. It is dull in colour, and it is still alive. He places it in front of us with a flourish, and exclaims '*Souvenir*'.

In a little while, the crayfish moves off the saucer and begins to crawl about the table.

Late on Saturday night in Kiev, the streets and squares are still full of activity. People sit on rows of benches around the memorials or in front of the shop-windows. In the amusement park, under the illuminated ferris-wheel, some boys use the swingboats as an old woman at the turnstile watches sceptically. The sound of conversation can be heard from the ascending cars of the wheel. People sit on benches in the amusement park and in the public gardens. Some of them appear rather tipsy. A militia van passes casually along up and down, snapping them up in pairs and fours. At the subway-entrance, a group of men and women, bundled up against the east wind, sing community songs, stamping their feet on the pavement. A boy stands with a girl in the recesses of the colonnade. The boy glowers from a turned-up collar, with a cigarette in the corner of his mouth. The girl holds a little bunch of red carnations.

At midnight, a master-switch is thrown. The city is empty. A machine moves slowly along the kerb, discharging water upon the pavement from a hose.

1976

Sharp Guys in Zion

The Utah sun shines on Salt Lake City with a strength that could dry clean the soul. This is the miraculous city of Mormons, settled a century and a half ago by pioneer zealots wheeling handcarts into a salt lake basin in which there then grew only a single cedar tree. The miracle is renewed each noontide as the sun glints off the skyscrapers, and sparkles on the drinking fountains, and lights up the gold angel among the Temple spires, and makes silvery waters of water endlessly sprinkling over the well-annointed lawns.

Below the angel, on Temple Square the gates of Mormondom stand open with vehement offhandedness. Tours, which include the Tabernacle and a feature-film of Heaven, begin at the monument to a flock of seagulls. Heaven dispatched the gulls, it is said, to rescue the pioneers' first crop from a plague of grasshoppers. To the Mormons, it is one of many proofs that God in the American continent has provided a Gospel at least the equal of the Holy Land's. Joseph Smith is their Messiah, Brigham Young their Moses and each of four million of them in that transplanted Heavenly realm is a Latter-Day Saint. Their Deity is jealous and imminent, as He was to the chosen of Israel. Equally He is love, and light and air-conditioning; His Power is AC/DC. Before speaking to the tourists, the Mormon elder plugs a small microphone into the monument.

The elder is 19, with a smile of unwavering happiness. For Mormonism is the religion of smiling young men. That it also should be governed by a sad old man of 96 is merely the introduction to its paradoxes; The Founding prophet, Joseph Smith, was only 14 when the angel first appeared to him, and directed him to the *Book of Mormon*. Only a very young man, and his young friends, could have established that odd, ersatz Bible around the figure of a 'lost' prophet named Mormon. Only young hearts, lungs and sinewy arms could, in the next hundred years, have shoved and buffeted their giant-killing faith through Indians, fire and famine westward to its air-conditioned Zion.

A century and a half later, Mormonism has still a young man's ambition: to convert the whole world. Fast. Every day, somewhere, a new chapel is dedicated. Smith no sooner found adherents than he scattered them as missionaries. There is no professional clergy. Every

Mormon boy is eligible to be ordained at 12, in a vehement pressing-down of hands, and, at 19, to be flung out in the steps of those first Apostles. He serves in a mission for two years: in Korea perhaps, or only Wyoming – 'It comes under Inspiration of the Lord,' an official said. 'That's where He wants 'em to go.' For each it is the summit of happiness, but not always for his mother. 'My son, Jim Kimball laboured in Leeds, England,' one missionary's mother said. 'He was very pale and frail of skin. I couldn't sleep nights, thinking of him under those black, overbearing buildings.'

The missionaries go lightly equipped. For eight weeks beforehand, scores of tender zealots sit in the Language School at Brigham Young University, knees constricted by kindergarten desks, interminably reciting the six lessons of Mormonism: in German, in Spanish – the largest source of annual conversions – in Navajo, in French. A classroom repeats *'Nouse deve-nons semblable a notre Pear Terrest'* with such steadfast incomprehension, one quakes to imagine its first application on a street in Paris. During this relentless pursuit of the Gift of Tongues, they may not telephone their families nor receive calls; they are thrown to the winds by a system that would be heartless and horrible were it not for their deep joy in submitting to it.

Anyone visited by Mormon missionaries in this country knows how difficult it is not to be charmed. Their eyes are clear, their mackintoshes white, their teeth innocent of cigarettes or coffee; there is a sweet reticence in the way they carry the dictatorship of the Word. Confronted by their wonderfully hygienic souls, one may overlook the darker, odder side of Mormonism; one simply wishes one felt as happy. In the hills around Salt Lake, a girl and boy were looking across the city spread on a cushion of night – at boulevards just as the master-coloniser Brigham Young laid them out: pipes of blue and sliding yellow beads with no red sacrilege from any strip-joint or bar. All from the sagebrush and one cedar, by God and ferocious application.

'If only Brigham could see it now,' the boy said.

'Oh, he can,' said the girl.

America's attitude is confused as one might expect of a land whose history is short and passing constantly under review. Their name is stamped equally on the terrible sin of polygamy and on a multitude of durably-manufactured articles. They were frontiersmen and heroes with the best, at the same time fomenting political malpractice, reigns of terror over non-Mormons by a holy secret-police, and not infrequent massacre: they were persecutors as well as martyrs and no doubt partly deserved to be burned out of their original capital, Nauvoo, Illinois. In Utah their early history culminated with all-out territorial war against the Government, at the conclusion of which Brigham Young was declared an outlaw. (He also was later offered a contract by the circus-proprietor P.T. Barnum.)

In the 20th century Mormons acquired the business arts of subtlety, discretion and benevolence. The trail they flamed over the old frontier, from New York to Ohio to Nauvoo and over the Rockies, is now an important tourist highway peopled by many waxwork angels. The majestic virtuosity of their Salt Lake Tabernacle Choir provides the longest-running American radio programme. Their welfare system of farms, factories, hospitals, schools, and employment exchanges is admired for its simplicity, efficiency and imagination. Above all – and this is a point which, in American minds, tends to excuse any amount of religious oddity – the Saints know how to turn a buck.

Downtown Salt Lake City shows Heaven's powerful holding-companies. Below the Church's new administrative skyscraper, white and keen like the raincoat of a good missionary, are grouped Zion's First National Bank, Zion's insurance companies and investment corporations, CMI, the far-West's oldest department store. The building which houses the Church's ruling authority, the First Presidency and Council of Twelve Apostles, itself much resembles a bank. And the minority of infidels – as non-Mormons are called – find it profitable to use the Mormon beehive symbol or 'Deseret', the *Book of Mormon's* name for the honeybee. From KSL, the Church-owned radio station, a glad voice exhorts 'Come and see the sharp guys at Zion Motors!'

Mormon captains of American industry include J. Willard Marriott the catering king; J. Lee Bickmore, president of the National Biscuit Corporation; Tolbert O. Kirkwood of Woolworth's. The Church is as proud of its capitalists as of Jack Dempsey or the two Saints who sat at once in President Nixon's Cabinet. Since Mormonism has only three set prayers but Mormons must needs pray aloud a good deal of the time, the Almighty is frequently called on to enshrine a business matter: 'O Lord in humility we bow our heads to Thee at the start of this executive meeting.' In many respects they have spiritualised Rotarianism; their belief in continuous revelation is easily interpreted as omniscient Chairmanship from the skies.

Yet they are pioneers still. A Mormon chapel may arise in the wealthiest neighbourhood – it is still called a 'stake', just a foothold, with armies of darkness beaten back all around. Mormonism is a man's life – a white man's life. Women, as well as Negroes, are excluded from the priesthood, although they may preach or work in the relief organisations, one of which Brigham Young founded to occupy his own polygamously-acquired daughters. For devout Mormon females, however, the emphasis remains on needlepoint and production of the great numbers of children for which the Church was always held in awe. A dozen households together at a Family Home Evening – basis of the excellent family-improvement programme – may collect together 90 heads.

The pioneer virtues of hard work and abstinence and thrift are everywhere encouraged. In the latter, a splendid example is set by the missionary authorities, which send the young men to who knows what tribulation entirely at their own expense. For bodily health the strict Mormon abstains not only from tea and coffee, but every one of their many substitutes, even from Coca-Cola. Brigham Young University had a million books and also facilities for a student, if he wishes, to keep his own cow. The most prosperous Saints are encouraged to keep a year's store of food against the possibility of famine. Not that it is common to meet an ill-fed Mormon. All the Church's factories, fruiteries, pecan-nut ranches and waffle-iron foundries compose a welfare system of beatific simplicity. By volunteer labour they fill their supermarkets with their own Deseret-brand goods, and then simply give them away.

Socially they strike few discords, being Conservatives of the deeper kind, obedient to the Flag and the necessity to shake hands on all occasions. The zealots droning out their catechism at Brigham Young are forbidden moustaches or light-coloured trousers; all art on the campus is invigilated. Nor does Mormonism object to military engagement in Vietnam (though in recent years the Draft has somewhat curtailed the missionary programme); nor have its sanctions against all wickedness restrained one Mormon from devising the Browning machine-gun or another from manufacturing one of the longest gambling neon-signs in Las Vegas.

They are in many ways the most attractive Americans. They have the ability, miraculous in that firebombed country, to assemble peaceably and happily. Each summer near Palmyra, New York, the students act a pageant depicting Joseph Smith's meeting with the angel and the glimpse afforded him of what ancient religion once flourished coast-to-coast. Below the hillock on which the oracle appeared, a hundred thousand people watch. There is no mass catering. The contentment, in the drizzle, is strong as champagne.

'Wonderful Brigham!' the a cappella girls group sing, lauding the fierce Mormon Moses whose name for the villa where he kept his harem – and the quartermaster store which clothed them – was 'The Lion House'. It is hard not to like Mormon singing, and Mormon services, in which the congregation remains seated, babies borne on laps, fingers and arms entwine contentedly, hour after hour ('Wonderful Brigham!') as a solemn 17-year-old in baseball boots administers the Sacrament.

Death is regarded as the most minor inconvenience. All families will be reunited, Joseph Smith taught, when the Heavens descend. In preparation for this, a formidable genealogical society is at work, searching dozens of old countries for Mormon ancestors. Unnumbered family-trees, retracing all the paths by which the Church assembled in Zion, are held on microfilm in refrigerated vaults in a

209

canyon outside Salt Lake, so that the Millennium shall be properly indexed, and the dead may be 'sealed' in baptism with their living descendants for all eternity. The perishing of the body is therefore considered a trifling inconvenience. 'We just feel a little sorry for ourselves,' a missionary said. 'It's like "see ya later".'

This summer the death occurred of the wife of the head of the Church, the Prophet and Revelator 96-year-old Joseph Fielding Smith. Mrs Smith had been adored for her temperament and for the thrilling contralto she gave to the Tabernacle choir. Frail as President Smith himself was, he had spent almost the last month continuously at her bedside.

Sun glanced into the Tabernacle from its side-doors, and down from the TV lights in the dome, designed by Brigham Young – apparently without *amour propre* – to resemble the roof of his own mouth. Such Apostles of the Council of Twelve as were in town sat in the wine-coloured plush below the great organ like a walnut Kremlin supported by gold pen-nibs. Between Apostles and organ, the choir rose in tiers of blue and salmon-pink. The congregation was in shirtsleeves. A snapshot occasionally flashed. There was not a black garment (or black face) to be seen.

President Smith's deputy President, Harold B. Lee, gave the funeral address. It was the best of prayers, directed not upwards but to President Smith himself, sitting very thin and still inside the ring of his own stiff collar. 'May God comfort you, Pres'dent Smith – I know He will. And when your time comes, Pres'dent Smith, may you too draw the draperies of the couch around you and sink down into pleasant dreams.'

Mormons acknowledge Christ – for did He not also reveal himself to Joseph Smith. One cannot help puzzling over this youth from 'the Burned Over District' of New York state (no relation to the incumbent Prophet) who, having done nothing remarkable up to the age of 14, was suddenly visited by an angel and led to buried tablets he successfully claimed had been buried by 'lost' Holy Land tribes after their migration to the American continent. To the cynical infidel, young Smith may have had something in common with Thomas Chatterton, a brilliant but slapdash juvenile forger, the success of whose productions now seems mystifying. For, compared with the King James Bible, Smith's chronicles of the prophets Mormon and Moroni – and such hitherto unrecorded Old Testament tribes as the 'Nephites' and the 'Lamanites' – have all the celluloid bogusness of angels along the present-day Mormon tourist-trail.

As one inquires deeper into Mormondom, the smiling, touching openness gives way to secrecy and obsessive ceremony still redolent of this rather shifty suspect Messiah. Thus, while everyday singalong

210

Mormon worship happens in a 'tabernacle', special forms of devotion withdraw into a 'temple', and remain assiduously shielded from infidel eyes. A marrying couple, for instance, can undergo a rite called 'The Endowment Ceremony' in which – according to Catholic scholar Thomas O'Dea – the couple have their genitals anointed, put on special apron-like garments and utter 'blood-curdling' threats to anyone who would question the sanctity of the occasion. Temples also perform the 'sealing' – the official consignment of souls, living and dead, to the Mormon's well-tabulated Eternity. The overtones of Freemasonry are no accident. Joseph Smith believed Freemasons to be descended from an ancient priestly order in the Holy Land – an ironic circumstance since he was assassinated by Freemasons in Illinois.

As well as the great granite Salt Lake temple, there are six more implanted throughout the world. With a smile and a pat, the Elders insist they are not secret places. Before a new temple is consecrated, parties of infidels are taken round to view the chambers of lavendar and powder-blue, the brass ox-borne fonts and Disneyesque frescoes depicting Heaven, Eden and Mormon conquest. The temple doors are then closed to outsiders. Even senior Mormon officials can enter only by special pass, the validity of which is carefully reviewed each year.

There is also the racial question, complicated by the fact that Mormons have traditionally been good to the American Indian. Joseph Smith taught that Indians were descended from that ancient tribe he identified as 'Lamanites': it was the Church's duty, therefore, to ignore their dark skins and raise them to the station of 'a white and delightsome people'.

By the same token, black people bear the Curse of Cain and so are disbarred from holding Mormon priesthood – which, in effect, means membership. The edict remains in the granite in which it was etched half a century before the American slaves were freed. It is where all Mormondom's open-faced, sunny logic and practicality leads at last into a blind alley. Why are black people cursed? Because the Lord said so. To whom? To Joseph Smith. How long can you do on believing that? Until the Lord tells us otherwise. How can He do that? He can do it only by a sign to our Prophet and Relevator, President Joseph Fielding Smith.

So all the fresh-faced young men lead back to that sad old man of 96 who is led into the Salt Lake City boardroom of 'The Council of Twelve' by his dapper and aspiring deputy, Harold B. Lee. If God relents toward blacks, He can declare the fact only through President Smith, seated there at the end of the huge, polished table, frail and motionless within his while collar, as unaware of the great world of Mormon acquision as of the question he had just been asked. 'I remember when they were building the Temple right out

211

here,' the Prophet says dazedly, for the second time. 'They brought the stone down on flatcars from Little Cottonwood Canyon . . .'

As President Smith begins to tell the story for the third time, deputy Harold B. Lee stops him by placing a well-manicured hand on his arm.

The philosophy towards Negroes is perfectly easy to accept, says President Lee, if you believe as Mormons do in 'continuous revelation'. Otherwise it is not easy to accept. Is revelation sometimes a warning? Possibly. Is not the race situation in America therefore of the nature of revelation? For answer to this and all points, President Lee turns to the *Book of Mormon* rather as a businessman might consult the Yellow Pages. 'You ask me when we're going to change our policy. I put that back to you as "when is the Lord going to change His policy". We don't try to second-guess the Lord. We regard it as a seller's market in the Gospels. We're not about to alter it to suit you.'

Yet there are some who think this has already happened; that, in its zeal for perfect corporate identity, the Mormon Church has already pre-empted Heaven. 'These are not Mormons, nor "Jack-Mormons" – smoking, drinking sympathisers – nor even people of the Reorganised Mormon Church, the splinter that remained in the East after Nauvoo was abandoned. Officially the dissenters do not exist at all, save in the banter of Jack-Mormon taxicab drivers. 'I was walkin' out with a gal last week,' one driver said. 'She told me that a feller in Davis County'd proposed to her to be his *fifth* wife. And he was righteous.'

The Church's most notable feat of public relations has been in removing from its person the stain of polygamy. The correctness of plural marriage was among the revelations of Joseph Smith, sanctioned by the *Book of Mormon,* made practical, like most of their pieties, by frontier life when often there were not enough men. In the 1890s, the frontier flattened and Utah anxious to win full statehood in the Union, Heaven strategically repealed it.

Despite the threat of excommunication, the polygamists were hard to stamp out completely. They are still acknowledged to exist in remote parts of Southern Utah, cut off from the clean-living highways by impassable roads of dirt; but they are also closer to the air-conditioned Zion than that, they are barely out of earshot of the sharp guys at Zion Motors.

In a normal Salt Lake suburb the houses stand close with the needle of a church spire stitching them up every few hundred yards and lawn-sprays moving together in the concert of faith. Out here all the buildings are back from the road and hidden. In the dust of the path, riding bicycles, sitting on swings under lean-tos, playing with rubber tyres, there are children – suddenly, more yellow-haired children than the eye can take in at a glance. 'We put 'em to school,' the woman said. 'The School Principal says "Oh don't worry 'bout him, he's one of *them*".'

She sat under a tree holding an ear of corn and a tomato, having been disturbed at preparations for lunch, but in perfect tranquillity. 'We believe that the established Church is out of order,' she said, 'and that Joseph Smith will be resurrected to put his Church in order. That goes for Jesus Christ the Lord.'

This small fundamentalist community are about to be evicted from their home, to make way for a car park. As Zion Motors move in, no noticeable effort is being made to re-house the woman and her family. 'They persecute us. They persecute us through our loved ones. I have seen my own dear father go to jail for obedience to the Law of Plural Marriages. Sex – sex-life is all they think of, but our law of chastity is strict. You got to have clean channels to give birth to valiant spirits.

'You can say,' she added, 'we follow Mormonism all the way.' She did not regard it as a seller's market in the Gospels. 'I hope you find the religion of your heart,' she said as we left. Her manner was hard and strict; better that, perhaps, than to be patted by smiling businessmen until you bruise.

1972

213

The Longest Show on Earth

When Dharmendra awoke this morning, after barely two hours sleep, his first thought was that he had dropped off in front of the camera. Fatigue and bewilderment are inevitable consequences of being an Indian movie idol, starring in so many 'Filums' at once that one loses count. His first words to the guard who awoke him were a panicky 'Where are my dialogues?'

Like most Indian matinee idols, Dharmendra does not look Indian. His height, muscular arms and slightly credulous face recall the kind of Hollywood Samson who would have all his hair cut off by Hedy Lamarr. He emerged from his bungalow on the outskirts of Bombay, and got into the car for his first day's shooting 'shift' at Filmistan Studios. On the way, we passed three huge hoardings advertising Dharmendra films currently showing in Bombay. The star smiled and dabbed at his eyes, which were pink and raw with fatigue as uncooked bacon.

Filmistan presents the normal aspect of a Bombay film studio – a melange of bungalows and builders' rubble, little boys, tea-glasses, a few chickens and old men of apparently sacred designation. However they try, movie moguls cannot prevent the studios from absorbing a little of the street. It is as if the very beggars have got in, and gaze down from the unguarded catwalks through the high elevation of their knees.

This film starring Dharmendra has the Hindi title *Yadon Ki Barat* (Down Memory Lane). It is, typically, an involved tale of heroism, vengeance, familial obligation and melody; a young man, hunting his parents' killers, is reunited with his brothers – by a song. In the part of the young man, Dharmendra is required to sink into a chair in a paroxysm of rage. Behind the camera the director's betel-orange lips whisper, 'You hate him. You will kill him.' Dharmendra, standing on a set that looks half like a hotel bedroom and half like a smuggler's cave, grapples with this emotion. The take ends. He goes to the side to dab his sore eyes and run a comb through the wig that is identical to his real hair underneath. The lights go on. The boy with the microphone boom stretches it out.

'Silence!' the director shouts.

'Silence!' Dharmendra shouts.

214

'Silence!' everyone shouts.
'*Action!*'

Earlier that week, in downtown Bombay, I had attended the premiere of one of the 300 Hindi language movies annually released into
the subcontinent. Premieres here are common as in Hollywood,
although the Bombay police have not quite learned to distinguish
them from political demonstrations. Tonight, however, the great
Dilip Kumar was rumoured to be there. In the stone cinema foyer,
hundreds of long, brown fingers grasped the staircase ceiling as
ushers thrust the crowd ruthlessly backwards.

The film *Roop Tera Mastana* (Fabulous Beauty) had been
completed in barely four years. It concerned a murdered Princess
and a poor girl, her exact double, compelled to impersonate her.
The bloodiness of the opening sequences thus quickly turned to a
jaunty if shrill re-enactment of *My Fair Lady*. Its heroine, Mumtaz,
was also at the premiere seated in the audience beside the protective
figure of her aunt. Throughout the performance, with little chinks
of filigree, she sniffed. Like many queens of the Hindi camera, she
had a nasty cold.

In the picture, meanwhile, a Prince had arrived. He wore a Ruri-
tanian uniform. At the sight of Mumtaz, his eye grew moist. So did
the entire screen, soft focus being the essential element in depicting
such moments of truth. As in a light fog, a song duet now began
which was to last several hours and be diversely prosecuted: across
a terrace, through foaming fountains, once even from a pair of
trotting ponies which the director had not been able to prevent
from defecating briskly the while. In all this, the single point of
development was Mumtaz herself, who, in four years of production
had grown so fat within the same costumes, her Prince could not
unfasten her corselet without holding on tight against the whiplash.
All these lengthy manoeuvres were designed to compensate for the
one missing – and forbidden – element of romance. In Indian movies,
men and women are not allowed to kiss.

India's one true surfeit is of reality. So the Hindi cinema justifies
its handiwork: it is escape from that unpitying realism beneath the
skies. People go to a film when they cannot afford to eat. They see
it again, up to 50 times. But, with that national impatience, they
require all the parts of the illusion to be offered to them simultaneously – violence, farce, murder, dancing. And everything spun
out to inordinate length by that weaving, feinting, dodging dalliance
that insinuates – but cannot consummate – a kiss. B. R. Ishara, a
Goth-like young man directing his first big budget production would
love to go straight to the point. 'We show love by the boy singing

215

to the girl, he chases her through three reels and then – they dance!'

B. R. Ishara extinguished his cigarette under his bare heel.

'Five thousand feet of film,' he said, 'you could cover by one kiss.'

Raw materials are scarce, both for the dream and its weaving. That camera beneath the quilt at Filmistan Studios is older than the nation herself; the entire film industry has the odour of unplaned wood. With no modern literature in any of the native languages there is also a famine of plots, but happily the government of Mrs Gandhi has not yet put a tax upon plagiarism. Each Hindi production will bear traces of one, or several, box-office spectaculars from the West, with *The Sound of Music* ever uppermost. Or they merely remake their imitations. An Empire endures, too, in borrowed works of Victorian literature. Those mahogany emotions seem to find cease-less response in the Indian soul. There has been an Indian *Oliver Twist,* an Indian *Wuthering Heights* – renamed *Give Your Heart and Receive Only Anguish* – and several versions of *The Hound of the Baskervilles.* At Guru Dutt Films, the proprietor's young assistant is preparing to direct his first feature, *The Woman in White* by Wilkie Collins. The young man said that it would be the fourth remake of that romance.

His employer, Atma Ram, is meanwhile at a story conference beside the sea. Atma Ram is a gentle person who once worked in England with the Shell Film Unit. He and his scenarist sit barefoot on the floor of a small drawing room; beyond its lace curtains are dark rocks and a violet-coloured sea. The writer Dr Rahi Masoon Raza (D.Litt.) is working on seven scripts at once. He removed his pipe from his mouth. 'There is no copyright,' he observed, 'on Shakespeare; we could, if we chose, make *Macbeth.* But we improve on Shakespeare. We do not call him Macbeth, we call him Ranesh.'

The hero is important as in any myth. His name alone initiates a film, he appoints his heroine and rewrites the dialogue to suit himself. The dozen most adored Indian matinee idols are working on as many as 30 productions each – usually in double roles, so that their faces never leave the screen – dealing with them, as Dharmendra does, in two, or sometimes three, eight-hour shifts a day. Dharmendra became a star a decade ago but does not yet feel secure enough to slow down. He dabbed his eyes again, appreciably worsening their condition. 'I sometimes feel ashamed, you know, to be so busy. I ought to be strict, but the producers come and they tell me sad stories. I have promised myself: from next year it will be different. I will make no more than six to eight movies and I will have my Sundays free.'

Production is fitful. The hero is so busy that he can work for each director only a few hours of the month. Often the producer will have raised only sufficient production money to pay for the *mohurat,* the

216

Hindu ceremony which inaugurates the first day's shooting, so certain of Dharmendra's commitments are films abandoned or postponed for want of finance. All day the crowd that collects about him, the children, old men, chaperones fluttering in the electric fans, will include a producer or two entreating Dharmendra's return to a project they have managed to reactivate. There was once a film, *Pakheeza*, which took 10 years to make. 'But unfortunately,' its producer said, 'before we finished shooting, the heroine, Meena Kumari, expired of cirrhosis of the liver.'

Dharmendra was moving on to the next shift of the day. He plunged into his car and thankfully shielded his raw eyes with sunglasses. Before the door could be shut, a supplicant producer had slipped in to join him.

Overwork has not killed him, he says, because he is a Punjabi; he would work with the same intensity on a farm. A Sikh is not musical, however, and Dharmendra finds the song-and-dance sequences trying. He is none the less perfectly content. 'I am the only hero who gives the chance to new girls. With heroines, too, I am very popular.' Here Dharmendra winked.

At home, in the beach mansion he occasionally sees, there is a combined family of his wife's relations and his own, and nine children. Wherever it occurs in India, good fortune creates encampments.

'When I come home late, sometimes I wake them up,' Dharmendra said. 'I go to my wife, I make love to her, I make her happy. I take her with me on my outdoors. I talk with her on the telephone sometimes an hour at once.'

'Does she like you on the movies?'

'She loves me!' he answered radiantly.

The producer who travelled beside him was in fact responsible for *Roop Tera Mastana*, that love-story including inadvertent horse-manure. His silver rim of hair blew down across his face, and English grew a little wild on his tongue. Suddenly he exclaimed: 'He is my actor! He is my brother-in-law! He is my friend! I have three-three four-four relations with him!'

'Three-three four-four relations!' Dharmendra laughed and smote the other on the knee. 'He has influence with the Customs – you bastard! He's a very nice person actually.'

'He is the only he-man in our filum industry!', the producer shouted. 'He is a gift from God! He is God-gift!'

Dharmendra winked. 'He is buttering.'

'He is a God-fearing man!' the producer said.

Outside in the Bombay lanes it was noon. The sky beat full on their moving labyrinth; on the peal, the press, the one-way street of

217

faces in which only dogs can sleep; on the hunger that exists in smells of frying batter; the shifts, the rags, the settled flies, pan-stalls, grey crows, lunatic cycles among the tired, loose fawn velvet of the wandering cows, the slums old as mud and slums newly-built of brilliant yellow straw; the sun revealed all of the colliding horizon, and the reason why even Dharmendra can never feel safe enough to stop working.

The situation of a heroine is peculiar – to the Indian mind, normal. Worshipped, they are still somehow obliquely disregarded. On the sets with their jewels and persistent head-colds, they seem to occupy a kind of rheumy purdah regulated by their mothers, their aunts or governesses. Dharmendra's wink was to suggest, however, that this chaperonage need not be absolute.

Asha Parekh, his latest co-star, has a face somewhat too flat for perfection; the halves of her sari release evidence of an appetite not stinted. She got into pictures by way of traditional dance which, somewhat heavily, she still executes. 'I was Ramonen Sagar's first heroine,' she says. 'And Premod Chakravarty's, and these movies went up woosh like a sputnik. The producers call me The Lucky Star.'

Between an Indian and his screen heroine, complicated emotions flow. 'They want to marry me or be my brother. I get a lot of letters that say, "Marry me or I'll murder you." There was a Chinaman!' Her kohl-blackened eyes wriggle with the memory. 'He sat outside my gate for six months. My servants gave him money to go away and he got out his little penknife at them. I used to see his little Chinky eyes looking at me. And there was an Army officer, a Major Gupta, and a gentleman from Bihar who came with *veni,* the flowers that a bride will wear in her hair. There is one crazy guy who sits by the dictionary each week and writes to me, He is a MA BA(Econ)LL.B. My Mummy says, "Do not try your eyes with reading such things".'

Miss Parekh's house, off a clamorous alleyway in Santa Cruz, is the marvel of the film colony. A semi-circle of rooms half-open to the beach, its mock stonework, narrow interstices and naked fuse-boxes give it somewhat the air of a ruined Welsh castle keep. Jets, as they approach Bombay, almost touch the palms encircling it, so that the very trees seem to shriek. Here The Lucky Star lives, with her father and her mother, a considerable lady in white, wearing a bunch of keys. The message of the keys is clear – few swains could brave the stardom and the obedience which she still owes to her parents; she seems to indulge no sensual tastes stronger than the pickles of her native Gujerat. Only when she comes downstairs, decorated for the premiere, can one see what became of the wealth that was formerly the princes'. At her ears, her wrists, her throat, she pulses with 18-carat gold.

If an important star signs to a production for five lakhs of rupees – a lakh is £5,000 – he will then probably receive 12 lakhs more 'in black' as money is called, which will not be declared to the Income Tax authorities. Life in the Bombay movie colony is seldom dull, thanks to the Revenue Department's 'Enforcement Squad', which conducts sudden raids upon the homes of the stars, ripping out walls and floors, sometimes exchanging pistol-shots with those attempting to make off with cash-books in speeding-cars.

S.R. Mehta is a financier – self-evidently so, for he sits in a darkened room in Bombay scrutinising cheques, touching a bell under his foot for a servant to bring in more or take away those he has scrutinised. S.R. Mehta is one of those in Indian business who finds the film business unstable.

'The picture is shown in the dark,' said S.R. Mehta. 'Also, they produce in the dark!'

He was visibly affected at the recollection of a producer who approached him for finance, and who was revealed by subsequent investigations to be a Bombay waterfront crook.

'Producers! They are nincompoops!' said S.R. Mehta warmly. 'Night is day to them and day is night. They do not rise until the afternoon!'

He touched the bell; a servant brought in more cheques; S.R. Mehta studied them.

'Stars! Consider Kishor Kumar the play-back-singer!' S.R. Mehta was referring to the owner of the unearthly voice dubbed over Dharmendra's and almost every other unmusical screen idol's. 'He is paid a lakh of rupees to sing one song! When he is working at the studios,' said S.R. Mehta incredulously, 'he goes to his house seven miles away just to make water!'

Not everyone in the industry is content with the standard it sets Sheik Mukhtar, one of the few character actors – 'I am more of Vallace Beery than Wictor McLaglen – shuts his eyes in simultaneous contempt for the modern screen and rapture for his idols in Hollywood.

'Clark Gable! Paul Muni! I have looked at them from all the angles God has given! Such handsome and beautiful personalities! *Rebecca – The Informer – va va subhanallah! Citizen Kane – Rear Vindow – va va – Goodbye Mr Chip!* I have come out of the cinema and I have vept! I have felt God has forgiven me my six-months sins! They have only to laugh and they fill the screen. Hallyvood! I would not go there! I hate that place! Sacks and voilance! When I see that *Easy Rider,* I want to throw my shoe at the screen! Charles Laughton – va va – *Mutiny on the Bounty* – va *subhanallah!* Marlon Brando! He have voice like that of crow! That Trafor Howard! I send him to kindergarten to learn how to speak! When I hear they are making new *Goodbye Mr Chip,* I know it will be nothing. That one was intended by God! Robert Donat! Va va va!'

In Bombay, there are real directors to be found languishing in crystal, silver paper and scattered stage-impedimenta that was auctioned off by the British Empire. Their burden is considerable. As well as the vanishing heroes, the bronchial heroines, the scuttling producers, there are financiers who, wishing the film to show a tax-loss, will seize it and show it half-finished. Even as they direct they are surrounded by the corpses of colleagues who dared move an inch from the common formula; yet still they direct. Is it slow death in compromise or nourishment on some queer, incorruptable seed of vocation? Dharmendra works the afternoon shift for Vijay Anand, who is tall, studious, sensitive and winningly honest about his perpetual compromise. 'Total satisfaction is not possible,' Vijay Anand says. 'Satisfaction in certain sequences is possible.'

Disgust transfigures the face of Hrishikesh Mukherjee recalling some of the trash he has to shoot. 'I am a prostitute!' he snaps; the betel nut he is chewing shoots from one cheek to the other; his very pith-helmet seems provoked. On the contrary, 'Rishi' is the most senior and principled of Hindi directors, whose contempt of the general mould has often been expressed in cheap films about real people. He works with a testy benevolence which makes him adored by his four assistants and sometimes gives a jolt to his star. Lately he was irked by Rajesh Kanna, the busiest of male juveniles. 'He arrived three, four hours late! I wrote him an open letter. "I don't care about you, get off the set, get out!" '

Even Rishi must occasionally work on something that appals him. Today he is completing *Phir Kab Milogi* (When Will You Meet Me Again?), an addition to the existing burden of romances of mistaken identity based circuitously on an O. Henry story which for different reasons has been seven years in production.

To pep up the final sequences, Rishi has added a guest appearance by the great Dilip Kumar. Kumar plays a dashing young horseman; his horse-riding is the subject of this afternoon's sequence in parkland outside Bombay. Rishi has left the horseriding scene to his four assistants and retired to play chess, near a little group of technician's wives, mothers and aunts.

'I am basically,' Rishi said, 'an angry man; I am terribly tortured, really.'

He paused as the 'horseman' approached. Dilip Kumar in an embroidered costume sat astride a saddle mounted on the broad boot of an old Packard convertible; the cameraman was lashed to its running-board, and, at all angles, in painful contortions as of worship, other men hung with sheets of tinfoil to augment the sunlight upon the face of the hero.

Among the onlookers was Reanjan, the Indian Errol Flynn. He is a tiny, smiling, learned walnut of a man in a swaggering Panama. In his day he did all his own stunts, even wrestling with wild beasts. 'My mother said, "If you are killed fighting a lion, I don't mind".'

Rishi pointed to the old man who was looking after the riding whips and picking his feet.

'For directing a picture I am paid two lakhs of rupees [£10,000]. He is paid fifteen rupees [60p] a day. We spend the most of every day together. Why he cannot share my joys? Why I cannot share his sorrows? How can I speak of standards when those in the country do not have enough food? How can I press the demand that there should be ten art theatres in every city when there is drought in Maharashtara and in Bihar?'

He was joined under the tree by Dilip Kumar's brother, Nasir Khan, a man as mild and soft as a baby, smoking a pipe. Nasir was himself a film hero once, before alopecia took every hair from his body.

'I have received the President's Medal for two, three years,' Rishi said. His face showed no reverence for this, the single accolade from Government to cinema industry. 'The last time, I did not even trouble to collect it.'

'There is a cash award, too,' Nasir Khan reminded him.

'Yes,' Rishi said disgustedly. 'In savings certificates!'

Mainly at the spur of Rishi's irritation, the Indian Government has set up a Film Finance Corporation for low-budget projects. Even the kiss will be legalised – should the report which recommends it ever find its way out of Parliament. Rishi himself has made a film about cancer that was a success. Truth remains, none the less, a volatile ingredient. Both men under the tree fell silent at the memory of what befell Raj Kapoor. He is the Indian D.W. Griffith and the Indian Charlie Chaplin; these elements he injudiciously mixed in the spectacular *Mera Naam Joker,* the cast of which included Dharmendra and an entire Russian circus. It died, gigantically, for one mistake. It had an unhappy ending.

'Once when I was acting,' said Nasir Khan, 'the Government wanted to deport me to Pakistan because my family are Pathans. I was then making seventeen pictures. I had to complete them in seventeen days. I saw only the windows of the car between the studios.'

That set Rishi off again about heroes. 'They do three shifts a day. They come on to the set and do not know at which film they are! I say, "You are no use to me in this condition. Do your work!"'

221

'They make fifteen,' said Nasir Khan, 'in the hope that one will click.'

'It is a vicious circle,' said Rishi morosely.

'Only a Bengali would put it like that,' Nasir Khan told him.

'It is a vicous *centre*,' Rishi said.

Darkness intensifies the raw wood smells round the studio and the mist of the giant fans. Dharmendra's afternoon shift has far advanced. His role now is of a husband who has sworn to abstain from his wife, a condition to which the red eyes lend credence. He waits for hours against a stage-wall, beyond which is a sunken bath filled with water the colour of pale ale. There is a bedroom, too, with some carpenters asleep on the quilt. During an interlude, Dharmendra crosses the yard to complete some dubbing on another production – his third today. The director Vijay Anand, meanwhile, lies back on a sofa. His film has no title yet. It is a story without embellishment, without any madness, he said, just a story of a husband and a wife.

Another set is entirely mirrors; shards that leap and flash around two buccaneers fighting with a pasteboard clap of weaponry in an almost overpowering aroma of feet. The pair of houris in orange drawers who, somewhat drily, attend them, turn out to be English girls, Penny and Rowena, recruited by a talent scout at Stiffles', the hippy boarding house. Neither has relished the attentions of the studio makeup-men.

'First they stuck cotton wool down our fronts,' Penny said.

'Then they threw water over us,' Rowena added peevishly. 'Of course they had to do that by hand.'

'We've got our money put up anyway; forty to sixty rupees a day and a rupee for the canteen.' Penny indicated the prancing pirate whose fans equal, at least, the population of her native Home Counties. 'So now we have to drape ourselves across the throne and kiss Fat Freddy's feet.'

Asha Parekh is appearing in a programme of traditional dance. She wears a Moghul costume, the jewel-encrusted bridle of which so constricts her abundant frame that her breasts assume the sudden defiance of diverging torpedoes; she performs without the benefit of intense rehearsal, giving many huge sniffs. As she leaves the stage, an admirer is waiting. So is her mother. The boy has a gift for her, a pen that is also a torch. His name and address are wrapped round it, in English and in Hindi. His thin frame, proffering this, shakes.

'Thank you,' The Lucky Star said coldly.

And Dharmendra may now go home. To what? All his joint family are asleep. In the feeling of release from lights and sweated powder, one may not in any case desire the society of nine children. There is a chair, to sit down. There are the brothels of Bombay, bright gashes among the sleeping limbs of night, with tiled walls, yellow beer and the song of a creaking harmonium. There is Scotch whisky, into the small hours. Friends who bear Dharmendra company in this recreation are known as *chamchas*– spoons.

The set is prepared for shooting tomorrow, a Sunday. It is a pattern of huge spheres, such as people of the past believed would constitute the future; a mad laboratory with a Victorian spiral-stair, which would all seem unrelated to Vijay Anand's simple dream of husband and wife. The director himself is lounging nearby.

'The husband is also a scientist,' he explained. 'He makes some supernatural experiments.'

At Rishi's location, Dilip Kumar got down from his mount on the Packard. He has been a star of the Hindi cinema for a phenomenal time – 25 years, but, at almost 50, is still dashing: India's John Wayne. He peeled off one curl of his false moustache, then the other.

'Our industry,' he said, 'is related to the condition of the whole country. I told Mr Nehru so once. I told him, there is no point in having first-class roads if you have bad houses or first-class education if your people are starving. You cannot have one thing in a vacuum. So you cannot have fine films here.'

A servant knelt before him and began to wash his feet.

'It is necessary only to believe,' said Dilip Kumar, 'that all will some day improve together, and therefore I should not worry over the circumstance that my work does not bear the ultimate stamp of merit.'

'All they want,' Rishi said bitterly, 'is four hours of make-believe.'

'Four hours of make-believe!' Nasir Khan exclaimed. 'I would call it four hours of redemption!'

1972

223

PART FOUR

Personal

Starring with Pharos and Miss Radar

When my fat Uncle Phil became landlord of the Star Hotel, a gloomy grey stone pub in Ryde, Isle of Wight, he did not foresee the duty that would devolve on him in addition to pulling pints, 'bottling up' and throwing drunks out into Ryde High Street. Next door to the Star stood the Commodore, largest of Ryde's three cinemas, a sumptuous place with a ticket office shaped like the sterncastle of Nelson's *Victory*. As well as its film programme, the Commodore presented regular variety shows, music hall, opera and, each November to February, the most lavish pantomime to be seen on the Isle of Wight. Uncle Phil's Star Hotel, for all its (and Uncle Phil's) lugubriousness, was where pantomime people from the Commodore always stayed.

My lovely cousin Dina first told me of Uncle Phil's new occupation as theatrical landlord, somewhere around 1953. 'We've got Leon Cortez staying with us,' she whispered to me through the Off Sales hatch. 'And some of the Vesta Beecher Dancers are in the Snug.'

I imagined Leon Cortez to resemble the conqueror of Mexico, striding the Star's Dettol-impregnated corridors in breastplate, knee-boots and treacherous Spanish beard. As I learned with disappointment, going in to see *Cinderella* on Uncle Phil's permanent free pass, he was a Cockney comedian who wore a small trilby hat, even as Buttons, and bawled out the same radio show catch phrase: 'You're higgerant!' But the Vesta Beecher Dancers were wonderful. To reach the stage, each of them slid down a tightrope from above the Dress Circle. They then sang 'All The Nice Girls Love A Sailor', high kicking along a special walkway beyond the orchestra pit. For the second 'Ship ahoy!' they substituted 'Naughty boy!' wagging their forefingers reprovingly. I felt certain one of them – if not all of them – must be pointing straight at me.

Pantomime and pre-pubic sexual excitement had been synonymous for me since, as a toddler in arms, I was carried into the circle of the London Hippodrome and looked down at a stage filled with half naked men, flinging pale pink women up into the air and catching them. Dandini in *Cinderella* became the cynosure of my fantasies. Sex to a child is fascinating puzzlement. What character could be more transfixing a puzzle than that jaunty figure, ostensibly male yet obviously female, in feathered hat and thigh-slapping gauntlets and

227

nothing below a foreshortened doublet but long, active, thigh-booted legs?

It was my longing to meet Dandini – and the equally compulsive all female 'Boys and Girls of the Village' – which, time and again, led me to the same exhibitionistic folly. Midway through each Commodore pantomime, when the chief comic character advanced to the footlights and invited children from the audience to go up on the stage, I would be foremost in the pounding rush down the centre aisle.

I never saw Dandini but Dandini, assuredly, saw me, turned into an unwitting stooge by a cracked and leering orange-pancaked face thrust down close to mine, or – horror of horrors! – hoisted up by strange hands to roll over a set of acrobat's bars. So mortified was I by my performance that when the acrobat tried to give me a prize, I felt I must say I didn't deserve one. To his roguish 'Do you like pink rock?' I tried to answer both 'Yes' and 'No, that's all right . . .' thus creating one of the show's best comedy lines.

'Yes thank you no!' my inquisitor repeated, as laughter rattled out of the huge dark with its tiara of green Exit signs. *'That's* a funny thing to say, isn't it, ladies and gentlemen? "Yes thank you no!" '

At the Star Hotel, I did not meet Dandini or, for that matter, Prince Charming. I only met Bobby Howes and Ruby Murray and Semprini and the Three Monarchs and a boys' choir, mysteriously added to the plot of *Mother Goose*. Upstairs in Uncle Phil's rather grim sitting room, I was once sent to fetch a gin and tonic for Joan Hurley the comedienne, currently appearing as an Ugly Sister. A serious, even morose woman, she seemed far from the glorious personage who, on stage the previous night, had removed layer after layer of vests and striped bloomers, each layer revealing a placard inscribed 'No Coupons!' or 'Blimey!' or 'I Can 'ear Yer!'

Between shows, the stars kept to their rooms or withdrew into the downstairs bar where I could not follow them. My cousin Dina, who worked in the Saloon, collected their autographs for me as I waited at the Off Sales hatch. She would sidle up in her barmaid's black dress – she was all of 14 – talking from the side of her mouth as if we were both engaged in espionage. 'Richard Murdoch's in the Snug. He's ordered a pink gin and a Tio Pepe. Give me your book quickly. And if you make a sound, I'll *pulverise* you.'

Pharos and Miss Radar first occurred in this way, as a scribble across one light green page of my autograph book. I did not see them in the flesh until halfway through a highly enjoyable performance of *Jack and the Beanstalk*, when the plot was abruptly suspended and Pharos and Miss Radar walked out on to an empty stage. Pharos was a neat gentleman with a goatee beard, wearing tails and an opera cape. Miss Radar was a slim woman in a long silver dress, conventionally elegant in every detail save for the short pole and black radar scanner fixed to the top of her head.

I had seen mind reading and telepathy acts before but never one so bizarre yet elegant. Pharos, speaking in what seemed to my childish ear an exotic Levantine accent, introduced Miss Radar as a being of supernatural origins whom he alone, exercising great persuasion, might persuade, just this once, to demonstrate her powers. Pharos would then blindfold Miss Radar with two pieces of baker's dough and a white bandage. People from the audience would be brought up on to the stage and asked to lend various personal items, like watches and lighters, to Pharos. Turning to his partner, he would then command 'Scan.' Sure enough, the scanner on top of Miss Radar's head would slowly begin to revolve.

Miss Radar would then tell Pharos what article he had borrowed from each audience volunteer, and answer various questions about their dress and appearance. The secret was, of course, not radar but a fairly simple verbal code. 'Can you tell me what this is?' would mean a watch. 'I wonder if you can tell me what this is?' might mean a handkerchief. The tension came from Pharos' cut glass formality, preserved until his final and climactic question to Miss Radar: 'Can you tell me, please, where this gentleman was born?'

I was able to see *Jack and the Beanstalk* an indefinite number of times, on Uncle Phil's free pass. I felt sure that Pharos and Miss Radar had noticed me, especially after I approached Pharos, in Abell's Gift shop on Ryde Esplanade, and asked him for a second autograph. 'By all means,' he said tersely, signing for himself and a silent and scannerless Miss Radar. I did not at the time reflect that Abell's Gift Shop was an odd place to have found them, among the postcards and cheap souvenirs.

In the end, my free ticket brought me a seat in the very centre of the Commodore front row. When Pharos selected his audience volunteers – which he did by tossing out ping-pong balls for people to catch – I was directly in his sight-line. I caught his eye and, audaciously, mouthed 'Here!' He threw the ping-pong ball directly into my cupped hands.

I was last of the group to be subjected to Miss Radar's telepathic power. As further proof of Pharos' inscrutable patronage, I also was the one chosen to apply the baker's dough to Miss Radar's eyes before he blindfolded her. I remember her finely-pencilled eyebrows, the little worry cleft at the bridge of her nose, the wonderful scent she exuded of theatres, glamour and late night. I remember how perfectly pleasant to it was to stand there waiting my turn, the footlights ablaze beside me like a white, fiery ditch and nothing beyond but tranquil emptiness. I must have understood that performance at its best is a rather private thing.

'. . . and lastly,' Pharos said, guiding me courteously downstage.
'Can you tell me where this young gentleman was born?'

And Miss Radar, with a shrug of her silver shoulders, prefiguring
the applause to come, replied: 'In bed!'

1982

On a Tide of Violence

Those who grew up in the fifties probably remember, as I do, the great hush that seemed to enfold the world. Time itself seemed to be running down to a stop. The Festival of Britain, the Coronation, the Vauxhall Velox car, the aircraft carrier cross-sectioned in my *Eagle* comic, each represented the apogee of existence: from here, though I myself still had to grow up, there was no real point in trying. I remember that sensation clearly at the age of 11, walking in sunshine down a steep hill strewn with sticky buds. My one regret was that 'history' had taken place before I could remember. I was sorry to have missed those days, penned up in all their colour and clamour behind 'the War'. I wished I had seen the kings and knights, the feasts and coaching-inns. But I was thankful to be here in 1954, with the sun, the sticky buds, not back there, being killed in so many horrible, sudden ways.

Like most children, I was afraid of the dark. I imagined, lying in bed, that 'murderers', were coming up the stairs. In time, I was comforted to realise my own insignificance. Who would want to be bothered to murder me? Murderers, I saw thankfully, belonged to a distant, highly idiosyncratic class, like Christie, or Ruth Ellis, the 'Mews Murderess' whose execution took place just before our school Assembly. I know because a boy came up to me, looked at his watch and said, 'That's the end of Ruth Ellis'. Obscurely but powerfully, I felt the night was safe again.

Now I know it is my destiny, and yours, to live in a world grown infinitely more terrifying than childhood's worst nightmares. I know that, on the contrary, almost anybody can be bothered to murder me. The victims of murder are not, as 20 years ago, a blurry-faced species, found generally 'on waste ground'. Their faces are terribly clear and unlike their fate. There is the face of the 10-year-old paper boy, tied up and shotgunned in a dew-dappled English village. There is the face of the smart London girl, abducted and murdered as she slipped out in her Mini for late-night shopping. There is the face of the judge, the antique-dealer, the opera singer, the man who co-founded *The Guinness Book of Records*. Each was a dreadful, memorable case. Yet who today can put a name to any of the victims I have mentioned?

Amnesia protects, but also threatens us all. Until I began to write, I had forgotten that, in the past three years, two people close to me have been attacked by an intruder and might have been killed. My response in each case was, I think, sensible and logical; it was to hustle the victim with all speed from the present into the future. The strangest symptom, I now see, was my vehement swearing to silence of everyone concerned. Suffering, however innocent, carries a stigma with it. A president, a pope, can far less afford to admit such disgrace. Huge forces are employed instead to persuade us the outrage has not mattered. And so, less than a week after what happened in St Peter's Square, I found myself believing it had not really mattered.

We speak of civilisations that 'toppled'; of the 'fall' of Athens or Rome; of a 'Dark Age', dropped over Europe like a sack. We choose not to recognise that, wherever chaos and terror have triumphed, it was slowly, through the bewildered acquiescence of millions of people like ourselves. They, too, tried not to worry; to get on with life. They moved, as we are moving, unconsciously with the tide of murder, from disbelieving horror to dazed unshockability.

The special paradox of our Dark Age is that it should have grown in the tatters of an era when 'peace' and 'love' were words in serious, widespread use. Today's urban terrorist wears the blue jeans and amulets of yesterday's smiling liberal. The Maze 'hunger strikers', those empty, almost ectoplasmic faces, wear their hair long the way young men did as a plea for tolerance and a declaration of non-violence. The contagion took root, not in Dallas in 1963 but in California, in 1969. We are menaced, not by the children of Marx but of Manson.

Our blindness is increased by our gigantic power of sight, through television: by habituation to terrible sights and, equally, by the growing adeptness of those responsible in hiding their crimes within language of perverted blandness. It strikes no one as strange any more when three madmen, machine-gunning an airport lounge, call themselves a 'popular front'; when a hostage is butchered by a 'people's court'; when those who use children to plant explosive term themselves 'freedom fighters'; when innocent shopping crowds are 'targets'; or when the 'Provisional' IRA, after ambushing a milk float, claim 'responsibility'.

In the age of the bloody mind, I can feel my own mind growing as bloody as the next. When I read that a bomb-maker has blown himself up, I feel quiet satisfaction at Fate's occasional symmetry. Not only to IRA terrorists but also muggers, vandals and those who cause suffering with their callous, self-righteous 'industrial action', I wish the corrective of actual physical pain. I have come to believe in the death penalty, as a deterrent to those many crimes based on pure cowardice, and to eradicate – as has been justly done before –

self-evident, unmitigated evil. I remember the words of Dr Herrema, the Dutchman whose intellectual toughness all but mesmerised his Irish kidnappers. 'Don't you realise?' he asked them at one point. 'These conditions are worse than in Belsen.'

As a child, my worst nightmare featured men wearing hoods, with holes cut for their eyes and mouths. The fifties melted them at dawn, into sun and sticky buds. The eighties legitimise them, slow-marching in Ulster. They are death embodied – perhaps yours, perhaps mine. I myself fear death as much as in childhood. But I see now what people throughout 'history' must have seen in their own terror times: that death can be something you choose. It is preferable to the suffering of my family, or to life in any world where the hooded ones hold power.

1981

Red, White and Blue in Manhattan

Flinging in the rain

I counted twelve of them in one corpse-strewn block between 85th and 86th Street: poor little draggled shapes trampled on the sidewalks or kicked into the gutter, their fragile wings crumpled, their brittle spines bent and protruding. The saddest orphan of a New York storm is the New Yorker's puny, pusillanimous umbrella.

This city of boundless technological expertise apparently can construct no better protection against its gargantuan cloudbursts than a cheap, dismal melange of too-prompt spring and too-accessible spike whose behaviour under stress resembles nothing so much as a feeble-minded and hysterical bird. Like a pigeon or senile parrot, the New York umbrella has only two basic reactions. The first is to be startled into premature flight. The second is to turn inside-out from heart failure. Small wonder that so few receive anything approaching decent burial.

In general America's best products are clothes and devices that shield one from the elements. America bows to no one in the manufacture of woollen jackets, fleece-lined boots, ski coats, mittens, goggles, groundsheets and windsurfing shoes.

But let Manhattan start sending down the storms that are not so much drops as lumps and crowbars of rain, and the national weakness declares itself. Grown men stumble along, trying vainly to shelter under bucking scraps of black cloth already pulverised into grotesque shapes or extruding rods more lethal than Boadicea's chariot-wheels. Smart women cower under exiguous coloured canopies that positively romp for joy at their power to ruin hairstyles or sabotage shoes. At corners, savage collisions – sometimes out-and-out fights – erupt between tormented souls goaded to frenzy by these instruments of betrayal and self-loathing.

New Yorkers, in their deepest psyche, must hate and despise the umbrella. If this were not so, umbrellas would be manufactured from stout American timber and hardy American fabric, and offered proudly for sale in stores alongside work shirts and boots. They would not be these furtive, dwarfish objects, most commonly obtained from street hucksters who spring up as instantly as the showers. One I have seen on Fifth Avenue seems not to possess English even as a second language: his chant of 'ombray-la, ombray-la' sounds like some invocation to voodoo. I would not suppose that man to be much interested in repairs or after-sales service.

Most New York umbrellas proclaim their unreliability even as they lie there on the peddler's mat. There is, however, an insidious model with certain superficial resemblances to the British multi-coloured golf umbrella – the kind that, in its pure, steel-shafted form, can withstand the fiercest gales sweeping over Gleneagles. Duped by the colours and metal stem, I bought one of these impostors during a Tribeca monsoon. I realised my mistake as soon as I tried to roll it up. You cannot, of course, roll up a New York umbrella. You can only grab at it, twist and bunch and stuff it round like the leg of one garish gaiter. Within two days it had given up the ghost of whatever golf was ever in it: I abandoned it to the sidewalk charnel house without a qualm.

It is not just for theatre that New Yorkers flock to London, I now realise: it is also for James Smith's splendid Victorian gold and glass umbrella emporium on New Oxford Street. I have seen them there often enough, ogling the City Gent models with whangee handles, the rainbow-hued golf umbrellas, the great monochrome fishing umbrellas, not to mention the silver-topped canes, ebony cudgels, even swordsticks. ' . . . yes, sir, *just* like the one Sherlock Holmes used,' the assistants murmur. 'I believe they *are* illegal in many parts of the United States . . .'

Each time the TV weathermen start grinning weakly and mentioning 'some precipitation', I am tempted to write home for my good old golf umbrella with its trusty Fox frame. Then I reflect that New York cannot long permit any vacuum; that, some day soon, a book will appear entitled *Tough Times Don't Last But Tough Umbrellas Should,* that 'real' umbrella shops will appear down in SoHo and the Village, and classes in umbrella-rolling be begun on spaces once occupied by Yoga. (The two might even be combined.)

Meanwhile, the skies are darkening. From a Fifth Avenue corner, I can hear that voodoo chant, 'ombray-la, ombray-la', mingled with the falsely cheerful click of many a spring-loaded handle. Once again, the casualties are bound to be tremendous.

Waiter, there's a ham in my soup

The truest thing I have heard about eating out in New York was said by an editor of *Rolling Stone,* after the recitation was over and the menus had been melodramatically snatched away. 'There are no more waiters left in this town,' she remarked glumly. 'They're all actors now.'

The complaint will be familiar if you have ever dined in those smart little restaurants, south of Houston Street, where the bar, visible through a large picture window, already reveals people in poses as multifarious as the first number in *South Pacific*. Such establishments have exaggeratedly modest and artless names like 'Bumbo's – A Seafood Place', emphasising that no one within serves food and drink as a first choice of career. The aura aimed at is that of theatre workshop or rock rehearsal room. The very cashier often seems only minutes away from breaking out on to Broadway.

You have passed the chorus-line bar, into the Stygian dark beyond, and are gathered with friends around a table which, in fairness, will probably be laid with a crisp pink cloth, festive with silverware, a carnation and abundant sesame breadsticks. It is, for me, the best part of any meal – the sitting down, the drawing close, the study of menus at leisure while breadsticks snap and talk matures deliciously into conversation. This is precisely the moment when your waiter arrives, interrupts whoever is talking and asks if he can run through the specials they have on tonight.

'Specials' are the main reason that so many New York waiters come on as cabaret stars. The theory is that restaurant dishes will seem more elegant if recited as a dramatic monologue. It is an idea born of nothing but the race for gastronomic trendiness. Everyone I know in New York finds the 'specials' interlude unnecessary and annoying. The consequence is particularly sad for a city whose cuisine was once famous for combining the fantastically varied with the gloriously matter-of-fact. A meaningless ritual is begetting its own meaningless food.

One would imagine a 'special' to be some simple peasant dish, like cassoulet, run up by the chef in an excess of high spirits and sold off in generous job lots so that people can enjoy it fresh. 'Special' in this context, however, refers chiefly to price – a detail often omitted from your waiter's monologue. It also denotes something so far from the mainstream of good cooking that its name alone will be incomprehensible. Hence the rambling verbal footnotes. ' . . . that's sautéd with mushrooms in a white wine sauce and served on a bed of fluffy rice with a *pisse-en-lit* salad . . .' (I do not exaggerate. That's what the pretentious places call dandelions.)

The list is always long, imposing the dual strain of memorising half a dozen arcane recipes while simultaneously maintaining one's face in the required look of suspended greed. Generally, by the time the recitation ends, you have forgotten everything but the *pisse-en-lit* salad: you can only watch your neighbour order, then, mutter, 'I'll have that, too.' The result is apt to be not a surprise so much as an ambush.

I have a nostalgic early memory of New York waiters as elderly men in short, mustard-coloured jackets, lugubriously but kindly

236

explaining how my choice of entrée would trigger off entitlements in *hors d'oeuvres* and dessert. Those comforting, flat-footed figures seem to have disappeared as completely as the wonderful dolloping New York portions of yesteryear. That which is sautéed in white wine sauce as a rule would be hard put to fill a dessert spoon. Scallops form frugal foursomes on sheets of raddichio *trompe l'oeil.* Even the hamburgers come naked and ashamed.

Catering in America has, admittedly, always owed a powerful debt to show business. In my time, I have sat in restaurants decorated to resemble Swiss chalets, enchanted grottoes and millionaires' railroad cars; I have been waited on by people dressed as cowgirls, twenties vamps, Italian tenors and 18th century highwaymen. I have watched counterhands in ordinary luncheonettes act out cathartic dramas with a compression of dialogue that Samuel Beckett would envy. Whatever the visual or verbal extravagance might have been, the keynote was always steely, speedy professionalism.

Your thespian waiter, by contrast, often affects a bobbing *faux naiveté* – 'Oh-oh! I just *knew* I'd leave out the Veal Parmigiana!' – and seldom has a concentration span lasting much beyond his initial big number. The misanthropic – no doubt disappointed by some recent audition – assail their clients with subtle manifestations of the Theatre of Cruelty. I am thinking of a particular Upper West side bistro, where the menu tells you who designed the waiters' shirts. I have never, in the course of one meal, been bludgeoned by so many raised eyebrows and petulant tosses of the head. Eventually, our waiter retired some distance with his colleagues for what looked like a tap dance rehearsal. My companion, having tried to attract his notice by all normal means, tentatively raised an arm. Our waiter replied by raising his own arm satirically.

I know from experience that it is tough being a waiter, and that one of the job's few unalloyed pleasures is to spoil a customer's story on the very punch-line. I realise that to earn tips in the labyrinthine hierarchy of New York restaurants, a waiter must project his personality by any possible means. My objections founder when, as often happens, I see specials recited with charm or notable cunning. I remember once overhearing a Sardi's waiter sell one special to an entire table, using the same blend of threat and promise that has made the restaurant itself immortal. 'It's an acquired taste . . .' he said silkily. 'Personally, I *love* it . . .' I am likewise all ears in a little trattoria on 81st Street where the pudgy-nosed young head waiter can make the night's specials sound like names of people who will be joining you in a jewel heist tomorrow.

Nostalgia is always a banana skin. I thought I had discovered a true old-fashioned New York waiter recently, at an elderly restaurant high on Madison Avenue. He wore a mustard-coloured jacket; he was, indeed, grey-haired, lugubrious and kindly as he explained the distinction between the western omelette and the Spanish. He took our order and left us with the heavily quiet tread of a Benedictine on the way to evensong. I remarked to my friend how nice it was to meet a waiter who wasn't an actor, and what a quiet, restful place this was.

During our meal, a commotion broke out at the cash register. There was shouting, banging glass and what sounded like a pistol shot. Almost at once, a police car slewed across the pavement before our eyes and four leathery officers ran in. A man in a blue raincoat accompanied them outside, talked to them for a few moments and was then abruptly hurled against the police car and searched. Paramedics arrived with a trolley and straitjacket. The man was overpowered, trussed, laid on the trolley feet uppermost, and removed. We saw it all through the window as we finished our omelettes, surrounded by a hubbub of Spanish-speaking kitchen workers.

Our waiter alone did not pause to stare or comment, but continued plying his fatalistic route, soliloquising in the voice of one long inured to anything that could happen around here. 'Crazier and crazier it gets . . . Guy stabs himself first, in the men's room, then *he* calls the cops . . . Now there's blood all over the men's room. Can I bring you folks some coffee or dessert?'

He was, of course, a consummate performer. The difference was that, after a long diet of trendy prima donnas, we had stumbled on King Lear.

Double-insulated Hokum

Last summer when we lived in a loft near Chinatown, surrounded by semi-pornographic sculpture, plagued by heat and roaches and shaken by heavy trucks thundering below to the Holland Tunnel, I would sometimes feel the wellspring of literary inspiration start to fail. In time, I evolved a remedy more effective than simply sitting, sweating and raving. I would seize a big, red, tasteless New York apple, pour myself a glass of salt-free seltzer, switch on the TV set and await the galvanic presence of Stephen R. Pacca.

Stephen R. Pacca is not an evangelist. He is president of the Aalco double glazing company of Lodi, New Jersey. He is a thickset, Sicilian-looking man crammed into a mid-seventies suit as rigidly-contoured as one of his own window frames. Like many another self-made American businessman, Stephen R. Pacca appears on TV to sell his own product, despite being not naturally endowed with what one might call thespian grace. In looks and style, Mr Pacca may have his shortcomings. But he can sell double-glazed window units like P.T. Barnum.

Stephen R. Pacca's oratorical power lies in his ability to speak from one corner of his mouth, gangster-style, while simultaneously bellowing as if hailing the foretop. 'Home-owners! Don't throw money out of old windows on high heating and cooling bills . . .' Beside him, a bespangled showgirl points to an 'old' – ie, not an Aalco – window, open to emit a fluttering blizzard of squandered dollar bills.

The efficacy of Aalco windows is then demonstrated by a series of vaudeville stunts which Barnum might have envied. For the line 'Aalco windows end draughts,' Mr Pacca is filmed on an airfield, standing between a glass-walled telephone box, with candles lit inside it, and a ferociously revving small plane. 'Even a propellor's power,' screams a tousled Stephen R. Pacca, 'cannot blow out these candles!' Cut to Mr Pacca, inside again, watching a circus fire-eater breathe flame at the same telephone box, wherein his showgirl assistant now theatrically cowers. 'Even a blast of fire,' he shouts triumphantly, 'cannot penetrate Aalco's famous double-insulated glass!

'Aalco windows end painting,' rasps Stephen R. Pacca, in close-up now. Behind him stands the showgirl, in classic Paris Lido pose, holding an outsize paintbrush. 'Throw away your paintbrushes!' The girl casts it aside. ' . . . Free alarm system with your order.' The alarm buzzer is heard. The burglar – a masked showgirl – is seen, roguishly recoiling. 'No money down! A hundred per cent financing!' The financial inducements are, indeed, so numerous that Mr Pacca can get through them only by the expedient of drawing no more breath. 'For every five windows you buy you get the sixth one free buy now and receive a free colour TV with your order call now for free estimate and free quartz watch!'

Tired writers can be revived by the spectacle of someone else working even more furiously hard. Last summer in SoHo, when I felt my resolution stiffen anew, and returned to my typewriter above the Holland Tunnel rat-run, it would frequently be thanks to Stephen R. Pacca's manic, contagious energy.

The doyen of these do-it-yourself TV hucksters is, of course, Frank Perdue, a chicken mogul whose fame derives in part from his eerie resemblance to the fowls he purveys. Frank Perdue's TV commercials, starring himself, have been shown for many years and now reach a level of artfulness rivalled only by the soft drink companies. An abrasive, humourless multimillionaire in private, Mr Perdue makes his TV persona folksy and jovial. In one ad, we see the chicken mogul – who is almost supernaturally lean and bald – standing in a tuxedo at the door of an elegant town house, winking saucily as several beautiful young girls arrive to sample his 'oven stuffers'. In another, he appears dressed as a hot dog seller, engaged in playful badinage with children about his fortuitously named 'Perdue Franks'.

The scripts are little masterpieces of cornpone good sense. 'The

Federal Food and Drug Administration tells us that a store-bought chicken can be thirty per cent bone,' Mr Perdue clucks drily in a head-cocked soliloquy to camera. 'That's a whole lot too much bone for one of my Perdue chickens. If you buy a Perdue chicken that's thirty per cent bone, write to me and I'll give you your money back. Who can you write to in Washington. What do *they* know about chicken?'

If Pacca and Perdue hold me mesmerised, there are other self-advertisers I cannot switch off fast enough. Chief among these is Tom Carvel, proprietor of Carvel ice cream, whose phlegmy voice-over, allied to the gruesomely-coloured panorama of his product, seems calculated only to deepen brand loyalty to Haagen Dazs. Mr Carvel's publicity mania often leads him into conduct unbecoming an elderly (Neapolitan?) gentleman. In some new Carvel ice cream ads, he raps to a disco beat. In others, he tries to pass himself off to children as 'Cookie Puss', a celestial – or, as Mr Carvel unluckily pronounces it, *cholesterol* – visitor from outer space.

At the other extreme, Joel Bogart makes a virtue of being barely communicative. 'I just got back from my greatest buying trip ever,' Mr Bogart pants, leaping from his car outside Kaufman's Carpet Center. 'Now I find I gotta clear all my best broadlooms to make way for the new stock. You folks don't come here to Kaufman for my autograph. You come for a great bargain . . .' On the eve of national holidays, Joel Bogart leads a full dress drum majorette parade towards the camera, then suddenly darts off left, to slash the price of another broadloom.

Not all these self-made men seem to have entered the limelight willingly. The president of Eldee Appliances Inc, I would guess, was brought to the studio in a straitjacket. One can almost hear the last desperate pleas to him to smile and gesture naturally. He stands there, bulky, white-haired and terrified, roaring tonelessly, his large hands spreading and retracting, always one syllable out of synch. 'At Eldee,' the unhappy semaphore stutters, 'buying an appli-ance is ee-zee . . .' He should indenture himself forthwith to the modest man in overalls who invites enrolment at Apex Technical School, and is among the most accomplished performers I have seen on American television. 'Now – I can't phone you,' this utterly charming personage says with a tolerant chuckle. 'You have to phone us. The lines are open. Give us a call . . .' Many times, he has almost had me on the phone, enquiring about the welders course.

Returning to New York this summer, I found Stephen R. Pacca's Aalco Windows ad still playing on three channels a dozen times a day. But there is also a revised version. In this, some meddlesome TV charm school has persuaded Mr Pacca to drop the money blizzard, drop the propellor's power, drop the blast of fire, drop the giant paintbrush, drop the showgirl and, worst of all, drop his voice.

'Double-insulated glass, eliminates storm windows,' Stephen R. Pacca now says, almost mildly, as if they were the most ordinary words in the world.

Myths of the Big Apple

A year and a half of living in New York has constantly shown me how gross were my misconceptions about it all the times I came here as a wide-eyed visitor. Someday I will collate an alternative guide-book from the notes (and furious exclamation marks) that chart the loss of my illusions. Meanwhile – as a solace for those at present unable to brave the horrible exchange-rate – I offer some footnotes to the larger myths of Manhattan.

In New York everything happens fast

America is among the slowest, most bureaucratic nations on earth. In New York that slowness is intensified by fear and suspicion. Basically, every shopper is treated as a potential thief. On entering most stores, you must register your bag or briefcase with a guard. Often you must ring a bell or buzzer to enter and leave. Buying anything in a department store takes inordinate time and effort, owing to cash registers that wheeze and chatter interminably to themselves. Production of a cheque book induces the same trauma as a crucifix in Transylvania. Over-population is another chronic cause of delay. An average restaurant meal is a ritual involving five rigidly demarcated attendants: the 'hostess', the 'captain', the waiter, the sommelier and the 'bus boy'. All will usually have disappeared by the time you want to pay and go.

New Yorkers are impatient, aggressive, snappy go-getters

New Yorkers of all classes are uniformly bovine, as they reveal in their willingness to form queues meekly on any occasion. At cinemas, it is thought quite normal to be herded brusquely into three different queues before being permitted to enter the auditorium. You can arrive at the smartest restaurant, your table booked, and still be required to 'wait in line'. Many hotels now corral arriving guests in roped enclosures, calling them forth to register one at a time, like Pavlov dogs. Ripping off this unprotesting public is an industry sanctioned by government. When you put 25 cents into a stamp machine, you receive 18 cents worth of stamps. I asked a fellow expatriate once why the city had no equivalent of *Private Eye*. 'It would have to be as thick as the Manhattan phone book,' he said.

241

The streets are dangerous

They are – but not, as visitors expect, because of muggers. They are dangerous because air-conditioning units hurtle down from 20th-storey windowsills, construction cranes topple over routinely, cyclists go through red traffic lights in the wrong direction, the pavements are scarred and pitted like elephant-traps and nobody looks where they are going. Vigilance spent on guarding one's valuables is better exercised in taking care not to fall off a kerb-edge and break a leg. In Britain we worry about always wearing clean underwear in case we suddenly have to go to hospital. In New York, rather worry you hold enough credit cards to make it worth a doctor's while to save your life.

New York is an all-night city

Away from Times Square and parts of Greenwich Village, New York after midnight is mostly battened-down, steel-caged and burglar-alarmed. The only true 24-hour phenomena are the half-nude street-walkers on Park Avenue South, and the Korean greengrocers who, as a rule, speak only one English phrase: 'Twenty dollars, please.'

You cannot use the New York subway

You can, provided you close your eyes to the graffiti and your nostrils to the smell, provided you avoid eye contact with the many commuting beggars, provided you do not ride after midnight and make sure you get off well before 125th Street, where Harlem begins in earnest. The trains are wonderfully quick – especially the non-stop expresses – and are, in fairness, not so much dirtier than taxis. An unexpected plus is the presence of smart-uniformed, helpful guards. Since the system has no logic and maps, if not obliterated, are baffling to read, I recommend the No.6 Lexington Avenue local as suitable for most English people's journeys up or downtown, and the 'N' train ditto, because for some reason 'N' trains are always cleaner.

New York is a city of miraculous technology – especially the bathrooms

The bath in our apartment is too small to lie in, and empties by means of an archaic column and plunger device which, I believe, disappeared even from British seaside boarding houses before the Great War. Showers may be equipped with fine tuning controls worthy of interstellar travel, but they still dispense only two temperatures, freezing or scalding. Most electrical wiring looks wickedly

242

dangerous. The city that perfected the dry Martini has yet to invent a serviceable umbrella or lavatory paper that does not auto-destruct on contact.

New Yorkers' wit is dry, quick and caustic

New York wit has become virtually extinct through dependance on psycho-analysis, and the changing phobias about cholesterol, caffeine, sodium and salt. Products should carry an additional label: 'Guaranteed not to contain irony.' Reading the *New Yorker*, like *Punch*, induces only a fretful melancholia. Humour comes best in its unconscious forms, like the listening device currently advertised under the name 'Little Bugger', or the TV announcer who recently said, 'This dramatised life of Pope John Paul the Second is made possible by Xerox.'

All New Yorkers are rude

They are until you expect them to be; then they suddenly become old wordly polite. In a chaotic jeans-and-sneaker store recently, I stormed up to a young black asistant and asked heatedly where I was supposed to pay for my purchase. 'Sir,' he replied, 'it would behove you to wait over there for a moment.'

New York is a city of fierce egalitarianism

You will never have seen so many butlers, maids, doormen and uniformed flunkeys of every type. The gulf between rich and poor, and the indifference of the former towards the latter, recalls such Third World cities as Bombay, Jakarta and Bogata. The human debris commonly to be seen on smart Fifth Avenue recently inspired Tiffany's the jewellers to a little joke. They filled their windows with dummies dressed as female derelicts and draped in Tiffany jewels.

New York wages are stupendously high

I heard a girl cashier in a Lexington Avenue supermarket tell a colleague that her wage was $1.50 per hour. The publisher's copy editor whose rewriting largely brought the success of a current multi-million dollar grossing book, earns $16,000 per year. Employees in service industries frequently end up paying their bosses owing to the practice of making them financially responsible for their merchandise. A Post Office clerk, refusing to take my cheque, explained, 'If it bounces, I'll have to pay the amount out of my own pocket.'

New York has the best Chinese laundries in the world

So far, during these 18 months, my worst New York battles have
been with launderers named Cheng, Chang, Ang, Lee, Ley and Loy.
I have stood in steamy, subterranean cockpits all over Chinatown
and Yorkville, screaming at men in white underpants (the usual
Chinese launderers' garb) or at impassive crones, the same hysterical,
fruitless words: *'No starch!'* When you come to New York, call me
and I'll show you my collection of free-standing shirts.

*New Yorkers are upfront. They say things to your face. They tell it
like it is*

My experience of corporate life here has given me the idea of
rewriting Shakespeare's plays in New York dialogue. In *Julius
Caesar,* just as the assassins surround Caesar, someone will be heard
to say, 'We want you to know, Julius, we really *love* your work.'

Roaring noon in the tuckshop

This 'roaring noon', as Scott Fitzgerald aptly called it, I have been
reading the very best thing to take my mind off East 85th Street,
the shrieking horns, the wildcat burglar-alarms, the human and semi-
human cries and the intermittent cacophonous excursions of the
Gracie Station fire engine:

> Mr Quelch frowned.
> He frowned because Billy Bunter grinned.
> The Remove were on 'con' in third school that morning, and if
> there was anything in the deathless verse of Virgil to cause a fellow
> to grin, the Remove master was unaware of it . . .

I have never lost my weakness for Billy Bunter books, though I
know they are full of flagellation and racism. I read them now as I
did aged 11, when Greyfriars, that mythic public school, was my
main refuge from the claustrophobic tyranny and scatology of the
real thing. I still have the habit, when eating alone, of imagining
myself at a terrific feast with Harry Wharton & Co in Number 1
study. I find myself doing it even here in midtown Manhattan,
mentally substituting jam tarts, sardines and ginger pop for my deli
egg salad, pumpernickel bagel and salt-free seltzer water.
    Books one can re-read endlessly, with the same eyes with which
one read them first, are among the most comforting, reassuring
things on earth. They are slippers and Ovaltine for the mind. I only
wish that, when packing for this trip, I had left out a few suits,
medicines and letters of introduction and included a few more such

good old well-thumbed friends from my shelves. They are among the things about 'home' I find I miss most sorely. I miss my Wodehouse, my Hornblower, my *Diary of a Nobody,* my *History of Mr Polly,* my Jennings and Darbishire.

The bookshelf I have acquired in 18 months is, I suppose, a typical expatriate's. That is to say, it consists mainly of books bought to satisfy an urgent passing need and, somehow, not thrown away afterwards. There are travel guides to places not yet visited, and thick paperbacks, dog-eared by domestic air travel. Halfway along, and painfully conspicuous, are the light green and the faded red cloth spines of the two books I re-read when I want to go home: *Billy Bunter's Brainwave,* and *William the Good.* I have loved William books even longer than Bunter books. This is a particularly good one, containing the story in which William disguises himself as a fortune-teller and tells even more terrible lies than usual.

Real books – as I now thing of hardbacks – have crept in here and there, almost by accident. A friend in London sent us the 1939 New York guide, written by a 'project' of first-rate authors including John Cheever, and almost heart-breakingly evoking the vanished New York of the Biltmore Hotel and the elevated railway, when lunch at the Russian Tea Room cost 50 cents. An American friend gave us *Vanity Fair* in an ornate Random House edition of the mid-fifties, with fancy chapter-headings and coloured plates. When I returned to London last, I could not resist bringing back a Shakespeare and the collected libretti of the Savoy Operas.

For all the high production standard and resiny voluptuousness of new American books, I feel oddly little compulsion to acquire them. Here, the act of buying a book is considered no different from that of buying groceries. I cannot, and hope I never will, get used to bookshops where an armed guard watches the door, travel from the fiction to non-fiction department is by escalator and to pay, one must wait in a queue. The solitary exception seems to be Scribner's, on Fifth Avenue, whose elegant gold leafed black facade has not changed since Mr Scribner's protégés Hemingway and Fitzgerald dominated the window displays. At Scribner's one can – almost – browse. Inevitably, the place is under threat of extensive 'remodelling'.

When I lived here first, I was hungry only for American writers. I gorged myself on Willa Cather, A.J. Liebling, O. Henry, Ambrose Bierce and Bruce Catton's studies of the Civil War. As homesickness took root, so did a growing need for Elizabeth Bowen and Barbara Pym; an increasing tendency to read *Billy Bunter's Brainwave* in the middle of the day. Then, on impulse, I turned to the writer through whom, I remembered, England – especially London – could be seen and felt with special intensity. I began to read Dickens.

I had, of course, read much Dickens – re-read, in my obsessive way, *Great Expectations, Oliver Twist,* the picnic and Christmas scenes in *Pickwick.* Now I set myself to travel methodically through the titles I was accustomed to regard as No Thoroughfares. On holiday in Hawaii, I read *The Old Curiosity Shop.* On assignment in Palm Beach, I read *Our Mutual Friend.* On a book publicity-tour, travelling between Detroit, Minneapolis and Houston, I read *Little Dorrit.* And last summer, living in a rented house on Shelter Island, with a friend's sheepdog for company, I read *Bleak House.*

It is strange, at the age of 41, to discover one's favourite books so, in reverse order. It is as strange to reflect on the circumstances that prevented me from discovering my favourite book in the world as on the surroundings in which I finally did discover it. I remember, a few years ago, standing on Broadstairs beach, looking up at the yellow clifftop villa where Dickens wrote *Bleak House,* still not knowing it as the greatest, tenderest, funniest, saddest portrayal of the state of being English. I had to wait until this American front porch, with cicadas starting up their night's din, to read passages like:

> It is the long vacation. The good ships Law and Equity, those teak-built, copper-bottomed, iron-fastened, brazen-faced and not by any means fast sailing Clippers are laid up in ordinary . . . The Temple, Chancery Lane, Serjeants' Inn and Lincoln's Inn even unto the Fields, are like tidal harbours at low water; where stranded proceedings, offices at anchor, idle clerks lounging on lopsided stools that will not recover their perpendicular until the new term sets in, lie high and dry upon the ooze . . .

My great-grandmother's collected Dickens, unexplored these many years, are among the friends I now think of, awaiting my return on shelves in Bayswater. Some day – perhaps when I am deep in the Isle of Wight or Oxfordshire, with not a siren or shriek to be heard outside my window – I must get started on his *American Notes.*

Mogging the juggers

My apartment on East 85th Street is only three blocks from Central Park where it meets the Metropolitan Museum (irritatingly called by some 'The Met'). Running my regular three miles is as easy here as in London and from one point of view, notably pleasanter. New Yorkers, unlike Londoners, allow runners to be part of the landscape. You can see them on the busiest midtown avenues, wired into their Sony Walkmen, with their hand-weights and small haversacks. No one smirks at them, or shouts 'Hup-two, hup-two!' Even my favourite Hyde Park run was never free of that satirical element.

'Aren't you afraid of muggers?' my English friends say. The answer is, yes, constantly, but less so in Central Park, where I am shod for flight and carrying no valuables other than a latch-key. Some muggers are said to prey exclusively on joggers (could they be 'juggers?') carrying off keys, watches and Sony Walkmen. A mugger in Central Park these days would be hard put to choose among the multitudes of runners, skateboarders and roller disco virtuosi who have opened the place up like a new frontier. The most insecurity I ever feel there is when a blue and white police car comes idling through the glades, packed with shotguns, wire netting and challenging, adolescent faces.

Each midday, therefore, I set off down East 85th, threading my way through the crowd of chain-smokers, trainee break dancers and leather-skirted vamps, disgorged at this hour by the York Preparatory School. Smells of fried chicken fat and rapid building hang feverishly in the air. My objective is to cross Park Avenue before the WALK signal changes to DON'T WALK, or in the few seconds' grace before DON'T WALK ceases its admonitory flash. Big checker cabs hurtle uptown, clanking over the brow of Lenox Hill. To my left, 40 blocks south, the Pan Am building shimmers like fish scales in phosphorescent sun.

The West Side declares its superiority even to a runner – leveller pavements, less slippery garbage, a scent of flowers planted recklessly in ground-floor window boxes. As I pass the multi-million dollar duplex apartment houses on West 85th, glass doors, held open by frock-coated porters, release other figures in creased shorts and scruffy sneakers, with little orange buttons screwed into their ears. I cross Madison Avenue, where every other shop window seems to display a small Picasso, and a fancy French loaf can be bought for as little as $7.50. More runners issue from their mansions to jog, lope or bound ahead of me. By the time Central Park comes into view, I have ceased to be a lone eccentric and become part of a mass pilgrimage.

My fellow runners are bound mostly for the Reservoir, a one-and-a-half-mile circuit famed as a pick-up place, and intermittently menaced by a personage known as the Reservoir Rapist. Others peel off to left or right along the six-mile outer ring road. I cross this at the point where I stood last autumn, watching the firstcomers in the New York Marathon cheered on by a girl personifying New York enthusiasm at its best. For each runner who passed, she managed a different cry of congratulation. 'Go for it, 27! . . . Yay, 91! You look great, 106! . . .'

More introverted, less amorous runners like myself prefer the Delacourt Oval, just south of the Reservoir, a wide grass expanse set aside for organised ball games. At one end there is a lake on which perches a small, synthetic château. Famous old West Side buildings like the Beresford show their Egyptian towers above the

247

encircling trees. Behind the lake the skyscrapers of north Manhattan rear up together, silver and black, like so many frozen waterfalls.

At midday, no baseball teams are practising on the Delacourt Oval. There is the odd skater, the odd unicyclist, the odd group of dusty black youths tuning up their pantechnicon-size ghetto blaster. There may be a troop of little boys from some exclusive local prep school, outfitted in uniform red tracksuits, exhorted by pedagogic cries of 'Nice job, Earl . . . Go for it, Brandon!..Okay guys – everyone go run after Mr Lazarus.' Squirrels dart everywhere, twirling the feather lariats of their tails.

The running-path, 880 yards in circumference, seldom reveals more than a couple of figures to disturb my thoughts and sightline. My most irritating rival is a man in a grey nylon tracksuit who comes scraping up behind me, then stops square in my path and chops at the air with loud samurai bellows. What Nobel prize-winner or captain of industry can he be? There is also, occasionally, a man of about 80, in everyday clothes, heavy shoes and a Lenin cap, wobbling slowly but indomitably round the inside track. Most others I meet are Sony-wired and expressionless, their brains aswim with the 'tish-tish-tish' of that ubiquitous disco drumming-machine.

Pounding my five circuits, I have watched the seasons change. I ran here even on last winter's coldest day, when Central Park was a featureless tundra, traversed by cross-country skiers, and I, alone among Manhattan's male joggers, remained insensible to the perils of penis frostbite. The ice on the lake that day actually steamed. I was utterly alone but for the skyscrapers and three black men with a chain saw, attempting to remove what they evidently mistook for a Christmas tree. Later, among some saplings, I glimpsed a charming sight. A group of Mountie-hatted park rangers, their wives and children were hanging presents on ice-petrified branches and singing 'Good King Wenceslas'.

I come to Delacourt Oval, in fact, whenever I need to feel better about living in this city. Five circuits are sufficient to quiet the clangour of sirens, road drills, Pepsi ads, analysts and caffeine phobia. I remember that New York is also a place of dog-owners, babies in push-chairs and people who sit quietly, reading books.

I remember my first naive sense of Manhattan being somehow cosy and welcoming, as I run round Delacourt Oval in autumn dusk, watching lamps twinkle on in the twin towers of the Beresford building. And running after dark reminds me of something else, each time those northerly sky-scrapers swing into view, shining all together like gold leaf half rubbed off the night. I remember that New York is the most exciting place I know.

The drudgery of the disc

The most persuasive TV ads here at present – more persuasive even than those for fizzy brown soft drinks – are the ads which tell Americans that if they care about their children's education, their financial future and the destiny of Mankind on earth, never mind keeping up with the neighbours, they cannot any longer postpone the purchase of a home computer.

The world of the home computer owner, as depicted by these ads, is a place from which no one would wish to be excluded. It is a world gauzed over with domestic happiness rivalling that suggested by ads for toilet paper. It is populated by wise young parents and angelic-looking children whose learning difficulties are all now at an end. Machines which in the seventies were targets for regular scorn and execration have somehow metamorphosed themselves into household pets. Faces young and old shine in the reflected glow of marvels wrought by those jolly green digits as they frisk across those homely little screens.

Several of my friends in novel writing and journalism now work entirely on computer word processors, and raptly tell me – and anyone else who will listen – how it has transformed their lives. One can understand why. Equipment of any kind is a time-honoured palliative both for the writer's loneliness and his chronic fear that what he does isn't 'real' work. The computer offers multitudinous escapes and diversions from the recurrent nightmare of sitting and staring at a blank page.

My friends have taken me into their once lonely studies, now bustling word process centres, and have proudly shown me the instrument of their redemption. I have watched as the little screen displayed English prose rendered into phosphorescent green columns as malleable as an airline departures board. I have seen that clever digit dance along to perform the amendments and erasures which I still stubbornly carry out by hand. I have seen the lightning swivel action whereby whole paragraphs can be moved forward or backward in the text. At such times, I forbear to remark that in well thought-out writing, paragraphs do not trundle about like so many spare bits of furniture.

As a beginner in journalism, I followed the general example and worked straight on to a typewriter. Journalists do not speak of writing but of 'bashing' or 'hammering' things out. The typewriter induces a shallow trance in which tired thoughts and second-hand phrases flow from the memory through the fingertips, seldom detouring to the mind. I weaned myself from typing, first of all, to give myself time to think.

The disadvantages of writing by hand are obvious. One feels perpetually engaged in school homework, and one develops blisters.

The advantage is that I can earn my living anywhere in almost any circumstances, using the merest stubs of pencil and old envelope. I can write in taxis, in airport lounges and while being kept waiting by inconsiderate people. I can turn the most empty boredom to profit, and endlessly defeat the world's conspiracy to waste my time. Now they tell me I should give up all that and voluntarily shackle myself to two thousand pounds' worth of plastic.

But consider, my friends say patiently – consider the computer's power of information storage. You can put all your background material, research and interviews, on to floppy disks and thereafter 'call up' anything on to the screen at the touch of a button.

It happens that I already have a perfectly good information-storage system. It is called the notebook. Its contents can be 'called up' by consulting the index label on its cover, then opening it. It can be aesthetically pleasing, a companion on difficult journeys, a hoard for triumphs, a pocket confessional for inadmissible mistakes. I keep all my old notebooks and enjoy re-reading them, savouring the past projects they evoke. There is the black police notebook I used for my Beatles biography; the red and black Chinese notebook in which I recorded my first year in New York. There is the chic brown Italian notebook, with the sales receipt still inside, I am keeping for my new novel. Where is the friendliness or tactile pleasure in a floppy disc?

The clinching argument for the word processor in my friends' minds is its print-out mechanism. 'No more typing out fair copies!' they say triumphantly. 'You make all your corrections on the screen, then you tell the computer to print and it prints.'

Typing, for me, is no drudgery: it is an emotional climax in which all those handwritten drafts, made in airport lounges and waiting rooms, achieve legible – will it be also plausible? – form. I enjoy my wrestling bouts with the Adler portable I bought for £20 12 years ago, whose keys punish my fingers like miniature push-ups. (I'm enjoying it now as well as taking the opportunity to give the words a final polish.) And if I should make a mistake, I have five totally mobile and versatile digits on each hand with which to correct it.

I suspect that my friends, for all their transformed working lives, are vulnerable to a trance more insidious than any mere typewriter's. It is easy to tell which books or articles have been written with a computer's aid. They read in a strange, glib, flat, floppy discy way, and every paragraph seems loose, as if you could move it forward or backward. I imagine it will not be long before computers come preprogrammed for literary composition, and are able independently to rattle off anything from a Jeffrey Archer-style bestseller to a profile for *Rolling Stone*. Indeed, judging by the recent output of both the foregoing, I think it may be happening already.

There is one aspect of my prejudice for which my nonliterary friends can bless me. I am not a word processor bore. When people at parties learn I am a writer and ask if I have a word processor, I always give the same answer. 'Yes,' I say, tapping my head. 'In here.'

Cabbie takes the cake

When we arrived here a year and a half ago, we promised each other faithfully not to be drawn into New York manners and customs like other expatriate Britons we know. We vowed we would never give up caffeine, visit an analyst, address mixed company as 'you guys' or leave laid-back, jokey messages on our telephone answering machine.

From our Chinatown loft to our present apartment in the old uptown German quarter, we have remained thoroughly – one might say, farcically – British. We travel miles on awful subway lines to buy leaf tea, digestive biscuits or the *Times Literary Supplement*. We will watch any old British movie on TV, however execrable, just for a fleeting glimpse of a London bus. Recently at a smart Manhattan dentist's, my friend was able to filch a six-month-old copy of *Country Life*. We read it all – the features on horse trials and old silver, the ads for Cotswold cottages and special blankets to dry your gundog – practically in tears.

We have a mutual English friend here, a woman whom we like partly because she responds as emotionally as we do to words like Marmite, Chilprufe and Ovaltine. She is a delightful person and when she got married recently to a New York playwright, we felt we knew the kind of wedding gift she would most appreciate. We decided to bake her a real Dundee cake with almonds on the top.

Gathering the ingredients was extremely pleasant. We bought fruit and glacé cherries on 86th Street, an area thickly populated by German bakers and *konditorei* where one could grow fat just from inhaling fumes of vanilla and caterers chocolate. More fruit, almonds and a good size cake tin came from an old Hungarian grocer's on Second Avenue. In both places, my friend asked for angelica and sultanas and received looks of total mystification. The latter turned up eventually under their New World name of 'white currants'. But you cannot get angelica here at all.

The mixing also was pleasant though, admittedly, somewhat one-sided. I have the good fortune to live with a past winner of the fruit cake class at Llanfair (Powys) annual fete. My own culinary adventures have so far been limited to pasta, hamburgers and – on one disastrous occasion – my face flannel. My role in the cake operation was to stand by, ready to give whatever help I could.

For six hours that following Wednesday, the inconvenient stove

251

in our minuscule apartment breathed out a smell of country kitchens, Christmas Eve, summer holidays near Penzance. At 9 p.m., my friend left our party at a smart restaurant amid cries of American wonderment. 'She's gone to take a *cake* out of the oven!' Several people came back with me afterwards to see it as it cooled. With its great dark circumference, its irradiating pattern of close-set almonds, it might have been a window in some famous old Spanish cathedral. It was indeed a beautiful, very heavy, real Dundee cake.

Fine as it looked, my friend worried it might seem too British and downbeat for a wedding cake. She therefore decided it must be iced. The bride being English and her bridegroom unrepentantly American, a characteristically bold plan suggested itself. 'I could ice one half of it like a Union Jack and half like the Stars and Stripes . . .' 'Good idea,' I said.

Icing began late on Saturday afternoon, the eve of our friends' wedding party. I stood by, as before, ready to give what help I could. What with one thing and other, I regret to say, the Cornish holiday atmosphere began to dissipate. The dialogue moved away from rosy cheeks and kitchen dressers. ' . . . why can't you be a bit less clumsy!' ' . . . all this fuss over a damned *cake* . . .' ' . . . If you do that again, I'm getting straight on the first plane back to London . . .'

Just before midnight, the supply of icing sugar ran out. I said I would find more somehow and plunged away to 86th Street. All the caterers and *konditorei* were long since closed. The only supermarket still open was a Grand Union, down near Second, where each cash register speaks your bill aloud. 'Icing sugar!' I called to several attendants desperately. They looked blank. At length, comprehension dawned. 'Oh – you mean *confectioners* sugar.' I bought the last two bags in stock. 'Four dollars, fifty-four cents,' the cash register croaked apathetically.

By Sunday morning, the kitchen was in a state of emergency. My friend had iced the cake and sketched on it her design of the newlyweds' conmingled flags. She was now using vegetable dye to give each half-flag its red and its blue. The difficulty was that when she got the dye dark enough, it became too runny. The blue on the Union Jack half was still only baby blue. The red on the Stars and Stripes half kept leaking over into the white. My friend went on heroically mixing and painting, stemming each blot with her artist's scalpel and cotton wool swabs. I stood by, ready to give what help I could.

The design was finished to her satisfaction half an hour before the wedding party was due to begin. There remained the final problem of transporting a Dundee cake, iced as a Union Jack and the Stars and Stripes, from East 85th Street across Central Park to our friends' apartment on West End Avenue. Glancing outside, I saw that it had begun to rain heavily. 'You could go and find a cab and bring it here,' my friend, somewhat pointedly, suggested.

Lexington Avenue was full of cabs, all occupied. I found a free one at last outside Gimbals – a big, clanking Checker, driven by a black man. In my present state, I felt more than a match for surly black Checker-drivers. 'Go back to Eighty-fifth at Lex,' I said. 'I need to pick someone else up.' Without a word, he did so.

My friend was waiting outside the front door of our building. On one hand – don't ask me how – she balanced the cake. In her other hand she carried the miniature bride and groom to be set on top of it, some red, white and blue streamers to be wrapped round it, sticky tape and cotton wool for last-minute repairs, and a bag containing her best high-heeled shoes. Otherwise, the rain would have ruined them.

My friend got into the cab, still balancing the cake, hauling red, white and blue streamers in after her. I felt she had not appreciated my heroism in procuring transport. Over the cake, the streamers and the shoe-bag, we began to have a fierce row. Suddenly we became aware that the cab was still stationary. Our driver had turned round and was watching us with interest.

'Where do you wanna go?' he said.

An extremely young, good-humoured black face took in the state of our overwrought white ones.

''s okay folks,' he added kindly. 'Be cool now – I'm waitin'.'

When the cab moved off, each of us steadied the cake as if the other had deliberately jerked it.

'It's all stress in this city,' our driver said over his shoulder.

'It certainly *is,*' I said meaningly.

'Yessir, it's a-a-all stress. But you cain't do that. You gotta stay cool. Go with the flow.' His voice had the soothingness of a fresh feather bed. 'Me, I didn't have no sleep last night,' he added.

We looked out at Central Park, locked in furious silence and steadying the cake. Our driver shouted back a question that sounded like 'Do you know Portnoy?'

'Portnoy?'

'Putney,' our driver said. 'It's in London, England.'

'Yes, we know Putney.'

'My sister lived in Putney,' our driver said. 'She's a doctor. Me, I'm into structural engineering.'

The cake notwithstanding, each of us very nearly smiled.

'It's all stress, man,' our driver resumed. 'I got four cabs. Last night, ten o'clock, one guy I got calls in. He's broke down in Queens. Callin' out the tow truck cost two hundred dollars. I say "Don't move. I'll come get you myself." My girl's waitin' on me three hours. She wants to go dancin' at '54. Then my other guy calls in. I put my girl on hold. *He's* in Astoria with two flat tyres. I say "Okay, man, wait there . . . " My girl gives me shee-it. I say, "Relax baby. I'll give you money, go get your girl friend and go dancin' with her. Let me *sleep!*" '

By the time the cab drew up on West End Avenue, all three of us were laughing.

' . . . I had to quit engineering school for one semester,' our driver said. 'I'm so tired, studyin' and drivin' a cab, I'm goin' uptown when I'm s'posed to be goin' downtown. White passengers say, 'Er, pardon me, you goin' the wrong way . . . " A black one say, "Hey man, what's happenin' with my *money* . . ." '

I got out first, with the cake. As my friend paid the driver, he repeated, 'Be cool now. And take care o' that gentleman.'

We were restored by kindness and humour as we carried the cake upstairs to our friends' wedding party. We were back to our normal, sensible British selves.

1984

Cruising to Extinction

Assuming that our final self-incineration will not mean the end of life in this galaxy, and that wiser beings will one day examine the steps by which we approached our collective suicide, one question about the human race, above all, will be asked in bewilderment.

How could we have lived under so ghastly a threat as nuclear destruction, and not been perpetually terrified? How did the majority of us contrive to put the subject so totally out of our minds?

The answer will come partly from etymologists of the future as they study the multifarious ways in which our fears, our sensibilities and our animal wits were dulled by our leaders' systematic undermining and perversion of our language.

Those future etymologists may note, for instance, that from the time mankind's weapons entered on their last lethally efficient spiral, officialdom was permitted to mask their disgusting purpose behind glamorous pet names. It will be noted that, over the years, we killed each other with the Centurion tank, suggesting Roman dignity, the Spitfire fighter, suggesting madcap youth, the Phantom and Mirage jet, suggesting ghostly romance, plus a wide assortment of missiles and genocidal systems named – affrontingly – after wild animals. It will be noted how the final, pre-holocaust phase produced the ultimate obfuscation of the 'Cruise' missile, mind-bogglingly equating Armageddon with a picnic on the river.

Students of our moral code will surely find it strange that, while taking infinite trouble to prevent tobacco and alcohol from being made attractive to our young, we never thought to apply the same advertising rule to nuclear armaments. They may wonder how different our attitude to war might have been under governments compelled to label weapons honestly – the People-Exploder, the City-Pulper, the Orphan-Maker, the Skin-Shredder, the Bone-Mangler.

Reading the final speeches of our leaders, future etymologists will note how, time and again, a decent, explicit English word had been corrupted to mean something diametrically opposite. Thus 'defence' became a synonym for 'war' or 'counterattack'. Thus 'freedom' became the accepted term for our bondage in a lemming-like arms race. Thus that strangest of all warmongering vaguenesses, the nuclear 'capability'. 'But surely . . .' someone in the future may remark. 'That was Man at his most *in*capable.'

Special study will doubtless be given to the mid-1980s, when life and cheap pulp fantasy became so instantly interchangeable that the latest terrifying leap in nuclear proliferation could be dubbed with the name of a high-grossing Hollywood movie. Visual records will certainly survive of the *Star Wars* president himself, grinning his B-Western grin as he walks away blameless yet again – perhaps indulging in one of the sit-com analogies with which he was always accustomed to deal with questions of life and death. 'Well . . . all you folks know how it can be around the house when something goes wrong . . .' No doubt Mr Reagan will have compared Doomesday itself to a leaky faucet or an overflowing drain.

Closest lexicographical study of all, however, will be devoted to a single word on which Western man, in his final terror, leaned like a crutch – that blind, arid little word whose magical effect, when applied to any man-made catastrophe, was to remove all sense of responsibility or blameworthiness. Doubtless, in the seconds before the terminal flash, a human voice will have been heard to say, 'Er – we've got a little *problem* . . .'

It may be the only explanation that future beings can find for man's disappearance from the earth. He had this little problem.

1984

An Indian Ghost Story

The continuing popularity of film and television dramas about India under the British Raj reminds me how close I came, 17 years ago, to becoming a pioneer scenarist in the genre. You producers of *Gandhi, The Jewel in the Crown* and *A Passage to India* little realise what seminal influence I almost had on your work. Riches and Academy Awards might be mine today, if only I had succeeded in devising a happy ending for the massacre at Cawnpore.

In 1968, newly launched as a London journalist, I found myself, one Chelsea pub Saturday morning, talking to just the kind of young man about town I had hoped to meet. He wore a Beau Brummel jacket and a bright green shirt, and held a burning joss stick in each hand. His sidewhiskers climbed down to almost touch under his chin. His name was Stephen Weeks. He was 19 years old and, he told me, a film director.

Back then almost everybody of 19 one met, especially in Chelsea, was likely to claim as much. But Stephen Weeks seemed to be genuine. I learned that he had already financed and directed several short features and that he ran his own company, 'Cinetrend Motion Pictures Ltd'. He used impressive words like 'neg' and 'rushes' and spoke airily of 'my musical director' or 'my lighting cameraman'. Though, like me, he lived in a bedsitter – his in a 'squat' in Bloomsbury, near the British Museum – he exuded an aura of entrepreneurial confidence. The joss sticks he burned in his little attic smelled as potent as any Hollywood mogul's cigar.

Stephen Weeks, I concluded, must be one of the 'young meteors' I had read about in *Queen* magazine and elsewhere. When he said he liked my work and could use me as a scriptwriter on various projects he had in hand, I was naturally excited.

Two subjects dominated Stephen's imagination: the 1914-18 War and the Indian Mutiny. For a 19-year-old director, trying to raise finance from a Bloomsbury bedsit, the latter, oddly enough, looked more viable. To make a Great War picture, one would have to go on location to France. But to depict the sepoy uprising of 1857, Stephen told me, one need go no further than his home town of Gosport in Hampshire. Apparently, during the imperial age, military buildings in prefabricated form had regularly been shipped out to

India from nearby Portsmouth. Around Gosport Stephen had found Moghul-style army barracks, civil buildings – even a complete railway station – assembled 100 years before but then, somehow, never dismantled and exported. And parts of the quiet Hamble river, he thought, could easily be made to impersonate the Ganges.

With these locations in mind, Stephen was attempting to finance a full-length film drama based on the Mutiny's most notorious episode. In June 1857, the British garrison at Cawnpore was persuaded to surrender by the local rebel leader, Nana Sahib, after promises of full military honours and safe passage by boat down the Ganges. Emerging from their entrenchment, men, women and children were ambushed by Nana Sahib's native cavalry. The few survivors were locked up in ghastly conditions, then butchered and their bodies thrown down a well.

On notepaper grandly headed The Cawnpore Mutiny, Stephen had produced a brief synopsis focusing on a British officer named Colonel Mowbray, one of the massacre's only two survivors. The other main character was Nana Sahib, an English-educated psychopath who used to play himself at billiards while his Scottish manservant read aloud from *The Times*. 'I think I can get David Hemmings to play Mowbray,' Stephen said. ' . . . or maybe Richard Harris. The main thing first is to bash out some sort of script.'

Stephen's energy and enthusiasm were infectious. I wrote the script in five days, using as my sole reference source a book called *Regiments and Uniforms of the British Army* which my father had given me on my eleventh birthday. This battered old friend provided, not merely the sequence of events at Cawnpore and thumbnail sketches of the main characters, but also a helpful glossary of Indian military terms like 'sowar' and 'subadar'. I had a vague notion of Victorian English and a vague facility for keeping characters in balance. I typed while Stephen paced to and fro, suggesting additional dialogue, occasionally crossing to the bed where his French fiancée, Joëlle, was recovering from influenza.

At intervals, I would become alarmed by the thinness of my characters and their adventures. 'Don't worry,' Stephen repeated firmly. 'The important thing is just to get it all down.'

My rough and unready scenes were then retyped by a script agency, impressively bound in dark green cardboard covers and 'messengered', with the required keen urgency, to several prominent British movie bosses. The response was instantaneously favourable. Bryan Forbes, at that time head of the Associated British Picture Corporation, wrote back to Stephen that he liked the idea and that 'several sequences' contained 'great dramatic potential'. Stephen was already talking to a musical director, a lighting cameraman and David Hemmings. We adjourned to the Pizza Express in Coptic Street, feeling well and truly on our way.

The Cawnpore Mutiny did not go to Bryan Forbes. It went to Tony Tenser, head of Tigon British Pictures, a company known chiefly for low budget horror movies. The fee for our story and first draft script was £3,000 of which (remember this was 1968) I immediately received something over £1,000. Though Tony Tenser might be lacking in artistic prestige, he had, at least, undertaken to make the film basically as we had written it and with Stephen, not his own appointee, directing. And Tigon had a reputation for putting properties into production with minimum delay.

Mr Tenser interviewed the two of us in the back of a taxi speeding towards Parsons Green. He was an elderly but exotic-looking man with a white moustache, white sideburns, white trousers and white shoes. He did not conceal his enthusiasm for a film about 19th century India that could be shot on location in Gosport, Hampshire.

'There's just one thing, boys,' he said. ' . . . the ending.'

'The massacre?' I said.

Mr Tenser winced.

'No, no, no, boys,' he said. 'No, no, no. Little kids being massacred by native cavalry? No, no, no.' (This may have been what people in the film industry call a no-no.)

We returned to the typewriter in Stephen's fiancée's bedroom to try to provide the happy ending for the massacre that Tony Tenser desired.

'Colonel Mowbray does survive,' Stephen pointed out.

'I know – but look what happens to his wife and children. And what about all those bodies that Nana Sahib throws down the well?'

'We needn't actually *show* the bodies,' Stephen said. 'We could just show a soldier from the relief column walk up and look into the well.'

'He could be a Gordon Highlander,' I said, consulting *Regiments and Uniforms of the British Army*.

'All right. Then, a moment later, he hears someone playing the bagpipes, and that cheers him up again.'

Our rewriting was cut short by a dispute between Stephen and Tony Tenser about the way the film should be directed. A week later, Stephen telephoned to tell me the script was no longer with Tigon. He had bought it back – for a sum appreciably larger than Mr Tenser had paid him – and now intended to produce as well as direct it himself. After what Bryan Forbes had said, finding a backer would be easy.

I know he tried – but, from then on, *The Cawnpore Mutiny* seemed doomed. Not even the promise of Indian locations in Hampshire and a potential happy end to the massacre could persuade any entrepreneur to come up with threequarters of a million pounds in finance.

Stephen turned to fresh projects; once again, his energy and enthusiasm were infectious. I found myself simultaneously writing a script about the life of Thomas Chatterton, the 18th-century boy poet, and concocting a 'treatment' from the medieval poem *Sir Gawain and the Green Knight*.

With the latter, Stephen again seemed to strike pay dirt. His idea and my synopsis were bought by Carlo Ponti. I received – and proudly framed – a cheque for £250 signed by the great man himself. *Gawain* went into production with Stephen directing and Murray Head in the title role. It was, I believe – for I never saw it – a medieval-Gothic fantasy much in the style of today's big box-office hits. In 1969, its distributors hated it so much, they ordered it to be recut with different music: it became in effect a comedy, a kind of *Carry On Up the Holy Grail*. It was eventually premiered as second feature to the Readers' Digest production of Huckleberry Finn.

In late 1969, Stephen had another idea. To give himself a track record, and thus more readily get backing for *The Cawnpore Mutiny*, he would make a quick, low budget, instantly commercial horror movie. The horror movie business was then booming – Stephen said one could raise finance on a good title alone. He therefore came up with just a title: *Asylum*. It worked. An American producer named Milton Subotsky agreed to underwrite, and let Stephen direct, a film called *Asylum*, on condition he could see the finished script within a week.

I protested that I was breaking up with a girlfriend *and* getting ready to move house.

'It doesn't have to be good,' Stephen urged. 'You can put anything down. Subotsky just wants to see *something* on paper.'

His energy was again infectious. I sat down and in six days managed to produce a screenplay to fit Stephen's title. It was set in the 1920s, and reeked of the influence of M.R. James. Three young men spend the weekend together in a mysterious old house in Surrey. One of them finds a Victorian doll, invested with supernatural powers. The doll transports the young man back in time to witness its former owner, a young girl named Sophie, being systematically driven insane by her incestuous brother, Robert. Sophie is sent to the neighbourhood asylum, which speedily catches fire, allowing its inmates to run amok over the countryside. Sophie returns to take bloody revenge on Robert, while the young man from the later era looks on, horrified.

It was all typed at breakneck speed, without a second's revision. For one scene, I simply wrote 'Young men go out shooting. Comic sequence?' At another point where inspiration failed, I put down a speech I had to learn in my school's amateur dramatic production of J.B.Priestley's *Laburnum Grove*.

The finished work, embossed with Stephen's Letraset Asylum logo, was messengered at frantic speed to Milton Subotsky. News quickly came back that Mr Subotsky hated it. He had even read out some of my 1920s dialogue (or it may have been J.B.Priestley's) in a funny voice to amuse his entourage. He still liked the title, but he wanted a different script. He would give Stephen another week.

Here the scriptwriter became recalcitrant. I had not been paid anything since the £250 from Carlo Ponti. For dropping everything to write the existing script, I was to have received £1,000 – clearly not now forthcoming. I told Stephen I had no more time to give away.

'You can just write anything,' he pleaded. 'It doesn't have to be good. All Subotsky wants is *something* on paper.'

Much as I liked him, I felt I must stand firm.

'You don't realise . . .' Stephen said dramatically. 'You're taking the tools of my profession away from me.'

'But you haven't *paid* for the tools yet, Stephen,' I reminded him.

My decision proved a wise one. Milton Subotsky, soon afterwards, decided not to produce our story, though his admiration for the title was demonstrably sincere. A few weeks later, Stephen telephoned to tell me that Mr Subotsky had begun production of his own horror movie called *Asylum*. Stephen, disillusioned with the London film world, had gone to live with Joëlle, now his wife, in a castle he had bought on the Welsh Marches.

We did not cease to be friends. I had a standing invitation to spend weekends at Stephen's castle. In 1972, he joined me in recreating Jerome K. Jerome's *Three Men in a Boat* for an article in *The Sunday Times Magazine*. Dressed in Victorian clothes, with a third companion and a ferocious little dog, we spent a week sculling up the Thames in the track of Jerome's idyllic comedy. Stephen rowed with a will. But at night, round our methylated spirit stove or under the skiff's hooped canvas, the atmosphere sometimes became charged with mutual reproach.

In 1974, Stephen came back to me with his consummate strategy. He had exhausted all avenues of potential finance for our (now untitled) ghost story in England. He had therefore decided to finance it, and if possible shoot it, abroad. He had in mind a country with a thriving film industry; one in which, he understood, materials and labour were wonderfully cheap and the weather was always reliable. He repeated that his ultimate aim was to make our Indian Mutiny epic in Hampshire. Meantime, he proposed to shoot our Surrey ghost story on location in India.

Stephen and his wife shut up their Welsh castle and journeyed to India. When they returned, the project was underway. Stephen had found an old hill station called Ootacamund which, with skilful set-dressing, could be made the very image of Surrey in the 1920s. The local maharajah's palace, built in mock-Gothic style and filled with Victorian furniture, would serve as the mysterious old house. Indeed,

Stephen said, there were English period details in Ootacamund that one could not find in Surrey. He showed me transparencies of wooded lanes, gravelled drives, half-timbered Tudor gables and, the pièce de résistance, a signboard in faded tennis club green, reading 'Savoy Tea Rooms'.

A stopover in Bombay, India's movie capital, had proved equally fruitful. Stephen had received several firm offers of financial support, and practical help in securing the multitudinous permits necessary to import a film unit into the subcontinent. The diversity of Indian manufacture would allow costumes and properties to be made there at a fraction of their European cost. Stephen had even obtained offers of concessionary plane travel from Air India. Jubilant with the ease of it all, he was now recruiting British actors and technicians. The only thing that remained, Stephen said – like one picking his way over stepping stones – was to do a little more work on the script.

His offer was that, for a complete rewrite, I should receive £2,000 'on deferment' – payable after the picture was released and earning profits. I said it was a ridiculous, and insulting, way to employ someone. Stephen replied that the actors and technicians he was recruiting would mostly be paid on the deferment principle. I told him it was unacceptable to me and that, furthermore, he had no right to use what I had already written without paying for it. We parted on bad terms. The next I heard was that Stephen had turned my script over to another writer – the historical novelist Rosemary Sutcliffe – and, satisfied with her revisions and some of his own, had gone off with a film unit to India to shoot it.

About six months later, Stephen telephoned me and asked me to spend the weekend with Joëlle and him at their Welsh castle. I went, resolving to put aside my grievance about the script. Stephen met me in the gateway to his castle keep. His complexion had grown much darker. He wore a thick, curly beard and a tweed suit so vehemently English, it could have been tailored only in Bombay. He smiled at me in that same sidelong way, under those shaggy brows. I felt myself warm to him all over again.

The story of Stephen's return to India, leading a company of distinguished British actors and actresses and a full film unit, emerged bit by bit that weekend. It was a saga which would have consigned a less robust or optimistic spirit straight to the asylum of my scenario. Making Ootacamund resemble Surrey had been the least of Stephen's problems. There had been bureaucratic nightmares. There had been chronic – sometimes epidemic – sickness. There had been open war on the set between Hindu and Muslim technicians. There had been bizarre assignations with the film's Indian backer to receive battered suitcases full of black market rupees.

Stephen's fortitude throughout had remained almost superhuman. At one point, with black market rupees running low, he had decided to return to England with the one can of completed film and on the strength of that raise extra finance from his London bank. The problem was that, when importing his film stock into India, he had signed a Customs undertaking to export only that precise quantity of exposed movie film. His solution was to go to Bombay airport and plead with successive shifts of Customs officers to let him leave India with just that can. One shift let him through, then relented and pulled him back off his plane just before take-off. A later shift said he could fly out with the film as long as it travelled as cargo. When Stephen reached London, he found the can had been removed from the hold at the last minute back in Bombay. He turned straight round, flew to Bombay again and began pleading with new shifts of Customs officers.

The irony – perhaps a common one among film-makers – was that, while living out this incredible day-to-day drama, Stephen had been obliged to concentrate his artistic faculties, and those of other highly talented people, on something irredeemably banal. For, despite subsequent tinkering, the script remained substantially the one I had scribbled down in six days, four years earlier, hoping to earn myself a quick thousand pounds.

The finished film – for patent lack of anything more inspired – was entitled *Ghost Story*. Its cast was certainly strong. Murray Melvin played the leading young man in the 1920s trio. Marianne Faithfull played Sophie, the girl in the Victorian flashback. Two future big names in TV drama, Penelope Keith and Anthony Bate, played the proprietors of the asylum. At the preview, I winced to see Anthony Bate recite the whole of the speech I had borrowed from J.B.Priestley's *Laburnum Grove*.

Alas, despite all Stephen's ingenuity, the Surrey village we saw on-screen could not help repeatedly betraying its true location in the north Indian foothills. The lawns over which the characters strolled were parched by an unrelenting sun. The sky above them squawked with ungainly buzzards and kites. The men's costumes were clearly the work of Indian tailors, unable fully to distinguish between 1920s plus-fours and Edwardian military puttees. Even the sugar packet passed round by the young men at afternoon tea bore an unmistakeable image of the goddess Kali. Stephen's direction did not hurry his characters through their surroundings but, on the contrary, prompted them to linger poetically, peering at furniture that could belong only to a maharajah, or pausing in the withered gardens to pluck a brilliant pink hibiscus flower.

The climax of the film came, not at its gory denouement, but, inadvertently, at the point where I had blithely written 'Young men go out shooting. Comic sequence?' There were the three young men advancing over an arid hillside, pointing their Indian 12-bores into the harsh white sky. As Murray Melvin shot his gun, an Indian property man was supposed to have thrown a model pheasant up, to land as if plummeting at the marksman's feet. Misplacing the model pheasant, the property man had substituted a rubber chicken. He had, moreover, tossed it up just a fraction too soon. Stephen, for some reason, had not reshot the scene. As Murray Melvin's gun went off and the rubber chicken instantly hurtled down, an otherwise indifferent preview audience evinced definite signs of emotion.

Ghost Story never did find a British distributor. Stephen kept trying, even after another film called *Ghost Story* (from the Peter Straub novel) began mopping up at the box-office. I thought no more about it, or my alleged 2 per cent equity in it, until four years ago, while listlessly glancing through Thames Television's Easter holiday movie guide. There was *Ghost Story,* directed by Stephen Weeks, described as 'a little-known British chiller, undeservedly denied a general release'.

I wrote to Stephen at his Welsh castle, reminding him I was a little-known British screenwriter who had been undeservedly denied payment. His reply, on a typewriter with Gothic lettering, came from an address in Hollywood. No doubt he thrives there.

1985

Why I Work

I started work at the age of 14 in my father's business during the summer holidays. My father was an impresario. His business was a large, damp, hollow, domed, wooden, slatted pink and grey structure at the end of Ryde Pier, the second longest pier in England. In my father's time, this structure did duty variously as a roller-skating rink, a ballroom, *thé dansant* and penny-in-the-slot arcade, all dependent on the ferries which brought the day trippers to the Isle of Wight during the six-week summer season. When I started work there, it had become a self-service cafeteria. My job was to push a trolley among the tables, collect the dirty plates and trays and, when the trolley was full, to wheel it into the wash-up. The hours were from 10 a.m., just after the first ferry arrived, to 6 p.m. after the last ferry had left. The payment, per week, was nothing.

I had not volunteered for this job. In accepting it, I was prompted by that instinct essential to hard work, a feeling of guilt. I believed that, if I did not devote my holidays to helping my father at the end of the pier, his entire enterprise would collapse and we should all be disgraced. He himself had intimated as much. I was also, at that time, passionately fond of a girl named Sheila (spelt 'Sheelagh'), who worked in her summer holidays in the inner part of the wash-up. Her white coat, her white shoes, the tantalising way she spelled her name, almost drove me insane, and I made many more journeys into the wash-up than were strictly necessary. Here, I was potently confronted with a model of relentless industry. My father himself, at the busiest times of the day, left his other duties and ceremonially worked in the outer part of the wash-up, drying plates and spoons. He had a special way, I remember, of drying spoons. They seemed to leap from the end of his teacloth like trout. His co-director and brother, my Uncle Phil, suffered no such compunctions. At the busiest times of day, Uncle Phil sat on a stool at the bar nearby, composing little descriptions of how busy we all were, in blank verse.

My job on the trolley, revolting as it was, gave me my first insight into the pleasure of work. Divorced from any feeling of achievement (or reward), I used to enter a zombie-like state. I became unaware of the crowds around me and their unspeakable habits; pushing, stopping, clearing, wiping. The repulsive little trolley with its

265

aluminium shelves, its hanging red plastic bucket, became transformed in my imagination to a noble three-decked ship of the Napoleonic period. The ranks of grey tables, with their slops and crusts, became hostile fleets to be slowly fought into submission; the trays retrieved were the spiking of their guns; the pile of trays, replenished at the start of the self-service line, seemed to symbolise my father's whole enterprise, holding on, stemming tides, gaining ground. The symbol, as it turned out, was deeply erroneous. But I had taken my first sniff at the narcotic which one day was to control me.

I am aware that to say I enjoy work is to run the risk of alienating my fellow man. How much more it would become me to describe my indolence, my love of luxury and hot baths. It was Dr Johnson who said that, if he could choose how to spend his time, he would spend it driving briskly with a pretty woman in a post-chaise. Dr Johnson's observation has endeared him to at least as large a public as his Collected Works. Energy, on the other hand, seems to be ostentation in its least acceptable form. Of all types of discursive article, the most nauseating must be those which Arnold Bennett used to write in the *Strand* magazine in the 1920s, entitled 'How to live on 24 hours a day'. Its equally nauseating modern counterpart, I suppose, would be the articles which still crop up in the daily Press, describing how many hours are spent each year in aeroplanes by David Frost as he pursues his vacuous errands about the world.

It is necessary to distinguish, however, between the pleasure of work and the pleasure of being busy. The two are utterly opposed and mutually inimical. Being busy is an enjoyable state, easily attained and just as easily relinquished. It is catered for by the manufacturing society in the form of dictaphones, motor cars, electronic calculators, parliaments and wars. It is open to everyone, being attained simply by a semblance of bodily momentum. In an office, for instance, one can achieve incalculable effect by running across the room, staring, hair flying, towards a distantly-ringing telephone. Being busy is essentially a sociable occupation conducted for the benefit of others. Work, in whatever circumstances it may occur, is the pleasure in wilful solitude.

My own ideal working day certainly would not furnish much for a discursive article. On most mornings, I have a telephone alarm-call at 6 a.m. I get up and spend a couple of hours at a typewriter. Then, I go to the job for which I am paid a salary and spend another six or seven hours in front of another, bigger typewriter. On returning home, I spend another hour or two in front of the first typewriter. Then, putting on a light blue one-piece thermal suit and a small olive-coloured hat, I go for a three-mile run around Hyde Park, via Speakers' Corner and the perimeter of Apsley House. I return along the south bank of the Serpentine, among nocturnally-promenading Canada geese. Then, perspiring with some violence, I retire to bed. Then I am awake again and the operator is saying in his butlerine way, 'Your alarm call, Sir'.

I am fully sensible that this life has made me, in some respects, not a very nice person. I confess to the exercise of a puritanical scorn directed at those whose compulsion to work is not so great. Because I am fortunate enough to enjoy working, I have a quite unreasonable expectation of professionalism from curry-waiters, house-agents, mini-cab drivers and public relations officers. I feel a specially enjoyable contempt in Italian restaurants towards those frequent young men with their jackets slung over their shoulders who come in merely to shake hands with the proprietor. I rarely shake hands. I do not take holidays. When I see my colleagues employed on the telephone in arranging holidays for the year still to come, I generally make some terse observation about living in the future. They, in return, call me a 'swot'. For reasons which I shall explain, it is an opprobium I relish.

And yet, if you were to question me closely, I would tell you that I do not consider myself to be a particularly hard worker. All those manifestations of hard work, which to some of my friends are puzzling and to others faintly repellent, seem to me to be evidence of my incurable laziness. I work in order to finish work; in the ever-receding hope of having no more work to do. My conceptions of idleness are no less grandiose for existing in a highly impacted form in the half-lit intervals between one alarm-call and the next. I believe that I have all the appetite for sloth in the world. I lack only the aptitude.

My own conception of hard work is idealised by one boy who was at my school. His name was Sanders. He came, I think, from St Helens. His head was unnaturally small and his ears stuck out; his pullover zipped up at the front, obscuring the knot of his tie. But his handwriting! At all stages of my school career, I can recall the handwriting of Sanders being praised and his exercise books held open aloft so that the rest of us might admire its perfect readability, its radiant blueness, its bulbous and invariable rise and fall. I can still conceive of no pleasure in work greater than that which Sanders then enjoyed, without stress, without anxiety or the need for decision as his careful pen multiplied around Simon de Montfort, around Pythagoras and the pluperfect and Ohm's Law, distinguished in his conformity and rewarded by his perfect anonymity. (I believe he is now in banking.)

How different was my own situation. I was the son, not of a respectable merchant with a local name, but of an impresario in manifestly reduced circumstances; through a gap in the playing field hedge, the tip of the pier could be seen, a constant reminder of my exceptionability. In my good subjects, I shone to such a degree as to arouse, not compliments but faint contempt. In my bad subjects,

I was past redemption. Not only scholastic considerations seemed to be at work: my helplessness at maths was somehow connected with the fact that my blazer lacked a badge; my inability to remember the towns of the Scottish Central Lowlands was a subtle consequence of my dirty PT clothes. *Try*, I was continually exhorted: *Try, try.* I would dearly have loved to try, but could find no way in, no handhold. I struggled most fruitlessly in front of the kindly-looking, shaggy eyebrowed master we used to call 'Sinbad'. 'Perhaps you *would* know', he told me benignly 'if you didn't spend your time hanging round street corners'.

My early dreams, nourished in the hope of achieving a Sanders-like safety and calm, were either to work in the BBC or as a publisher's manuscript-reader. I can see now that either would have brought starvation: the first intellectual, the second physical. Instead I have been lucky enough to enter a profession where one can enjoy all the pleasures of scholarship without the necessity of having, or acquiring, an education. In newspapers, there is the feel and odour of school and the schoolboy humour. There is the same necessity for ingratiating oneself with the givers of house-points, without their knowledge. Above all, in the urgency of publication, there is the feeling of homework, endlessly repeated.

I can think of no other job which brings one periodically into contact with pleasure so extreme or so lurid. It has paid me a salary, among other things, to visit Bali and India and America; to drink champagne on ocean liners and be held at gunpoint with Mr Richard Burton. In its most mundane form it has translated me from pushing the trolley at the end of Ryde Pier, into worlds which during my early life were not even rumoured to exist. It can also be a difficult, a tiring and worrying occupation. However hard the going may become, I can comfort myself that I am no longer sitting at my school desk of wood and iron, with 'Sinbad' before me, rocking slightly on his shoes, his nostrils, at my very existence, flaring with bushy disapproval.

I am sitting, instead, at my own desk with the hour-glass upon it. A clock is ticking, and a second clock is ticking, further away. Here, my journalistic pleasures must be expiated by writing, the pleasures of which are not so immediately apparent. V. S. Pritchett told me once that he never sits down to write without a feeling that he is completely mad. With me, the moment is heralded by instantaneous sweat. Writing is a disease with many manifestations. It can be, as with Simenon, a lycanthropic mania: its most common form, however, is a creeping paralysis wherein first the hand, then the arm and shoulder seem to develop intolerable weight; the fingers, arranged in their little shelter around the pen, thrill with horror at the acreage of white which must be traversed. Above all, there is that terrible knowledge that it cannot yet nearly be over since it has not yet even begun.

One attempts to surmount this moment by means of feeble and facile incidental pleasures. The room where I work I refer to, not as my office but as my 'study'. I cling to a romantic notion of some great shadowy space, full of the silhouettes of familiar objects, and in the centre, a single beam, equally mingling light and concentration. Most writers surround themselves with familiar objects of such diversity as were placed in the tombs of Egyptian pharaohs, with record-players, biscuit barrels, picture postcards, model soldier collections, hourglasses and P. G. Wodehouse novels, to bear them company in the land of the dead. Most writers have an unnatural fondness for stationery: for blocks of paper, pens laid out like a surgeon's tools, the flat red and silver boxes in which carbon paper is sold. My personal demon is that I cannot bear to make a typing error. Much-corrected handwritten manuscript, on the contrary, is pleasant, and hearteningly similar to that preserved in the Dostoevsky Museum. Recently, on settling down to write, I have found myself leaving the door of my 'study' open a little way and a light burning outside in the hall.

All this can only partly mitigate a process which, even at its highest moments, is completely without logic. Harold Ross, the founder of the *New Yorker,* once said that 'nobody gives a damn about a writer's problems except another writer'. That is not true: people would care about a writer's problems if only it were possible to explain them. But they change by the minute; they recur always in some fresh disguise; upon mastering the most fearsome equations, you can be floored by simple arithmetic. And, if a writer has any duty apart from writing, it is to prevent his quandary of simultaneous foolhardiness and fear from infecting the souls of decent folk.

My situation has become very much as it was when I worked on the trolley in my father's cafeteria. Once again, I find myself asking use of imagery – or, if you insist, self-deception – to live out a role in which I lack conviction. Scott Fitzgerald once said that writing was like swimming underwater. I prefer to view my projects, amorphous, unaccomplished, in rough physical terms, that I may accomplish them by muscle alone: by 'trying'. I imagine my work as a great overgrown garden in which there are brambles to be cleared, stones to be raised and marshes to be drained: with care, with infinite slowness, this expanse can be transformed into wide lawns and white paths and topiary; the hostile landscape becomes friendly and familiar, until at the last I am sad at leaving it behind.

And what of the consequences? I live half my life in another world; on returning to this world again, I feel a curious sense of nakedness, of incapacity; my very own name has an unconvincing sound. Summers have passed without my knowledge, and with them the accumulation of friends, children, holidays – forgone to what purpose? I cannot explain. I only know that I shall continue to forgo them. Nothing – however bright, however charming – has proved impenetrable by the knowledge that it must eventually be sacrificed. At the centre of my other world, sometimes I can feel the reverberations of doubt; the memory of sunshine which I ignored; the moments when I got too quickly out of bed, leaving somebody behind; the moments when I went out of the room, leaving somebody behind, and into the room next door.

Loneliness is said to be endurable if one has a genuine longing for immortality. Yet it is a fact that the most dedicated, the most prolific of authors seem to have found time to exist as humans, tempering their compulsion with love or perhaps golf. I am aware that leisure and its employment have been proved to be biological necessities. Cyril Connolly enumerated the enemies of artistic promise but, being unfamiliar with it himself, he neglected to mention the enemy of over production. A greater discipline than work is surely knowing when *not* to work. I cannot pretend that my work is a necessity. I know that it is a camouflage of necessity, protecting me against the things in life which I fear most. With me, therefore, work is pure indulgence: it is pleasure of the impurest sort.

And yet I know how I feel when, briefly, I emerge from the self-allotted span of this self-inflicted despair. I feel, however temporarily, like the sort of person I should most like to be. It is as if all the colours in the world have become lighter, sharper; I can see things in devastating detail – the top floors of tall houses, the play of sunlight across book-spines, the tender habits of the domestic palm-tree. Only now do I think that I can endure the other pleasures of life. I am ready to attack existence head-on: to hang pictures, fetch laundry, visit cheap china-bazaars. If I open a cupboard, and a candle rolls out and falls and smashes a dish below, then I can laugh.

And when life deals – as it still can – a blow which causes bruising to spread outward from the heart, I also know how I feel. The pleasure of work is not only the pleasure of having worked. One door, at least, remains open to me. Outside the garden waits, with all the work that is to be done. The trolley waits and the tables to be cleared. I go into my 'study'. I pull my chair back from my desk, noting that the curtain behind has a white mark where the chair has touched it. I sit, touching the curtain with the chair; tilt the hourglass and begin again.

1975